MIDDLE-CLASS JUVENILE DELINQUENCY

EDITED BY

EDMUND W. VAZ

UNIVERSITY OF WATERLOO

HARPER & ROW

Publishers

NEW YORK, EVANSTON, AND LONDON

Library of Congress Catalog Card Number: 67-10806

CONTENTS

FOREWORD

This small volume of articles and selections from books is intended as supplementary reading to courses in Social Problems and Juvenile Delinquency. Directed primarily at undergraduate university students, it tries to bring together some of the current theory and research on the topic of middle-class juvenile delinquency. If the findings are valid, many of the students, in retrospect, ought to find familiar some of the material discussed in these pages. It is hoped that this selection of readings will encourage them to think critically about the subject and perhaps challenge their developing skills at responsible speculation.

I am grateful to Professors Albert K. Cohen and Harold Fallding for their suggestions on various parts of this book, and I am especially indebted to my wife Cécile for her careful and patient assistance throughout its preparation.

EDMUND W. VAZ

Introduction

Delinquency is not new among middle-class children. Although it has long been manifest among these youths, there is a paucity of research on the subject. Early studies concentrated primarily on the urban slum—the "natural" habitat of the delinquent gang. Slums were thought to be socially disorganized, ridden with culture conflict, and were considered the breeding ground for crime and delinquency. Certainly delinquency among lower-class boys was public knowledge. Perhaps, too, lower-class boys were more approachable, and official statistics, albeit unsatisfactory, were available for purposes of research. For a long time delinquency among middle-class boys escaped scot-free from sociological investigation. Some early researchers had demonstrated the presence of "official" delinquency among the "best" families in "well-to-do" areas, and the suspicion existed that delinquency might even be widespread among middle-class youths. But knowledge of the informal handling and preferential treatment by officials of middle-class boys, the difficulty in gaining access to middle-class institutions, and the absence of a socially recognized image of the middle-class youth as delinquent, perhaps discouraged systematic research. In addition, the bellicose quality of lower-class delinquency often aroused public indignation and made any concern over behavior among middle-class boys appear misplaced. In any case, whether or not widespread delinquency among middle-class youths is a comparatively new phenomenon, as some writers suggest, we will never know.

We still do not know very much about middle-class delinquency. Speculation continues over the amount and quality of the behavior, but there is as yet little evidence to suggest that the rate of middle-class delinquency is increasing. To help overcome the bias of official statistics, much contemporary work relies on self-reported data—detailed information gathered from the general community of children in school. Increasing use of this excellent technique reflects the difficulty of obtaining satisfactory kinds of official statistics.

Moreover, it helps to explore the extent of delinquency not known to official agencies.

Recent studies have proved enlightening. The notion that delinquency is rooted somehow in the lower socioeconomic groups is much less tenable today than was the case previously. Rural and small town data (not all reported here) gathered from high school students fail to demonstrate significant differences in delinquency participation among social classes. There is good reason to believe that all children, rich or poor, engage differentially in varying kinds of delinquency, and that official statistics reveal only a fraction of the delinquency committed in any community. But more data are required to supplement this small but seminal body of knowledge. Urgently needed are data from large cities on the delinquency involvement of children from different social classes. Yet, it remains true that the more costly, victimizing types of delinquency (behavior that is apt to try any public tolerance), occur in gangs of lower-class boys.

The conception of adolescence as a period of emotional turmoil and behavioral ambiguity is well documented in the literature on youth. However, it is largely overlooked when an explanation is attempted of middle-class juvenile delinquency. Instead, the concept "youth culture" has captured the attention of sociologists. But there is not always consensus regarding the structure, organization, and content of the youth culture, and the terms "youth culture" and "subculture" are sometimes used interchangeably. Today it seems likely that adolescents do constitute a social system, something akin to a special world of their own. Common to this system of youths is a culture of relatively distinguishable values, attitudes, and norms. Since social class is an important variable accounting for behavioral variation among teen-agers, perhaps it makes sense to refer to a lower-class youth culture, middle-class youth culture, etc. Yet, each adolescent class culture is only partially distinctive and mirrors in part its parent class culture. Equally likely is the presence of adolescent subcultures, cultural pockets of norms and values sufficiently distinct to set them apart from their respective adolescent class cultures. But again the distinction is apt to be more a matter of emphasis than of kind. Although it is premature, perhaps, to talk of a delinquent subculture among middle-class youths, we talk with confidence of a delinquent subculture among lower-class boys.

Behavior in the youth culture is viewed often as irresponsible, defiant, and independent. Some sociologists challenge this conception of adolescence and doubt even the authenticity of the youth culture. They emphasize the "protective" nature of the middle-class home, and the continuity in the socialization of middle-class children. Family relationships are said to be closely integrated, norms are stable, and children often select parents as role models of behavior. In this family setting teen-age heterosexual relationships are prominent and encouraged, and children are taught the social niceties of conduct to prepare them for later adult roles. However, data are accumulating regularly on the theft, drinking, gambling, and sexual activities of these boys. Recent studies have shown that automobile offenses (which include drag-racing, driving without a license, etc.) are higher among "white-collar" than "blue-collar" boys. There are partially convergent findings that hint at a similarity between middle-class delinquency and what has been called, elsewhere, the "subterranean values" of society—a disdain for work, search for pleasure, thrills, adventure—a youthful version of which seems reflected in middle-class teen-agers' pursuit of non-academic, social, and athletic interests in high school and the youth culture. Perhaps this casts some doubt on the protective influence of the middle-class family socialization process. On the other hand, this kind of family environment does not preclude the existence of a middle-class youth culture nor widespread delinquency among these youths. Indeed it might encourage it.

One task is to establish the rate of delinquency among middle-class youths. Another is to determine what proportion of youths engage in what kinds of delinquent acts. To what extent are certain patterns of delinquency institutionalized in the middle-class youth culture? Some youngsters refrain from participating actively in youth culture events. Dances and girls, parties, sports, dating and going steady, "hanging around" and drive-in midnight movies are alien to their interests. To what extent do such activities constitute the content of the middle-class youth culture? How long can a city boy engage in these widespread respectable affairs and not violate the law? Driving without a license, "dragging," drinking beer at a party, feeling a little "high" occasionally, gambling, having physical intimacy with a girl, keeping late hours are, seemingly, behavioral variations on routine events among middle-class teen-agers. Our guess is that all boys who commit themselves to youth culture activities sooner or later break the law. Perhaps, too, the longer a boy remains in high school (the institutional catalyst for teen-age activity) and behaves in accordance with the adolescent role, the more apt he is to become delinquent. We ought to ask the question: in what ways does the high school contribute to delinquency among middle-class youths?

A related problem is to explain middle-class delinquency given the above kinds of data on the socialization of middle-class children. Interestingly, the daily activities of these youths are perfectly compatible with the protective type family socialization. Indeed, it is precisely these group-oriented activities (dances, parties, dating, socializing, etc.) that are encouraged by middle-class parents and teachers, and often serve as "dummy-runs" for later adult roles. The apparent inconsistency between the protective upbringing of middle-class children and their delinquencies is resolved, partly, when middle-class delinquency is viewed as a function of conformity to the expectations of the role of adolescent in the middle-class youth culture, and to parentally favored activities of teen-agers.

Among middle-class teen-agers sociability is the quickest route to acceptability and status gain. The recluse and the bookworm are seldom admired. Teen-agers expect enthusiastic participation from peers in youth culture events. But the pursuit of status and the pull of popularity may easily lead to novel kinds of behavior, variations on everyday games and practices. Perhaps much middle-class delinquency is precisely these kinds of acts. This suggests that certain kinds of delinquency are an unexpected result of institutionalized patterns of conduct, and that delinquency is spawned among the stable, cherished values, attitudes, and activities of the middle class. Much excellent work has been conducted on the legitimate interests and events of middle-class youths. The failure to envisage delinquency arising from these highly endorsed practices and social arrangements in the youth culture has obscured, perhaps, much of the delinquency that actually transpires among these young people. This is only a single perspective among others, however, and although some limited confirmatory evidence has been gathered, the other theories also require further empirical verification. Until this is done, each theory remains incomplete.

PART I

The Adolescent Youth Culture

INTRODUCTION

If we are to understand the culture of adolescents we must explore the things that they do, inspect their interests and activities, and examine the rules by which these events are practiced. One thing is certain, sports, girls, and cars hold high rank among middle-class teen-agers, and school is taken pretty much for granted. But teen-agers do not live only among their peers. In the first article, William Westley and Frederick Elkin report on the family training of adolescents in a semi-isolated suburban community. Their data point up the healthy continuity in the socialization of middle-class youths. Although these adolescents possess their own distinctive interests and customs, a happy congruence exists between their attitudes and those of their parents. Remarkably, perhaps, these youngsters are relatively sophisticated in evaluating their own conduct, and they soon appreciate the value of parental dictates.

In her excellent overview of the data, Jessie Bernard states that the teen-age culture is the product of a leisure culture and an affluent society. Teen-agers are big business today. Their patterns of insatiable consumption make the adolescent culture a significant part of the social and economic structure, and children are seldom able to escape its pervasive influence. Bernard indicates that soon the teen-age culture may include an even earlier age range of youngsters, which implies that the teen-age culture is here to stay for a while.

James Coleman's impressive study of adolescents makes clear once and for all the strategic importance of athletics for high schools and high school students. Coleman spotlights the time and energy devoted to organizing athletic contests, the salaries paid to coaches, and the special status of athletes among students and teachers. The data reveal that a function of high school is to increase the freshman's interest in sports while sapping his enthusiasm for academic matters. Athletic contests serve to cohere the student body and promote a collective identity for the school. Very likely athletes and athletics function as social catalysts that strengthen common values, beliefs, and behavior patterns throughout the youth culture.

Writing almost 20 years ago, Willard Waller saw dating among young people as a period of dalliance, and not as an integral part of courtship. And what he saw remains partly relevant today. It was a relationship of fun and thrills which included varying degrees of sexual experimentation—an experience to be sampled, but not taken too seriously.

Contemporary teen-age sex codes suggest that today dating is a more serious affair, and going steady is not unpopular among adolescents. Given the institutionalization of teen-age dating, it should not surprise us to learn that a network of norms regulates the sexual practices of adolescents. While emphasizing the variability in teen-age sexual codes, Ira Reiss suggests that the trend is toward greater permissiveness in sexual practices. If petting is permitted, perhaps even encouraged among young people, and going steady is a safeguard against an injured reputation for the girl who "goes all the way," sexual intercourse with affection is not discredited altogether.

The Protective Environment and Adolescent Socialization

WILLIAM A. WESTLEY
AND FREDERICK ELKIN

This article presents a challenge to a popular conception of adolescence. In the literature of psychology and sociology, adolescence is generally described as a period of severe storm and stress. As a consequence of psychological and institutional pressures, the adolescent is said to experience innumerable conflicts and tensions. He must resolve discrepancies between his sexual impulses and societal restrictions. His prolonged tenure in school prevents him from "trying his wings" and discovering his own natural abilities. He has strong dependency needs in the family while at the same time he is expected to choose his goals and become a self-reliant independent adult. As a result of his uncertainties about his status and obligations, he tends to identify with a youth culture and seek the solidarity and support of a peer group, a group in turn which makes its own strong demands for conforming behaviour. The following description of adolescence in the American middle class family by an anthropologist and psychiatrist is not atypical.

The wild fluctuations between extreme dependence and disdainful or defiant independence, the gyrations from idealism to cynicism, from lush romancing to hard-bitten, stripped-down sexual aims, and from cringing conformity to last ditch non-conformity are attitudes largely unique to our

Reprinted by permission of the authors and of the editor from *Social Forces*, Vol. 35 (March, 1957), 243–249.

All footnotes appear in the Notes section, grouped by article, at the end of this book.

own social system. Threaded through all the adolescent attitudes is the power of the gang, or the adolescent peer group with its own, unique and frequently spectacular behavior patterns.[1]

As dramatic and logical as is this explanation, the question remains—to what extent is the above adolescent pattern characteristic of all middle-class adolescents. The authors' study of one middle-class suburban community, characterized by relative social and vicinal isolation, suggests a quite different pattern. According to this pattern, the adolescent belongs to a small closely-knit family and participates with other family members in many activities. He internalizes aspirations for a professional or business career; he learns the expected patterns of language and breeding; he learns to resolve disputes by peaceable means; he learns to defer many immediate gratifications for the sake of future gains; and the peer group to which he belongs, rather than serving as an opposition group to the parents, tends to encourage and reinforce many values and patterns of the adult world.

This picture is quite at variance with the picture given by the authors cited above. While these findings must necessarily be restricted to the community under study and are closely related to its social and vicinal isolation, they should have wider relevance for the study of adolescence. The findings not only challenge the popular characterization of adolescence but also suggest the need for important conditioning data in reports on particular studies and in the presentation of generalizations. Specifically we would suggest that in any particular study, the adolescent pattern be seen as part of its community context, that data on discontinuities be balanced by data on continuities, and that any generalizations specify the extent of social insulation and control provided by the community.

Theoretical aspects of this problem have been discussed elsewhere;[2] it is the purpose of this paper to present some of the research case material which demonstrates the continuity of adolescent socialization in the suburban community and the process by which such socialization occurs.

COMMUNITY AND METHOD

Suburban Town is a suburb of Montreal with a population in 1951 of less than 12,000. The community has its own municipal government, police and fire departments, schools, churches, and recreational facilities. The average family size in 1951 was 3.5 persons. The family heads, over two-thirds of whom have managerial or professional positions, work in the City of Montreal and commute via a direct railroad line. Their median earnings in 1951 were over $5,700.

Twenty adolescents and their families were intensively studied. The adolescent sample, selected from lists provided by various residents of the community and community organizations, comprises approximately fifteen percent of those in the community who met the criteria of selection. All were ages 14 or 15, of English origin, Protestant, and members of families of professional or managerial status.

The average interview time per family was approximately ten hours. Following a preliminary interview with parents and child together, each adolescent was interviewed two or more times. These interviews were partially directed, the adolescent being asked to prepare a diary of day-to-day activities and to discuss certain activities, interests, and ideas. Finally, each mother and child separately was given an interview covering the same general subjects. These interviews were held on the same day, in succession, in order to prevent collusion. Supplementary data were also obtained from the life histories of approximately twenty post-adolescent college students who came from Suburban Town.[3]

The materials which follow may suggest that the children and parents of Suburban Town are paragons of adolescence and parenthood and have no serious psychological or interpersonal problems. No such implication is intended. The data presented focus on the behaviour and more conscious attitudes of the respondents and do not directly concern the psychological health or ill health of either adolescents or parents.

THE PROTECTIVE ENVIRONMENT

For the adolescent in Suburban Town, the environment is integrated and protective. Usually, we stress the heterogeneity of modern society, the alternative norms, conflicting patterns of behaviour, and institutional complexity. However in Suburban Town there is a generally consistent and stable set of norms and expectations and we find that the adolescent is protected in various ways from contact with alternative patterns of behaviour. This protectiveness may be seen in the effective isolation and social organization of the community.

Effective Isolation

The adolescent in Suburban Town has little opportunity to participate in, or become meaningfully familiar with, ways of life which differ greatly from his own. Within the community he has his school, community services, recreational facilities, and friends. Parental interest likewise functions as an effective control device since the parents, at any particular time, are likely to know what their children are doing and where and with whom they are. One mother says:

I make it a point of knowing what he is doing. If he can't be home one afternoon when he's expected, he'll leave a note telling me what he's up to. I like to know where he is. If, for any reason, he's going to be late, he calls and lets us know.

From the parents' point of view, isolated Suburban Town is a "good" environment for their children, one with "positive advantages" and without danger of contact with impolite language and behavior, improper sex play, or delinquent activity. One mother expresses this as follows:

You're lucky in an area like Suburban Town. All the activities have a religious bias and are under competent people. You don't have to worry about the children getting into trouble. All of John's friends are just impeccable.

The isolation of the effective environment is encouraged by the model of the parents themselves whose social life likewise tends to be circumscribed within the community. Through participation in local associations and activities, the parents implicitly define the community as a desirable area of delimitation.

Social Organization

The protective qualities of Suburban Town are further reinforced through the community's social organization. This is especially evident in the structuring of time of adolescents, the joint activities of adolescents and parents, and the collusive actions of parents in supervising adolescent behaviour.

The adolescent has little unstructured time. Typically, on school days, he spends his out-of-school hours doing about two hours of homework, helping in household activities, and participating in school organizations, directed sports, or church or "Y" activities. On week ends, he does have more free time, but even then he participates in some family projects, has certain household tasks, and often attends gatherings at which adults are present. In summers, he either works, attends camp, or vacations with his family at a summer cottage. Thus, much of the adolescent's activity has a productive or educative orientation, and he has little opportunity to "hang around" or devise "inappropriate" amusements. The following remarks illustrate this structuring of time.

Girl: *In the fall, sometimes we would visit each other's houses. Right now there is a keen interest in senior basketball and we stay and watch that. When I get home I practice the piano for about half to three quarters of an hour. Then I go upstairs and do my homework. After supper, I'll do the dishes so they don't pile up too much. After that I'll finish my homework. Then, if there is nothing else, I'll listen to the radio.*

Boy: *On Saturday morning I help my father around the house. We've been building the recreation room downstairs. We cemented the walls, fixed up a place for cold storage, and now we've just started on the furnace room. We're going to do the garage next and we're building a patio, too. We both get a kick out of it.*

In many areas no sharp distinction is made in the family between parental and adolescent activity. The adolescents, for example, participate with their parents in visiting relatives, team curling, work around the house, entertaining guests and other such activities, while the parents participate in many of the activities of the adolescents—they discuss their school courses and activities with them, attend the school's dramatic and athletic events, welcome their children's guests into their homes, and assist in their social gatherings.

The protectiveness of the setting is perhaps most evident in the joint actions of parents regarding the social activities of their adolescent children. Many instances were reported in which the parents, in collusion, decided how much allowances should be, the number of dates permitted per week, and the required hour of return from dates. In some instances, when a boy and a girl began dating each other steadily, the parents of the two conferred to discuss whether or not the relationship should be encouraged. The following statement of a fifteen year old girl cites one instance of such joint action.

I never go out on a week night. Last year our parents thought we were going out too much. They got together and they all decided that we were. Then they said we could go out one night every week end and we had to be in by twelve.

The protective environment is effective in Suburban Town because it has become the accepted pattern of life and because it is so completely accepted by the adolescents themselves. The adolescents accept the parents' prerogative of supervising their activities, willingly report the details of their lives,[4] and express little desire to participate in activities that take place outside the community. Such an internalization of controls on the part of the adolescents precludes any overt rebellion or any negative contrast with other patterns.

CONTINUITY OF SOCIALIZATION

This protective environment is of significance primarily because it encourages a continuity in socialization between adolescence and adulthood, a continuity which is especially evidenced in our research in the congruence of attitudes of adolescents and parents towards heterosexual relationships and economic matters.

Heterosexual Relationships

In such situations as party behaviour, discussions of marriage partner ideals, and dating, adolescents are being continually socialized for their adult roles and are internalizing the norms of the community. In giving parties, for example, the girls learn their proper hostess roles: they go over the guest list with their mothers and include those they *should* invite as well as those they *want* to invite; they are careful to have the same number of boys and girls; they send out formal invitations; and they make certain that the party guests mix. And the boys at these parties are so aware of their escort responsibilities that they may draw straws to decide who walks home with the less popular girls. The following statements illustrate how party behaviour is so functional to the roles the adolescents are expected to play in later life.

Mother: *In his own parties he knows that he has to see each of his guests to the door and to make sure that every girl has an escort home. I've told him that when he's the host it's his duty to make sure that the boys take the girls home.*

Boy: *Well, the girls always ask their friends to come to the party. But some of the girls' friends are not popular. Sometimes nobody wants to take them home. Usually what happens is that the boys draw straws. The hostess tries to arrange it so that everybody is taken home. It always gets worked out at parties.*

Girl: *Mom and I plan the parties. For balloons or anything like that, I buy them myself out of my savings. Mom encourages me to give parties because she wants me to be a good hostess. When you're married it's always better to be a perfect hostess. I find that I'm always a little bit afraid. Once everything gets going it's not too bad because you've got a chance to relax.*

Continuity is also evident in the ideas of the girls about marriage. Both mothers and daughters believe that the girls should have careers, since marriage involves risks and a girl should be prepared for whatever contingency may arise. Also, in describing the ideal marriage mate, the girls, in all but one instance, stressed not his physical attractiveness, athletic ability, and popularity, but rather his occupation, class status, religion, and character. The daughters are not so absorbed in "adolescent culture" that they lose sight of their long-run goals. The following statements are typical of the comments about marriage.

Mother: *I know Jane wants to get married, but she is not awfully definite just when. My own view is that she should finish her education before taking such a step. If she ever needed it in the future, she would have something to fall back on. . . . I would hate to see her marry anyone who is not on her own level, or who didn't have the same outlook. The only equipment I've given Jane is some sort of ability to discriminate. The rest is up to her.*

Girl: *The girls talk about it quite a bit. I don't care what he looks like. He must have the same interests as I do. He should also be able to support a family, though I don't care what he does. I wouldn't want a drunkard, of course, and I don't want anybody with dirty fingernails, for instance.*

Girl: *I want to get married and go into journalism. It's the type of career that you can work at and still run a home. I wouldn't want to marry until I'm 21. By that time I would be educated enough to take the responsibility. . . . He could be a teacher. Not a ditchdigger or somebody like that. He would have to be doing something constructive; I'd prefer a professional.*

Dating patterns, although obviously an adolescent activity, likewise evidence such continuity. "Going steady," for example, is not uncommon among the adolescents of Suburban Town. However, "going steady" is under parental supervision and the adolescents themselves are quite sophisticated about it. The following statements are typical.

Boy: *I figure this is the time to play the field. I think I'll stay this way until the middle of next year. Then it's a good idea to start going steady so you can be sure to go to all the important dances, like the graduation dance. It's important to go to that; so it's a good idea if you have a steady.*

Girl: *Well, going steady is all right, but it's silly to think of marriage at our age. You just stay clear of the subject. You might talk about getting married, you never talk about it as if you meant yourself. You know that you have to break up one day, but you just hope that that day will never come.*

Mother: *Norman went steady with Barbara Sloan. I didn't think it was a good idea. Mrs. Sloan and I had a talk about it. We were both against it. Then all the kids in the group stopped going steady and he stopped, too. Mind you, I suppose the boys and girls feel more secure when they go steady.*

Economic Life

A continuity of socialization is also particularly evident in the parental training devices, attitudes, and aspirations associated with jobs, careers, and finances. The parents are ambitious for their children; however, since the husbands are salaried personnel and the families have high expenses in maintaining their way of life, they cannot leave their children either independent businesses or large sums of money. The children, therefore, must be trained to attain social and economic success through their own capabilities and characteristics. Thus, the parents feel it is important to inculcate in their children the "proper" economic attitudes: that work and saving are virtues; that given occupations are associated with given social statuses; and that money is to be used not for conspicuous display, immediate gratification, or speculation, but to achieve one's economic and social goals. The continuity of socialization is evidenced in that the adolescents by the ages of 14 or 15, have already well internalized these values and ideals. Note, for example, the following comments of parents and children regarding career aspirations, part-time work, allowances, savings, and discussions of family finances.

CAREER ASPIRATIONS

It is assumed by all members of the family that the sons will attend college and attain upper middle class positions. Although specific occupations may not yet be chosen, a concern with careers is evident.

Mother: *I want him to go to college but I don't see the point in his just going for a B.A. I was hoping that he might be interested in becoming a Chartered Accountant. You know, I have been nothing but confused at the high school meetings. They advise that you put off any decision until they're in College. That seems a little late to me. I know that the whole business worries us and it worries Johnnie.*

Boy: *Around here, university helps in business. If you don't have a university education you don't get the jobs. I like to play sports and lead a gay life but I'll have to settle down to work soon. Mom doesn't want me just to be having fun all the time.*

Boy: *I haven't really considered it yet. I am hoping to go to college, but I haven't considered what course. I've been thinking about engineering and commerce.*

PART-TIME WORK

Part-time work has become the norm for the adolescent boys in the community and is not uncommon for the girls. To the parents, such work is a significant training device for character development. Work, it is said, teaches the children the necessity of labor, the value of money, and a sense of responsibility.

Mother: *I've always encouraged the boys to take any stray jobs—cutting the grass of neighbors, putting up storm windows, or even baby sitting. If I hear anyone say that he needs somebody to do this or that I immediately suggest the boys. It's not the money. They should learn that you just don't get money, you work for it. It develops a sense of responsibility.*

Mother: *I have encouraged baby-sitting jobs. I feel that it's good for Jill to take on responsibility and to feel that she is earning money herself. We've talked about it and she agrees to it.*

Boy: *It was my idea to take a paper route to help along with my pocket money. I wanted to take some sort of a job this summer. I even tried applying for farm work. Before taking the camp job I wrote to the C.N.R. through my father's friend. But they had a full staff. A lot of my friends have paper routes so I got one, too. I didn't really need the extra; I don't spend that much money.*

ALLOWANCES

All but one of the adolescents in our sample were given allowances, the allowances averaging $1.00 per week.[5] The allowance, to the parents, is a device for teaching the child that money is to be used carefully and wisely. The allowance "teaches" the child to save, to know the "value of money," and to distinguish important from unimportant expenditures. There are variations in the degree to which the adolescents themselves have internalized these attitudes, but they all recognize that these are the "proper" attitudes.

Mother: *Their father has given each of them three times the amount of their age. At 15 Louise is getting 45 cents a week. Now she supplements that with her baby sitting. She has done very well with her baby-sitting money. She has paid for her band lessons out of her savings. My husband has taught them not to waste money. Any jaunts that Louise takes she pays for herself. She even buys clothing for herself that she considers necessities.*

Girl: *Well, I get $1.00 a week. I don't buy lunches or anything like that out of my money; that all comes extra. If I go to a movie alone or with the girls I spend my own money. But most of the time, if I go, it's with a boy, and he pays the fare and for the movie. I can save most of my money. I'm not loaded or anything, but by this week end I should have $7.00 saved. I buy useful articles with it. Two weeks ago I bought a sweater, and now I want to get a cotton blouse.*

Boy: *I get $5.00 a month, but I have to pay for everything out of that. I have to buy my own bus and train fares, get a haircut, and all that. I have to get everything except my clothes out of that money. They are trying to get me trained. They give it to me all at once so I'll learn how to keep a budget. If I run short I'm just short. I have gone for over two weeks without bus money.*

SAVINGS

The puritanical attitudes of the parents toward money are also evidenced by their statements about saving. The parents wish to inculcate in their children the belief that money is not to be spent recklessly and, if not immediately necessary, should be put away for future use. The children are thus encouraged, and apparently successfully so, to view their economic lives as lives of continuity.[6]

Mother: *She gets a dollar a week. I started her off with fifty cents, then she graduated to seventy-five and now it's a dollar. I want her to save some of this, but I don't feel that she saves enough. She just uses it for pocket money. The thing I object to is that she doesn't save enough to buy things for herself.*

Mother: *We've always encouraged them to save. When they were little they had bank accounts opened for them. Whatever money they banked they got half again as much from us. Now Murray is going to Quebec, Ottawa, and Burlington with the school band. We'll pay for one of the trips, but he's got to have enough saved to pay for the rest himself.*

Boy: *I like to save money. I had about $25.00 saved up a little while ago. I don't know where it all went to. All of a sudden there was nothing left. My parents have encouraged me to save. They always say that if you learn how to save you have money when you need it. You realize it yourself when you see how fast $25.00 can disappear.*

DISCUSSION OF FAMILY FINANCES

Although the parents in our sample are most concerned about the expenditures of their children, they—with only one exception—strongly feel that the children should not know the family's financial position; consequently, they carefully avoid open discussions of family finances. This has two important implications for the socialization of the adolescents. First, by keeping the children from knowing the true financial position of the family, the parents are better able to rationalize the limited allowances they give and their demands for work and saving. Secondly, in their sensitivity to the subject, they undoubtedly suggest to their children that money is somehow important, mysterious and sacred.

Mother: *No, that is something we never talk to the children about. My husband feels that the finances of the family shouldn't be open to criticism from the family. For instance, he wants to be able to say that they can't have this or that without feeling that the children would be able to say, but why not? From my point of view the only danger is that they might talk outside the home about it. I don't know why it is, but that's the type of thing you don't even tell your best friends.*

Boy: *Mother wouldn't even tell me my father's salary, or how much the car is worth, or even what her fur coat is worth. If I asked her how much it's worth she would think I'm only a kid and be embarrassed. I'm never allowed to ask my father what his salary is. I couldn't do that. He never discusses money with me like that. I don't mind. I sort of think it's a good thing.*

Girl: *I don't know how much Daddy gets a year or anything like that. Dad feels that we shouldn't know things like that. They sometimes talk about it, but it's not really meant for me to hear.*

SOCIALIZATION AND THE PEER GROUP

We noted that the peer group occupies an important place in the popular explanation of adolescence, serving the function of emancipating the child from the family while giving him psychological support. The peer group is here described as an opposition group to the parents with a unique and immature set of interests and values. In Suburban Town, we find no such peer groups.[7] On the contrary, the peer groups in Suburban Town generally are committed to the values of the parents and further a continuity in socialization. The peer group, for example, views part-time jobs and allowances as the norm for its members; it encourages participation in school organizations; it rates its members in terms of school grades; and the girls, in their groups, discuss the proprieties of entertaining and the desirable characteristics of husbands.

Boy: *A guy should know how to dance and be in on the sports. Sports is very important. And something else: school work is very important too. You would be surprised just how much that counts for boys. I was at a party last year after I came first in the class. I could just stand there and not say a word all evening. Everybody came up to me and all that kind of stuff. Just because I came first in the class, I was the "brain" for the evening.*

Nor is the peer group isolated from the world of the adults. In fact, as we have observed, the peer group is almost completely under the observation of the community at large; and the family, in various ways, literally participates in its activities.

There are, of course, certain behaviour patterns distinctive of the peer group—the adolescents have their own dress and language styles; they have characteristic dating patterns; they "kid around"; they explore in the area of heterosexual relations; some collect popular records. However, it is evident that the adolescents are quite sophisticated about such peer group behaviour, and the parents, by tolerantly and flexibly accepting such activities, often manage to guide and relate them to the very goals they have for their children. Thus, in the context of Suburban Town, the youth culture of the peer group neither indicates discontinuity nor the rejection of the adult world.

CONCLUSION

Current writers continue to view adolescence of the middle-class child as a period of tension, distinct from childhood and adulthood. They likewise see a link between the needs of the adolescent for emancipation and the youth culture of the peer group. The adolescent, in becoming emancipated from the family, is said to participate in a conformity-demanding group of his peers, and this participation serves to balance his needs for independence and security.

The reported research asks to what extent this picture is true of adolescents in an upper-middle-class suburb of Montreal. The data suggest that it is not true. In Suburban Town, the adolescent does not manifestly experience much storm and stress, and the peer group serves to reinforce rather than oppose parental values.

In summary, the adolescents live in a protective environment: their lives are in full view of the adults; their world is relatively consistent and integrated; and they have little direct acquaintance with other patterns of thought and behaviour. In this environment, the adolescents, by the ages of 14 and 15, have already well internalized the ideals and values of the surrounding adult society. The adolescents appreciate the keen interest of the parents in their activities and feel that their parents are working in their behalf; they are in close agreement with their parents on general career and marriage goals and the manner in which these goals are to be achieved; they recognize the value of the parental attitudes towards financial matters and the specific training they receive in saving and handling allowances; they do not reject adult values or participate in an anti-adult "youth culture"; and they tend to look at their distinctive adolescent activities from a relatively sophisticated and integrated point of view.

Thus, the life of the adolescents in such an environment is both objectively and subjectively a period in continuity with the succeeding phase of life; it is the patterns of continuity in socialization which are dominant and striking rather than the patterns of discontinuity.

Teen-Age Culture: An Overview

JESSIE BERNARD

The 1961 teen-agers were born between 1942 and 1948. They are, therefore, the war babies and the postwar babies, the advance guard of the great baby boom. Many are atomic-age youngsters, born after Hiroshima and Nagasaki.

There were an estimated 19 million teen-agers in 1959.[1] About one seventh of them were nonwhite, mostly Negro. Most of them, over 57 per cent, lived in cities; only about 21 per cent lived on farms. The others, about 22 per cent, lived in rural nonfarm communities.

CHRONOLOGICAL AND CULTURAL TEEN-AGE

Not all teen-agers participate in the teen-age culture. Those who are in the civilian labor force (4,419,000 in January 1961), who are in the armed services (about 904,000), or who are married (about 1,206,000 in 1959)—something like 6½ million all told—are chronologically, but not necessarily culturally, teen-agers. They are neophytes in the adult culture of our society. They may share some aspects of teen-age culture, but, for the most part, they are expected to perform adult roles in adult dress. Teen-age culture is essentially the culture of a leisure class.

Reprinted by permission of the author and of the editor from *The Annals of the American Academy of Political and Social Science*, Vol. 338 (November, 1961), 1–12.

Class Selectivity by Age

The figures just given are important because they reflect a class selectivity in teen-age culture by age. Youngsters of lower socioeconomic classes are in the teen-age culture only in their early teens. They are more likely than children of higher socioeconomic class to enter the labor force or the armed forces or to get married soon after high school and, thus, to disappear into the adult world. This exit from the teen-age world by youngsters of lower class background means that those who remain are disproportionately from the higher socioeconomic class background.

TABLE 1. Proportion of Teen-Agers in School by Sex, 1959

	14–15 Years of Age	16–17 Years of Age	18–19 Years of Age
Males	97.8%	84.8%	45.6%
Females	97.0%	81.0%	29.2%

The drastic nature of this class selectivity by age in teen-age culture can be seen in the proportions of the several age groupings that are in school and, hence, able to participate in it. In 1959 the proportions of teen-agers still in school were as shown in Table 1.

Practically all children, then, regardless of class, are in the teen-age culture of the younger years; less than half are in the teen-age culture of the later teens. By and large, therefore, the teen-age culture of the younger years is more colored by lower socioeconomic class standards; that of the later years, by higher. And, as contrasted with, let us say, thirty years ago, the lower socioeconomic classes are of increasing importance.[2] It should be noted, also, that later teen-age culture is predominantly a male phenomenon. The teen-age culture of the early teens is, therefore, a lower-middle class phenomenon, in which girls are equally involved with boys; that of the later teens is an upper-middle class phenomenon, in which young men outnumber young women by about half. The differences are mainly in matters of taste. Money is required in both lower and higher class teen-age cultures. The differences arise in the ways the money is spent.

A PRODUCT OF AFFLUENCE

Our teen-age culture—in contradistinction to the teen-age culture of the past or of other societies—is a product of affluence. It is possible because our society can afford a large leisure class of youngsters not in the labor force but yet consumers on a vast scale, or, if in the labor force, free to spend their earnings on themselves.[3] And they spend it primarily on clothes, cosmetics,[4] recreational paraphernalia, records, cars, travel, and other leisure class goods and services.[5]

Material Aspects

Clothes are an important part of teen-age culture. Industry first discovered the profitable teen-age consuming market in this area. Clothes were once sized and styled very simply—little-girl dresses, for example, until about age thirteen or fourteen and misses' and women's thereafter. The common lament of mothers and their teen-age daughters was that there was nothing suitable for the in-between age—once called the awkward age—when the girl was no longer a child but not yet a woman. Once industry discovered this market, the teen-age girl became one of the most catered-to segments of the buying public. Deb, sub-deb, sub-teen, and scores of other categories were developed, sized, and styled—by the most talented designers—for her. Her figure, not that of the mature woman, became the norm of fashion. An analogous development occurred for boys, who once jumped from knickers to long trousers in one dramatic leap. "Ivy league" is now as important in clothes for teen-age boys as Jonathan Logan is for girls. Leather jackets and chinos are equally standard for the younger or lower socioeconomic class boys.

The importance of clothes in teen-age culture in the case of girls is illustrated by the following document:

A girl should dress as the other girls do but with just a a touch of individuality. If she is considered a good dresser, she wears labels. Her dresses are Lanz or Jonathan Logan. She wears shoes by Capezio for people who dare to be different. Her skirts are Pendleton and the right length and the sweaters to match are Garland. Her coat is a Lassie, and no good dresser uses any make-up but the current fad which usually alternates between Revlon and Coty. All of these labels show (1) that she has money, (2) that she is allowed to spend it on her choices, and (3) that those choices are ones of quality.

The automobile is another basic trait in the material culture of teen-agers. It is taken for granted that every teen-ager will learn to drive and that, if he does not have a car of his own, individually or as member of a group, he will certainly have access to one. In one community, a car-dealer takes it for granted that when a boy reaches the age of sixteen he will be in the market for a used car. There were some 1½ million cars owned by teen-agers in 1960. The number of licensed drivers was, of course, much greater—some 5.9 million in 1958, or 7.2 per cent of all drivers—and they did 5 per cent of all driving done.[6] The psychological and social problem aspects of the automobile are important but do not concern us here; the cultural aspect, however, is interesting and relevant:[7]

. . . automobiles have become a factor of great importance in adolescent culture. For example, in many cities it is an accepted pattern that in order to date a girl, a boy must be able to provide a car for transportation; she may not go in a cab or allow herself and her date to be driven by parents. To many boys the car itself becomes a dominant motivating force. Having acquired a car for transportation, socialization, and dating, a boy becomes so involved in its care and upkeep he has little time or interest left for other activities. . . . "For many, the clubhouse on wheels is a medium for holding a party. . . ."

Popular records—$75,000,000 worth annually—constitute another important trait in teen-age culture; the contents will be analyzed below. Bongo drums, athletic equipment, high fidelity phonographs, travel, camping are other elements which loom large in the material aspect of teen-age culture.

To get these clothes, cars, bongo drums, record players, and cosmetics to the teen-agers, an enormous market has developed. It amounted to an estimated $10 billion in 1959 and was expected to reach twice that amount by 1970.[8] The girls in this market have been called the "teen tycoons," the "more groups":[9]

They do and feel more *than anybody else. They eat* more. . . . *They wear* more—*high school and college girls buy 889 million dollars worth of clothes in the 60-day back-to-school period. They give* more *parties—at least once a month 7½ million girls get together for some kind of social event and spend over 432 million dollars a year on party foods. . . . These girls are a power to reckon with.*

". . . a power to reckon with"

The existence of this great leisure class with so much buying power at its disposal has had profound repercussions on the relationships between teen-agers and the adult world. They have had to be catered to. The values of teen-age culture become a matter of concern to the advertising industry. What teen-agers like and want, what they think is important. As contrasted with the traditional agencies charged with socializing youngsters, the advertisers and the mass media flatter and cajole. They seek to create desires in order to satisfy, rather than, as the parent, teacher, or minister must often do, to discipline, restrict, or deny them. The advertiser is, thus, on the side of the teen-ager. "The things bought are determined by what the child wants rather than by what the parents want for him."[10] Coffee is encouraged, as is smoking, if not—as yet—drinking. In fact, the rebound of the cigarette industry after the first cancer scare in the 1960's has been attributed to a big increase in teen-age smokers.[11] The teen-age press—to be commented on in greater detail below—reflects values and standards which teen-agers select for themselves, rather than those selected for them. They have the money to call the tune; they are "patrons" of the arts and must, therefore, be catered to.

The coalition of advertisers and teen-agers is, thus, buttressed not only by psychological props but also by economic ones. For, "if parents have any idea of organized revolt, it is already too late. Teen-age spending is so important that such action would send quivers through the entire national economy."[12] Many parents feel that they are dealing with a piper who, though never pied, nevertheless draws children after him. The teen-ager's "relentless consumption"—to use Keynes' phrase—is essential to the economy, and it is they who direct it, not their parents.

NONMATERIAL TRAITS

The language of teen-agers serves to maintain barriers between them and the outside world. This language may vary from community to community and from class to class. The following expressions were current on one campus in 1961: "clod," a person who is socially unacceptable by real collegiates; "tweedy," fashionably dressed; "tweeded down," dressed up; "rough and tough," well-accepted individual; "whip," to transport one's self; "roomy," roommate; "wheels," a car; "zowies," happy surprises; "tough dresser," a stunning dresser; "mickey mouse," anything easy, as a college course.

The values and preoccupations of teen-age culture may be discovered by analyzing those aspects of the mass media beamed directly to them: teen-age periodicals and popular records.[13] The "tribal customs" of teen-age culture can best be observed in the teen-age hangout.

Teen-agers constitute an important set of publics as well as of markets. Children who used to have a hard time coming by pennies now have quarters and half dollars to spend on a bewildering variety of periodicals beamed primarily at them. These range from highly technical magazines for hot rod and railroad buffs all the way to lonely-hearts-type magazines for shy little girls. Photography, sports, athletics, as well, of course, as pornography, have their publics also. The teen-type magazine, characterized usually by the term "teen" in its title, reveals the major positive—fun and popularity—and negative—overweight or underweight and adolescent acne—values of its readers. How to be attractive in order to be popular in order to have fun is the major burden of their contents. The teen-type magazine differs from its slick counterparts—*Seventeen* and *Mademoiselle*, for example—in a way analogous to the way true-story magazines for adult women differ from the service-type women's magazines. The class background of these differing publics is revealed in the relative sophistication of the contents as well as in the nature of the advertising. The values, however, are the same in both class levels—beauty, fun, popularity.

Popular songs, almost exclusively a teen-age cultural trait, have been subjected to content analysis by several researchers. One author finds that they fit neatly into what he calls the drama of courtship. There is a Prologue which emphasizes wishing and dreaming. Act I deals with courtship, and songs in this category constitute about a third of all popular songs. Five scenes deal respectively with: direct approach, sentimental appeal, desperation, questions and promises, impatience and surrender. Act II, contributing about 8 per cent of all lyrics, is on the honeymoon. The downward course of love, including about 14.5 per cent of the songs, is depicted in four scenes of Act III: temporary separation, hostile forces, threat of leaving, and final parting. Then, alas, Act IV concerns All Alone, about a fourth of the songs, in three scenes: pleading, hopeless love, and new beginnings.[14] He found remarkable similarities wherever he turned for materials, the Hit Parade, lists of Song Hits, Country Song Roundup, or Rhythm and Blues. In all categories, courtship and downward course of love songs accounted for well over half of all songs.

The values of teen-age culture are also reflected in what is rewarded among high school students. Schools differ markedly, but there is great uniformity in one respect: athletic ability is far more rewarded and prized than intellectual ability.[15] James Coleman believes one factor involved is that, when an athlete shows great achievement, the school and the community share the honor; when a bright student shows great achievement, he does it as an individual and he alone shares the honor; he may even be viewed as a rate-buster.[16]

TRIBAL CUSTOMS

Contrary to the pattern of past generations, present-day teen-age boys and girls do not pass through a stage of withdrawal from one another. It has been found that as early as the fifth or sixth grades the sexes are already interested in one another; dating may begin as early as age ten or eleven. This teen-age culture already has a set of sex mores of its own. Kissing games—spin the bottle and post office—are very old; they antedate current teen-age culture by many years. What is new is parental acceptance by many, grudging in some cases, but resigned. Kissing games are supplemented by parking as soon as the boys acquire cars. Along with parking goes the custom of "bushwacking" or "hunting"; peers find the parked cars and flash their headlights on the petting couple.

Group norms may be observed in the hangout, as values can be noted in the mass media. In the early teens, the hangout may be a local malt shop or soda fountain. If the community provides a canteen, it may take the place of a hangout, but it is not the same thing, because it is supervised by adults.

The hangout can be usefully analyzed in terms of the framework of "the establishment," as suggested by Erving Goffman:[17]

> *A social establishment is any place surrounded by fixed barriers to perception in which a particular kind of activity regularly takes place. . . . Any social establishment may be studied profitably from the point of view of impression management. Within the walls of a social establishment we find a team of performers who cooperate to present to an audience a given definition of the situation. This will include the conception of own team and of audience and assumptions concerning the ethos that is to be maintained by rules of politeness and decorum. . . . Among members of the team we find that familiarity prevails, solidarity is likely to develop, and that secrets that could give the show away are shared and kept. A tacit agreement is maintained between performers and audience to act as if a given degree of opposition and of accord existed between them. . . .*

In the teen-age hangout, the "teams" are likely to be the boys on one side and the girls on the other. One study found that going to hangouts—drugstore, fountain bar—almost equalled pleasure-driving in terms of numbers of participants involved.[18]

WORK IN TEEN-AGE CULTURE

The teen-ager participates in the economy primarily as a consumer. It is true that teen-agers work very hard—customizing automobiles, for example, or organizing and soliciting members for fan clubs—and it is conceivable that such work might have a market. But it is usually not marketed and, therefore, not subjected to the discipline of the adult work world. When the teen-ager sells his labor in the market, he is participating in adult culture, not his own.

When he does participate in the labor market, it is likely

to be as a marginal producer, usually in part-time jobs which articulate well with the other demands of teen-age culture and, therefore, do not remove him from it. Certain occupations are characteristically teen-age. The paper route, odd jobs such as cutting lawns and shoveling snow, and baby sitting are standard teen-age jobs. Between high school and college, summer jobs may be in the adult world and constitute a first introduction to its demands. Some kinds of jobs at supermarkets are sometimes reserved for teen-agers. But, for many teen-agers, the typical job is at a summer camp or resort; and most of these articulate well with the other demands of teen-age culture and, therefore, do not remove the worker from its impact.[19]

THE POLITICAL VALUES

Teen-age culture provides for an absorbing way of life. It is fairly well insulated against outside forces except those beamed directly at it. One of the commonest characteristics of American teen-agers, in fact, has been that, in alleged contrast to those of some other societies, they are politically apathetic. Interest in politics is not an integral part of teen-age culture.[20]

When pressed for opinions on political questions by adults, however, teen-agers reply in ways which reflect, as clearly as other aspects of their culture, a distinct class bias. Polls of high school students during the 1940's and 1950's with respect to political opinions and attitude corroborate with almost uncanny accuracy the conclusion which Seymour Lipset arrived at after analyzing adult voting behavior.[21] With respect to government control, that is, lower class teen-agers are more likely than upper class teen-agers to be "liberal"; but, with respect to civil liberties and race relations, they are more likely to be reactionary (see Table 2).

CLASS AND TEEN-AGE CULTURE

Hollingshead reported more than a decade ago on the pervasiveness of class in high schools in the 1940's.[22] Teen-age society is still stratified and class still pervades teen-age culture. By and large, the cleavage still divides high school

Table 2. Teen-Age Political Opinion Related to Socioeconomic Class

Issue	Per Cent Upper Income Group Teen-agers	Per Cent Lower Income Group Teen-agers
Civil Liberties and Race Relations		
Democratic institutions depend on free business enterprise	64%	54%
Democratic institutions depend on freedom of the press	47	42
Unwarranted search and seizure is permissible	11	26
Third degree is permissible to gain criminal confessions	53	59
Taking the Fifth Amendment is acceptable	28	39
Wire tapping is not acceptable	37	29
School desegregation is approved	46	38
Disturbances and pupil strikes to prevent desegregation are disapproved	70	50
Government Control of Economy and Private Ownership		
Government should have control of railroads and airlines	11	26
Basic industries should be owned by government	14	21
Large unused estates should be divided among the poor for farming	48	63
Slum clearance should be privately controlled	18	16
Private ownership and/or control is advocated for:		
Peaceful uses of atomic energy	25	13
Electric power from rivers and dams	26	18
Electric power from steam plants	55	38
Oil resources	53	49
Nativism		
Immigration should be restricted	35	42
Foreign countries have little to contribute to American progress	10	19

Source: H. H. Remmers and D. H. Radler, *The American Teenager* (Indianapolis: Bobbs-Merrill, 1957), pp. 208 ff.

students into the college preparatory or academic students and the vocational or commercial students. All aspects of teen-age culture—like political attitudes referred to above—differ for the different classes—taste in moving pictures and dress, hangouts, dancing, and dating practices. The ideal-typical girl is different. The following reports document these differences.

Class and Moving Pictures in Teen-age Culture

My town had three movies, two of which showed grade A movies while the third showed grade F—cowboy and horror movies. Two different classes of boys and girls attended these features. In the grade F theater one would find the "cats" of the town, mostly boys. Conduct in this movie could be characterized by whistling, throwing empty candy boxes, and placing feet on chairs. Loud conversations also could be heard.

In the grade A movie houses one usually saw the girls and boys of middle class families. Of course, while these individuals did not attend the horror shows in the other theater, once in a while the "other element" would attend the better movies. Personal conduct in the grade A movies was opposite to that in the grade F movies—no throwing boxes, placing of feet on chairs, engaging in loud conversations. Once in a while the boys might whistle, though.

Class and Dress

From my experience, I've found that the clothes a boy wears definitely elevate or lower his social status. When a boy dresses in the current fashion, it shows that he knows what's going on and is not "out of it." On first impression, a boy is rated on his appearance—either tweedy or cloddy, as the case may be.

To rate well socially, a boy should look as tweedy as possible. This means wearing tan raincoats, crew-neck sweaters, button-down oxford cloth shirts, khaki, corduroy or flannel pants, and loafers or sneakers. Not only must he wear these clothes, but he must choose the correct style in each. Sweaters should be in neutral or dark shades, shirts are white, blue, or pinstriped, and the pants are continental or at least tapered and slim in the legs.

A boy may be considered a clod if he wears flannel or non-button-down shirts, baggy pants or deviates from the traditional crew-neck style sweaters. Shoes with laces (oxfords) worn with casual clothes are also in poor taste.

A girl may also be socially rated as to the clothes she wears. Girls dress to look tweedy or collegiate. Tweedy girls wear button-down blouses or round or pilgrim collar blouses, pleated, bandstand, or flared skirts, wool crew-neck or fur-blend sweaters, knee socks and loafers. . . . Girls should beware of rayon-type or felt skirts which are too long, wing collar blouses, banlon sweaters, and low socks. Sneakers are being replaced by loafers in the really "in" groups. The goal is to look simple, the characteristic of tweediness. Most of the kids I know feel that sharp clothes indicate a hip personality.

Class and Hangouts

In my town of 20,000 people, there were two main hangout for the teen-agers. The YMCA recreation room was a place where one could snack, watch TV, play ping pong, and dance to juke box music. But it was more of a canteen, I guess, than a real hangout. It was considered a nice place for the kids to go. Most of the girls and boys would usually drop in after school for an hour or two in the evening. Since the canteen was a part of the Y, it was considered quite respectable.

Another gathering place for the students was a little drug store. The boys and girls who frequented this particular drug store were the smokers and drinking set of the school. They were considered to be off-limits by the more respectable students. Perhaps not strictly off-limits—one could talk to them, but, on the other hand, interdating would not occur. This element of our town, while they did attend the Y-teen dances, also had their own little restaurant dancing spot where they would go on weekdays and week ends. It was not considered such a good place to go. One needed transportation to get to this second hangout.

Class and the Ideal-Typical Girl

The girls who are high school cheerleaders and those who are high school majorettes differ markedly in background, appearance, and personality. The cheerleader is typically an academic student preparing for college and representing the middle and upper class. . . . She is a clean-cut, all-American girl. . . . She is not made up nor does she wear her hair in anything but a simple, classic, schoolgirl hairdo. . . . She is a breathing replica of a Seventeen *model. . . . She belongs to the right clubs and dates a football hero or the student body president. She is in the know but not conceited about her position. . . . As a rule she doesn't associate with the majorettes.*

The majorettes, who lead the band, seldom lead the school. They are usually commercial students who are planning to be secretaries. Most of them are from lower middle or upper lower classes. Their attitude toward school is poor and, as a result, their grades are low. Or, if their grades are good, they are discounted by the fact that they are in a commercial curriculum.

The twirlers are opposite in appearance, also, to the cheerleaders. They are pretty but in a gaudy way. Their hairdos and make-up are overdone and in poor taste, and they wear tight and often suggestive clothing that suggests cheapness. As a rule, they are not the popular girls nor do they try to be. Often being a majorette is their only activity. . . .

Because the cheering squad was so selective and enviable, many very capable girls who qualified were disappointed each year because they failed to make it. A group of these girls, who wanted to be in on things at school knew that they couldn't make cheering yet wouldn't settle for being a majorette. They began to organize a marching squad which would be chosen on the same criteria as the cheering squad except that these girls would do precision drills with the band. At first their group was small and only performed at talent shows and the like. But it soon became a part of pep rallies. . . . These girls formed their own in-group and at last have status almost equal to the cheerleaders and far above the majorettes.

Related to these class distinctions is the existence of alienation among teen-agers. There are the clods, the outs. And they constitute a sizeable proportion of the high school population. One study, for example, found that there were 22 per cent who felt left out of things, 11 per cent who felt "different," 44 per cent who seldom had dates, 13 per cent who felt they were not wanted, 20 per cent who felt lonesome, and 25 per cent who felt ill at ease at social affairs.[23] This alienation occurred in all classes, but it was more common in teen-agers with low income backgrounds than it was in those with high income backgrounds.

THE COLLEGE LEVEL

Up to now, the class selective factor has operated to weed out teen-agers with lower class backgrounds from the older teen-age culture, leaving the upper middle class teen-agers as bearers of teen-age culture at the college level. Typically, it took the form of the so-called "rah-rah" culture.

Today, however, many young people from lower socio-economic class background also go to colleges and universities. Some are absorbed into the collegiate culture. But many others have a strong vocational orientation. They do not participate in the old collegiate culture; they are preparing for adult roles. And even students from upper class backgrounds now find that they must take higher education more seriously. The tendency is, therefore, for teen-age culture to end with high school for an increasing number of young people. The forces at work making for this result have been analyzed by Clark and Trow, whose findings we follow here.

They distinguish four models of student cultures, namely: collegiate, vocational, academic, and nonconformist.

The collegiate culture is the world of football, Greek letter societies, cars, and drinking. Courses and professors occupy a dim background position. This culture is not hostile to the college; it is only indifferent and resistant to serious demands and involvement in intellectual activities. "This culture is characteristically middle and upper middle class—it takes money and leisure to pursue the busy round of social activities—and flourishes on, though is by no means confined to, the resident campuses of big state universities."[24]

The vocational culture tends to prevail in urban colleges and universities attended by the children of lower middle class families. Because many of these students are married and working hard, their culture is not teen-age in character. They are customers not in a luxury market but in a diploma market. "They buy their education somewhat as one buys groceries," to use an idea of Riesman and Jencks. "If the symbol of the collegiate culture is the football and fraternity weekend, the symbol of this vocationally oriented culture is the student placement office."[25]

The academic culture has learning and knowledge and ideas as a central set of values. "The distinctive qualities of this group are (a) they are seriously involved in their course work beyond the minimum required for passing and graduation and (b) they identify themselves with their college and its faculty."[26] No more than the vocational culture, therefore, is this one teen-age in its essential characteristics.

The nonconformist culture belongs to the intellectual, radical, alienated Bohemian. The authors who distinguish it concede that it is elusive, that it may be merely a residual category, difficult to distinguish from the academic culture. "The academic cultures we speak of include students with intellectual interests as well as grinds submissive to the demands of the faculty. When students' intellectual interests are not merely independent of but also at odds with the curriculum, they often form the nucleus of what we have called 'non-conformist' cultures, which however also include styles and interests that are by no means intellectual. In our typology, the members of the academic subcultures tend to link their interests to the curriculum; the non-conformist pursue theirs outside it."[27]

It is the conclusion of Clark and Trow that, because of the career demands in large bureaucratic organizations whose hiring staffs scrutinize transcripts and evaluate grades, the characteristically teen-age or collegiate culture is now on the decline. As more and more children of lower middle class background go to college and as the demands of society call for greater training, the vocational and academic cultures wax. "Both the vocational and the academic orientations are 'adult' in a way that the collegiate culture is not."[28]

ETHNICITY AND RACE

Our discussion so far has emphasized class and age differences in teen-age culture. Ethnicity and race are also significant factors, closely related to class. The child of the recent immigrant is pulled between the ethnic culture of his family, which is separatist in effect, and the teen-age culture of his peers. After two or three generations, the ethnic factor all but disappears. Not so the racial factor. The Negro teen-ager is in many ways an even newer phenomenon than the white teen-ager today. It is only very recently that a substantial middle class could afford to keep children in high school, let alone college. The upper level teen-age Negro finds himself caught in two intersecting cultures. The clash is between the traditional values professed by American society which he now studies in school and the discriminating culture he still sees in operation around him. In 1960 the Negro college student decided to do something about it.

CONCLUSION

This overview of teen-age culture is presented as an introduction to the papers which follow. They will develop in greater depth the meaning and significance of the several facets of teen-age culture. No forecast of future trends is attempted. The whole phenomenon of teen-age culture may be moving down, so far as age is concerned. As the collegiate culture of the eighteen- and nineteen-year-olds wanes, we note that entrance into teen-age culture occurs at an earlier age than in the past—cosmetics and brassieres at younger ages, for example, as well as dating. Teen-age culture may come to refer to those in the ten to eighteen age bracket rather than to those in the thirteen to twenty age bracket.

But so long as our society can afford a large leisure class, profitable to exploit, teen-age culture will continue. The specific contents, it may safely be predicted, will certainly change. And in 1981 many of the current teen-age generation will be bragging of their pioneer experiences in the Peace Corps and be clicking their lips in disapproval and harking back nostalgically to the good old days of the 1960's when the songs and dances were so much more attractive than those of today.

Athletics in High School

JAMES S. COLEMAN

The role of interscholastic athletics in high schools is a controversial one. Athletics is castigated as the antithesis of scholastic activity by intellectuals—many of whom have never taken part in interscholastic sports. It is defended and praised as the builder of men by coaches and athletes—most of whom have a vested interest in this proposition.

It is characteristic of athletics to provoke violent and lasting controversies, for it occupies a very special position in high schools. The amount of attention devoted to athletics would be most striking to an innocent visitor to a high school. A visitor entering a school would likely be confronted, first of all, with a trophy case. His examination of the trophies would reveal a curious fact: The gold and silver cups, with rare exception, symbolize victory in athletic contests, not scholastic ones. The figures adorning these trophies represent men passing footballs, shooting basketballs, holding out batons; they are not replicas of "The Thinker." The concrete symbols of victory are old footballs, basketballs, and baseballs, not works of art or first editions of books won as literary prizes. Altogether, the trophy case would suggest to the innocent visitor that he was entering an athletic club, not an educational institution.

Walking further, this visitor would encounter teen-agers bursting from classrooms. Listening to their conversations, he would hear both casual and serious discussions of the Friday football game, confirming his initial impression. At-

Reprinted by permission of the author and of the editor from *The Annals of the American Academy of Political and Social Science*, Vol. 338 (November, 1961), 33–43.

tending a school assembly that morning, he would probably find a large segment of the program devoted to a practice of school yells for the athletic game and the announcement of a pep rally before the game. At lunch hour, he would be likely to find more boys shooting baskets in the gymnasium than reading in the library. Browsing through a school yearbook, he would be impressed, in his innocence, with the number of pages devoted to athletics.

Altogether, this visitor would find, wherever he turned, a great deal of attention devoted to athletics. As an impressionable stranger, this visitor might well suppose that more attention is paid to athletics by teen-agers, both as athletes and as spectators, than to scholastic matters. He might even conclude, with good reason, that the school was essentially organized around athletic contests and that scholastic matters were of lesser importance to all involved.

To be sure, his impression would vary from school to school—but, perhaps surprising to him, it would vary little by the social origins and destinations of the adolescents served by the schools. In ten schools recently studied by the author, athletics was about as dominant, by any of several criteria, in middle class schools with a high proportion of their graduates going to college as in working class schools.[1]

Considering his impressions, such a visitor to American high schools might ask himself two questions: First of all, why is it this way? He had assumed, naively, that schools were for learning, yet his impressions led to a different conclusion. He had talked with educators about curriculum, new academic programs, and scholastic standards. Yet, upon visiting the schools, he found the adolescents' attention on athletics, and all the excitement and enthusiasm he found was focused around athletic contests. Why the discrepancy?

The visitor might ask another question: What are the consequences of the attention devoted to athletics? What are the consequences within the school itself, and what are the long-term consequencies for these adolescents when they have become adults?

It is to these two questions, the question of consequences and the question of sources, that this paper is directed. The examination will be based upon evidence collected during a study of ten high schools in 1957–1958. These high schools were located in the Middle West. Five were small-town schools with 500 or fewer students; one was a parochial school of 750 boys in a large city; there was a working class, suburban school of 1,000 students; two small-city comprehensive schools were included of 1,400 and 2,000 students respectively; there was an upper middle class, suburban school of 2,000 students. Unless otherwise noted, the generalizations mentioned below apply to all schools.[2] In fact, a striking discovery in this study was the similarity of all schools in the importance attached to athletics. Greater similarity among schools was found in this than in any other dimension of the research.

CONSEQUENCES

The more difficult question concerns the long-term consequences of attention to athletics. On this question, the study has no evidence, since adolescents were studied only during one year in high school, and there seems to be no systematic evidence on the matter available elsewhere. However, evidence from the research does show some of the short-term consequences, those manifest in the school itself.

Impact on Freshmen

The attention focused upon athletics in high schools directly affects the impact of the schools upon their incoming freshmen. Football, which is played in the fall as school begins, is especially important. A major element in the impact of athletics is the visibility of athletic stars. A boy who achieves something, however creditable his achievement, can be a model to emulate only if that achievement is made visible by the structure of activities in the school.

Some idea of the relative visibility of scholastic achievement and athletic achievement can be gained through a finding from the survey of the ten schools. About six weeks after school opened in the fall, each boy in every school was asked to name the boy whom he saw as the best student in his grade and the boy who was the best athlete. This can be a difficult task for freshmen, but it is less difficult in those areas for which school activities focus attention on achievement. Thus, a comparison of the proportions of boys able to answer the questions provides some guide to the relative visibility of scholastic and athletic achievements in each of the four years of school.

Table 1 shows this comparison. The data indicate, in general, that the best athletes are more visible than the best scholars. The difference is greatest for the freshmen—the best athlete is known 10 per cent more often than the best scholar in the small schools and 14 per cent more often in the large schools. Only in the junior and senior years does the visibility of the best scholars catch up with that of the best athletes. Thus, for the impressionable freshmen, the achievements that stand out most are those of the athlete, not those of the scholar.[3]

Assuming adolescents desire to be successful, known, and recognized, one consequence of the visibility of achievement

TABLE 1. Comparative Visibility of Best Athletes and Best Scholars to Their Classmates

	Freshmen	Sophomores	Juniors	Seniors
Small Schools				
Per cent naming best athlete	68%	75%	88%	85%
Per cent naming best scholar	58%	66%	83%	88%
Number of cases	317	292	214	205
Large Schools				
Per cent naming best athlete	54%	56%	48%	72%
Per cent naming best scholar	40%	47%	57%	68%
Number of cases	635	1,049	749	557

Note: Percentages are based on the nine public schools.

in athletics or scholarship would be the desire to achieve in these particular areas. Does the environment and climate of opinion in the school affect these desires? Boys were asked, in the fall shortly after school had started and again in the spring toward the end of the school year, how they would most like to be remembered at school—as a brilliant student, an athletic star, or most popular. One would suppose, if schools focus attention on scholastic endeavors, that the effect of the school year would be to increase the strength of the brilliant-student image relative to that of the athletic-star image. Yet, for the freshmen and sophomores of the schools surveyed, matters are quite different. Of all those responding either "brilliant student" or "athletic star," 44 per cent in each grade responded "brilliant student" in the fall and only 37 per cent gave this response in the spring.[4] Rather than increasing in strength over the school year, the brilliant-student image declined in strength relative to that of the athlete. It appears, then, that the very functioning of the school itself tends to reduce the initial interest of the adolescent in being seen as a brilliant student, or tends differentially to increase his interest in being seen as an athletic star.

Another effect of athletics upon the incoming freshmen concerns the "leading crowd" in school. Most high schools, other than the very smallest, have a leading crowd in each grade, though schools larger than about 2,000 in enrollment may have more than one. This crowd is recognized by other students and by its own members, and most students can name members of the leading crowd in their grade. This, in fact, was what they were asked to do in the research discussed above. In addition, all boys were asked to name their friends, so that it was possible to reconstruct the actual crowds or cliques in the school. Then, by identifying which of the cliques had as members boys frequently named as members of the leading crowd, it was possible to identify objectively the leading clique or crowd in each grade of each school. Having done this, the question then was asked: What do these boys, who constitute the leading crowds in their grades, have in common?[5]

Among the freshmen in each of the four schools studied for leading cliques, the one attribute shared by every boy in every leading clique—twenty-three boys in all—was being out for either football or basketball. Most of the twenty-three were out for both. No other attribute—in background, activities, or attitudes—so sharply distinguished the leading cliques. In the later years of school, the leading cliques were found to be less uniformly athletic, but, among freshmen, they were found to be totally so.

Athletic participation as a basis for membership in the leading clique is not, of course, characteristic of every freshman class in the country, but it seems likely that the general tendency is widespread. Athletic teams provide a basis for intensive and prolonged association, more than any other activity in school. Thus, the foundation is laid, from the very beginning of high school, for a cohesive, tightly knit group.

This, together with the attention directed toward athletic contests and athletic stars in high school, makes it very likely that the athletes will constitute the leading crowd among freshmen. Later, when other activities develop in school and groups form on other bases, there is less dominance of the athletic crowd. But, in the crucial first year, when a boy's aims and aspirations in high school are established, the athletic crowd dominates.

Altogether, then, athletics is a particularly important factor in the impact of the high school upon its freshmen. Through the several mechanisms discussed above, the freshmen get a picture of the school focused even more toward athletic achievement than it actually is.

Athletics in the Status System

One of the most important aspects of any social system is its distribution of status: the way status attaches to different persons and to different activities. The importance of the distribution of status lies partly in its effect as a motivating device, for it motivates people toward those activities which confer status upon them. To the extent that adolescents are concerned with status among their peers—and every indication suggests that the great majority of them are so motivated—their motivations and aspirations in various activities are shaped by the distribution of status.

It is important, then, in assessing the consequences of the attention to athletics in high schools, to examine the position of athletics in the adolescent status system. In the present research, this was done by several means.

Each boy was asked to assess what was required in his school to be a member of the leading crowd, and he was asked to rank various attributes for making a boy popular.

In response to the first question, the two attributes most often mentioned were personality—mentioned by 23 per cent of the boys—and a good reputation—mentioned by 17 per cent. Next in order, however, was athletic ability—mentioned by 16 per cent. This was followed by good looks and success with girls—mentioned by 14 per cent—and good grades or "brains"—mentioned by 12 per cent.

In ranking attributes for their effect in making a boy popular, six attributes were available to be ranked from first to sixth. These attributes, with their average rank in all schools, were the following:[6]

Being an athletic star	2.2
Being in the leading crowd	2.6
Leader in activities	2.9
High grades, honor roll	3.5
Having a nice car	3.9
Coming from the right family	4.5

TABLE 2. Average Numbers of Choices Received by Athletes, Scholars, and All Other Boys on Status Criteria

	Be Friends with or Be Like	Member of Leading Crowd	Number of Cases
Athletes	5.6	7.8	272
Scholars	3.4	4.9	278
All Other Boys	0.4	0.8	3,598

Note: "Athletes" and "scholars" are those named two or more times as best athlete or best scholar in their respective grades by other boys. Percentages are based on the nine public schools.

These answers show the great value that boys attribute to athletic achievement in gaining popularity. It is ranked considerably above any other item and far above good grades, which is fourth among the six.

In addition to these subjective estimates, it is also possible to determine which boys have highest status. In this research, it was done by asking each boy to name another boy he would like to be like, one he would like to be friends with, and who were members of the leading crowd. The status of a boy was determined by the number of such choices he received. Another question had made it possible to identify the boys seen as the best athletes and the best scholars. By comparing the likelihood of the best athletes to receive the status choices with the likelihood of the best scholars to receive such choices, it is possible to examine the objective status of athletic achievement. Table 2 shows the average number of choices on these criteria received by the best athletes, the best scholars, and all other boys in the schools studied.

As in various other tests, athletics scored higher than

scholarship, although both athletes and scholars far outdistanced other boys. Stated another way, the star athletes, only 6.6 per cent of the schools' male enrollment, received 47.4 per cent of the "be friends with" and "be like" choices and 36.5 per cent of all the leading crowd nominations.

According to all evidence, then, the status of athletic achievement in the schools surveyed is exceedingly high, considerably higher than that of scholastic achievement. Thus, the attention paid to athletics in American high schools, which would so puzzle an innocent visitor, is paralleled by the status of athletic achievement among adolescents.

Other Studies

Other research shows that these facts are not limited to the ten schools surveyed nor even to high schools in the Middle West.

In a large, predominantly Jewish, middle class high school in New York City, Abraham Tannenbaum studied evaluations of stereotyped, fictitious students.[7] These fictitious students were distinguished in short descriptive statements on the bases of intelligence, athletic ability, and studiousness. Juniors in the high school were then asked to ascribe traits—some desirable, some undesirable—to each of the eight fictitious characters. Tannenbaum devised a mean acceptability rating from the ascribed traits, and the fictitious students fell in the following order of acceptability, from high to low:

1. *Brilliant nonstudious athlete*
2. *Average nonstudious athlete*
3. *Average studious athlete*
4. *Brilliant studious athlete*
5. *Brilliant nonstudious nonathlete*
6. *Average nonstudious nonathlete*
7. *Average studious nonathlete*
8. *Brilliant studious nonathlete*

As the order shows, all athletes had higher acceptability ratings than any nonathlete. Brilliance apparently had little effect in increasing acceptability, and studiousness reduced acceptability. Thus, in a school in which, because of its location and student body, one would expect to find brilliance or studiousness outdistancing athletics, the results are otherwise—and consistent with the results in the ten midwestern high schools.

These data on the status of athletic achievement in schools of widely varying types raise even more insistently the question of why there is such a dominance of athletics. Athletics is wholly outside the focus of attention of many educators in schools of education, for whom curriculum variations have overriding importance. Yet athletics is central to the attention of adolescents, far more so than curriculum variations. And, despite educators' professional disinterest, athletics is an activity promoted by the schools themselves—not an outside interest like cars and dates. These inconsistencies and paradoxes all lead to the question: Why does athletics hold a place of such high importance in the high schools?

Athletics, Democracy, and Legitimacy of the System

The effect of athletics in forming leading crowds among freshmen was examined earlier; the formation of leading crowds among girls was left unexamined. The cliques of girls among freshmen reflect, much more than for boys, associations from earlier grades. Girls who travel together in the lower grades maintain their cliques in high school and often present an impregnable front to outsiders. Presumably as a result, the leading crowds for girls among freshmen are more completely middle class in background than for boys.

In effect, athletics provides for boys an interruption of this pattern, breaking down the organization based on common background and replacing it with organization based on common activity or achievement. Perhaps as a consequence, boys are more willing than girls to accept the status system of the school and view it as more legitimate. When asked to agree or to disagree that "There are a few who control things in this school, and the rest of us are out in the cold," 43 per cent of the girls agreed with the statement in the fall, and the number increased to 48 per cent by the next spring. Only 34 per cent of the boys agreed that the statement was true in the fall, and their number decreased to 32 per cent by spring.

Such a democratizing mechanism is particularly important for boys, who, to begin with, are less involved in school than girls and get poorer grades. If it were not for interscholastic athletics or something like it, the rebellion against school, the rate of dropout, and the delinquency of boys might be far worse than they presently are. This can only be a matter of conjecture. It does seem clear, however, that athletics introduces an important democratizing factor in the status system for boys in high school by undercutting social background as a basis for status.

SOURCES

Clearly, a part of the importance of athletics for adolescents lies in its compatibility with teen-age energy, enthusiasm, and explosive spirits. Were it not for this basic compatibility, the avidity with which teen-agers follow sports contests would be difficult to explain.

But the compatibility does not explain the special place that athletics holds in the activities of a school. As an innocent visitor might observe, the institution itself often seems more oriented toward athletic goals than academic ones. This can hardly be explained by the interests of teen-agers alone, for teen-agers are interested in many things—popular music, cars, dates—which have relatively little place in the high school structure of activities. Nor can the interests of teen-agers explain the fact that, in the ten schools surveyed, the strength of the athletic-star image increased during the school year and, apparently, decreased over the summer.[8]

Athletic contests in schools seem to serve an important function for the institution. Every institution depends for its survival upon capturing a certain portion of the energies of its members. In business organizations, this is done by pay, including incentive pay, and by opportunity for promotion. Among some members of an organization, identification with the achievements of the organization provides additional motivation. In unions, motivation derives from the common goals of the members, which can only be gained through concerted, collective effort.[9]

Schools, however, provide no comparable motivating devices for their students. Students are forced by family and by law to attend school, but this insures only their physical presence, not their involvement in school activities. The necessary motivation for the expenditure of effort in school arises naturally only for those students whose backgrounds and aspirations make good grades important for them. For some students, that is, grades are comparable to pay for workers in a factory. The crucial difference is that grades are important only for a part of the school population. For many adolescents, high school only delays their access to adult freedoms and pleasures and does not offer any unique and necessary benefits.

But, even for students with the right backgrounds, grades are a poor motivating mechanism, because they are unique to the school and useful only in comparison with grades of fellow students. This generates invidious comparisons, sets each student in competition with his fellows, and is a powerfully divisive force among the students. Direct incentive pay, or piece work, in factories produces the same effect and has sometimes been consciously used by employers to keep employees divided against each other.[10]

In the long run, this is a dangerous mechanism, as the history of incentive pay has shown. Under many conditions, it encourages informal norms restricting production—against the "rate-buster"—just as grade systems in high schools promote informal action against too much studiousness—against "the curve-breaker" or the "D.A.R.," Damned Average Raiser. Finally, piece work systems in factories have led to organized collective activity against the companies, unless the workers feel strongly identified with their companies.[11]

A much more successful mechanism of control in an institution is one which generates strong positive identification with the institution. Churches employ such mechanisms with their revival meetings and special holy day services. Associations and groups of all sorts do the same with rallies and collective events. But schools—apart from their athletic contests and similar activities—are peculiar institutions. There are no collective goals which the students share, and the institution is lifeless. There are only individual goals, individual scholastic achievements, made largely at the expense of other students.

Athletic contests with other schools provide, for these otherwise lifeless institutions, the collective goals that they lack. The common goals shared by all makes the institution part of its members and them part of it, rather than an organization outside them and superimposed upon them. The results are evident to any observer: The adolescent social system is centered at the school, not at the drugstore; the name by which the teen-agers identify themselves is that of the school ("Those are East High kids; I'm from Tech."); the teen-agers think of the school, the team, and the student body as one and use the pronoun "we" in referring to this entity ("We're playing Parkville Friday.")

Such effects are evident as well in the bases of alumni loyalty to many private preparatory schools and colleges. Athletic competition as a basis of loyalty is so dominant that the stereotypical alumnus is a man cheering wildly at a football game, waving a school banner in his hand. Colleges which dropped interscholastic athletics, like University of Chicago, or which never depended on them, like Johns Hopkins, thereby sacrificed the attention and support of many alumni.[12] Historians have noted that colleges in the United States, before the introduction of organized sports, were beset by student violence directed at both the college and other students. Sports seemed to transform the disorganized and explosive student body into a close-knit community with strong common goals.

Thus, the importance of athletic contests in both high schools and colleges lies, at least in part, in the way the contests solve a difficult problem for the institution—the problem of generating enthusiasm for and identification with the school and drawing the energies of adolescents into the school.

In the study of the ten high schools upon which much of this paper is based, all students were asked, "If school were not compulsory and it were completely up to you, would you stay in school until graduation, leave school before graduation, or are you undecided?" Very few students, only 3.6 per cent, responded that they would leave, and only 9.3 per cent were undecided. It is hard to imagine that the great body of adolescents in our society which has been brought into high school in such a short period could be so positively oriented to school without some mechanism such as athletic contests for providing common goals.[13]

Lack of Common Community Goals

A force which strengthens the emphasis upon athletics in the high schools comes from outside the schools themselves. Except in the very largest cities, a high school is a community or neighborhood institution. Many communities have only a single high school, whose name is the name of the town. In those cities with several high schools, each school usually represents a community area within the city and often carries the name of that community.

Communities, like schools without interscholastic games, have few common goals. They fight no wars, seldom engage in community rallies, and are rarely faced with such crises as floods or tornadoes that can engender a communal spirit and make members feel close to one another by creating collective goals. One of the few mechanisms by means of which this can occur is that of games or contests between communities. Sometimes these games are between professional teams representing the communities.[14] More often, there are high school games, and these contests serve the purpose admirably. The community supports the team, and the team rewards the community when it wins. The team is a community enterprise, and its successes are shared by the community, its losses mourned in concert.

The results of this are evident in many ways. One striking evidence is teacher salaries. The school board characteristically pays more to athletic coaches than to other teachers and, occasionally, to keep a winning coach, may pay more than to the principal. When a new principal is to be found among the ranks of teachers, the pattern is common for the athletic coach to be promoted to the job.[15]

Another indicator is buildings. It is often easier to obtain funds for a new gymnasium—especially in "basketball territory"—than for other buildings. In Paris, Illinois, for example, where the high school team won the state basketball tournament a few years ago, the community voted funds for a large new gymnasium, while the high school remained without a library. In one of the ten schools included in the survey, the author found, returning in 1961, that a new gymnasium and a new reading room had been built. Funds for the gymnasium had been donated by a member of the community; the reading room had been added by means of school building funds.

SUBSTITUTES FOR ATHLETICS

It is indisputable that the interscholastic sports function to give the school and the community a collective identity.

Few principals would seriously consider dispensing with these games. Yet, it is also indisputable that athletic contests create serious problems for schools. Perhaps the most serious problem is the change they engender in the institution itself. Their very importance to the life of the school transforms the school from an institution devoted to learning into an institution focused, at least partly, on athletics.

It is useful to wonder whether another mechanism might not give the school collective goals without effecting this transformation. Completely to replace athletic contests between schools with something else would possibly have ill effects. To reduce the dominance of athletics in high schools, however, clearly would be desirable. The most obvious course is to keep the game but to change the content in the direction of educational goals. Although it is true that athletics fits especially well with the interests and energies of adolescents, other games could fit equally well.

There is some experience with games and contests other than athletics, the most extensive being with debate. In a number of areas where debate leagues have flourished, these contests have generated some of the same community and school enthusiasm and involvement that is evident with athletic games. In a few states, interscholastic leagues promote competition in other fields than athletics: music, drama, mathematics. Although the effects of these contests have not been adequately evaluated, they do provide examples of what might be done.

There has very recently been another development which promises to make games truly educational in many areas. These are social and economic games which use a complex environment provided by electronic computers. The first to be developed were management games which involve teams of decision-makers representing competing firms. These games have been used by business and are coming to be used in graduate business schools. A political game, with teams representing political candidates in competition for votes, has been programed for a computer and is used in a college course at Johns Hopkins. At least one economic game has been developed—at Washington University in St. Louis—for teaching the course in principles of economics. Experience with these games shows that they generate a high degree of involvement and interest among players and spectators. It is possible that the most valuable use of machines in education will come to be their use for games, rather than programed learning.

These examples indicate that it is possible to change the content of games in an educational direction yet to maintain some of the values athletics provides for school. To do this, however, would require more than sporadic contests. To gain attention and involvement, leagues, schedules, and tournaments would be necessary. Through such means, it might be possible to transform schools back into the educational institutions they were intended to be. An innocent visitor to such an institution, upon examining the trophy case, listening to student conversation, and examining a yearbook, might well conclude that the institution was one devoted to learning.

The Rating and Dating Complex

WILLARD WALLER

Courtship may be defined as the set of processes of association among the unmarried from which, in time, permanent matings usually emerge. This definition excludes those associations which cannot normally eventuate in marriage—as between Negro and white—but allows for a period of dalliance and experimentation. In the present paper we propose to discuss the customs of courtship which prevail among college students.

Courtship practices vary from one culture group to another. In many cultures marriage eventuates from a period of sexual experimentation and trial unions; in others the innocence of the unmarried is carefully guarded until their wedding day. In some cultures the bride must be virginal at

Reprinted by permission of the editor from the *American Sociological Review*, Vol. 2 (October, 1937), 727–734.

marriage; in others this is just what she must not be. Sometimes the young are allowed no liberty of choice, and everything is determined for them by their elders. Sometimes persons marry in their own age group, but in other societies older men pre-empt the young women for themselves. Although there are endless variations in courtship customs, they are always functionally related to the total configuration of the culture and the biological needs of the human animal. It is helpful to remember that in a simple, undifferentiated, and stable society a long and complex process of choosing a mate is apparently not so necessary or desirable as in our own complex, differentiated, and rapidly changing society.[1]

The mores of courtship in our society are a strange composite of social heritages from diverse groups and of new usages called into existence by the needs of the time. There is a formal code of courtship which is still nominally in force, although departures from it are very numerous; the younger generation seems to find the superficial usages connected with the code highly amusing, but it is likely that it takes the central ideas quite seriously. The formal code appears to be derived chiefly from the usages of the English middle classes of a generation or so ago, although there are, of course, many other elements in it.

The usual or intended mode of operation of the formal mores of courtship—in a sense their "function"—is to induct young persons into marriage by a series of progressive commitments. In the solidary peasant community, in the frontier community, among the English middle classes of a few decades back, and in many isolated small communities in present-day America, every step in the courtship process has a customary meaning and constitutes a powerful pressure toward taking the next step—is in fact a sort of implied commitment to take the next step. The mores formerly operated to produce a high rate of marriage at the proper age and at the same time protected most individuals from many of the possible traumatic experiences of the courtship period.

The decay of this moral structure has made possible the emergence of thrill-seeking and exploitative relationships. A thrill is merely a physiological stimulation and release of tension, and it seems curious that most of us are inclined to regard thrill-seeking with disapproval. The disapproving attitude toward thrill-seeking becomes intelligible when we recall the purpose of such emotional stirrings in the conventional mores of courtship. Whether we approve or not, courtship practices today allow for a great deal of pure thrill-seeking. Dancing, petting, necking, the automobile, the amusement park, and a whole range of institutions and practices permit or facilitate thrill-seeking behavior. These practices, which are connected with a great range of the institutions of commercialized recreation, make of courtship an amusement and a release of organic tensions. The value judgment which many lay persons and even some trained sociologists pass upon thrill-seeking arises from the organizational mores of the family—from the fact that energy is dissipated in thrills which is supposed to do the work of the world, i.e., to get people safely married.

The emergence of thrill-seeking furthers the development of exploitative relationships. As long as an association is founded on a frank and admitted barter in thrills, nothing that can be called exploitative arises. But the old mores of progressive commitment exist, along with the new customs, and peculiar relationships arise from this confusion of moralities. According to the old morality a kiss means something, a declaration of love means something, a number of Sunday evening dates in succession means something, and these meanings are enforced by the customary law, while under the new morality such things may mean nothing at all—that is, they may imply no commitment of the total personality whatsoever. So it comes about that one of the persons may exploit the other for thrills on the pretense of emotional involvement and its implied commitment. When a woman exploits, it is usually for the sake of presents and expensive amusements—the common pattern of "gold-digging." The male exploiter usually seeks thrills from the body of the woman. The fact that thrills cost money, usually the man's money, often operates to introduce strong elements of suspicion and antagonism into the relationship.

With this general background in mind, let us turn to the courtship practices of college students. A very important characteristic of the college student is his bourgeois pattern of life. For most persons, the dominant motive of college attendance is the desire to rise to a higher social class; behind this we should see the ideology of American life and the projection of parents' ambitions upon children. The attainment of this life goal necessitates the postponement of marriage, since it is understood that a new household must be economically independent; additional complications sometimes arise from the practice of borrowing money for college expenses. And yet persons in this group feel very strongly the cultural imperative to fall in love and marry and live happily in marriage.

For the average college student, and especially for the man, a love affair which led to immediate marriage would be tragic because of the havoc it would create in his scheme of life. Nevertheless, college students feel strongly the attractions of sex and the thrills of sex, and the sexes associate with one another in a peculiar relationship known as "dating." Dating is not true courtship, since it is supposed not to eventuate in marriage; it is a sort of dalliance relationship. In spite of the strength of the old morality among college students, dating is largely dominated by the quest of the thrill and is regarded as an amusement. The fact that college attendance usually removes the individual from normal courtship association in his home community should be mentioned as a further determinant of the psychological character of dating.

In many colleges, dating takes place under conditions determined by a culture complex which we may call the "rating and dating complex." The following description of this complex on one campus is probably typical of schools of the sort:

X College, a large state-supported school, is located in a small city at a considerable distance from larger urban areas. The school is the only industry of the community. There are few students who live at home, and therefore the interaction of the young is but little influenced by the presence of parents. The students of this college are predominantly taken from the lower half of the middle classes, and constitute a remarkably homogeneous group; numerous censuses of the occupations of fathers and of living expenses seem to establish this fact definitely. Nevertheless, about half of the male students live in fraternities, where the monthly bill is usually forty-five or fifty dollars a month, rarely as high as fifty-five. There is intense competition among the fraternities. The desire for mobility of class, as shown by dozens of inquiries, is almost universal in the group and is the principal verbalized motive for college attendance.

Dating at X College consists of going to college or frater-

nity dances, the movies, college entertainments, and to fraternity houses for victrola dances and "necking"; coeds are permitted in the fraternity parlors, if more than one is present. The high points of the social season are two house parties and certain formal dances. An atypical feature of this campus is the unbalanced sex ratio, for there are about six boys to every girl; this makes necessary the large use of so-called "imports" for the more important occasions, and brings it about that many boys do not date at all or confine their activities to prowling about in small industrial communities nearby; it also gives every coed a relatively high position in the scale of desirability; it would be difficult to say whether it discourages or encourages the formation of permanent attachments. Dating is almost exclusively the privilege of fraternity men, the use of the fraternity parlor and the prestige of fraternity membership being very important. Freshman men are forbidden by student tradition to have dates with coeds.[2]

Within the universe which we have described, competition for dates among both men and women is extremely keen. Like every other process of competition, this one determines a distributive order. There are certain men who are at the top of the social scramble; they may be placed in a hypothetical Class A. There are also certain coeds who are near the top of the scale of dating desirability, and they also are in Class A. The tendency is for Class A men to date principally Class A women. Beneath this class of men and women are as many other classes as one wishes to create for the purposes of analysis. It should be remembered that students on this campus are extremely conscious of these social distinctions and of their own position in the social hierarchy. In speaking of another student, they say, "He rates," or "He does not rate," and they extend themselves enormously in order that they may rate or seem to rate.

Young men are desirable dates according to their rating on the scale of campus values. In order to have Class A rating they must belong to one of the better fraternities, be prominent in activities, have a copious supply of spending money, be well-dressed, "smooth" in manners and appearance, have a "good line," dance well, and have access to an automobile. Members of leading fraternities are especially desirable dates; those who belong to fraternities with less prestige are correspondingly less desirable. I have been able to validate the qualities mentioned as determinants of campus prestige by reference to large numbers of student judges.

The factors which appear to be important for girls are good clothes, a smooth line, ability to dance well, and popularity as a date. The most important of these factors is the last, for the girl's prestige depends upon dating more than anything else; here as nowhere else nothing succeeds like success. Therefore the clever coed contrives to give the impression of being much sought after even if she is not. It has been reported by many observers that a girl who is called to the telephone in the dormitories will often allow herself to be called several times, in order to give all the other girls ample opportunity to hear her paged. Coeds who wish campus prestige must never be available for last minute dates; they must avoid being seen too often with the same boy, in order that others may not be frightened away or discouraged; they must be seen when they go out, and therefore must go to the popular (and expensive) meeting places; they must have many partners at the dances. If they violate the conventions at all, they must do so with great secrecy and discretion; they do not drink in groups or frequent the beer-parlors. Above all, the coed who wishes to retain Class A standing must consistently date Class A men.

Cressey has pointed out that the taxi-dancer has a descending cycle of desirability. As a new girl in the dance hall, she is at first much sought after by the most eligible young men. Soon they tire of her and desert her for some newer recruit. Similarly the coed has a descending cycle of popularity on the campus which we are describing, although her struggle is not invariably a losing one. The new girl, the freshman coed, starts out with a great wave of popularity; during her freshman year she has many dates. Slowly her prestige declines, but in this case only to the point at which she reaches the level which her qualities permanently assure her. Her descent is expedited by such "mistakes," from the viewpoint of campus prestige, as "going steady" with one boy (especially if he is a senior who will not return the following year), by indiscretions, and by too ready availability for dates. Many of the girls insist that after two years of competitive dating they have tired of it and are interested in more permanent associations.

This thrill-dominated, competitive process involves a number of fundamental antagonisms between the men and the women, and the influence of the one sex group accentuates these. Writes one student informant, a girl, "Wary is the only word that I can apply to the attitude of men and women students toward each other. The men, who have been warned so repeatedly against coeds, are always afraid the girls are going to 'gold-dig' them. The coeds wonder to what degree they are discussed and are constantly afraid of being placed on the black list of the fraternities. Then too they wonder to what extent they can take any man seriously without being taken for a 'ride'." Status in the one-sex group depends upon avoiding exploitation by the opposite sex. Verbatim records of a number of fraternity "bull sessions" were obtained a few years ago. In these sessions members are repeatedly warned that they are slipping, those who have fallen are teased without mercy, and others are warned not to be soft. And almost all of the participants pretend a ruthlessness toward the opposite sex which they do not feel.

This competitive dating process often inflicts traumas upon individuals who stand low in the scale of courtship desirability. "While I was at X College," said a thirty year old alumnus, "I had just one date. That was a blind date, arranged for me by a friend. We went to the dorm, and after a while my girl came down and we were introduced. She said, 'Oh, I'm so sorry. I forgot my coat. I'll have to go get it.' She never came down again. Naturally I thought, 'Well what a hit I made!'" We have already seen that nonfraternity men are practically excluded from dating; it remains to note that many girls elect not to date rather than take the dates available to them. One girl writes as follows: "A girl's choice of whom to fall in love with is limited by the censorship of the one-sex group. Every boy that she dates is discussed and criticized by the other members of the group. This rigid control often keeps a girl from dating at all. If a girl is a member of a group in which the other girls are rated higher on the dating scale than she, she is often unable to get dates with boys who are considered desirable by her friends. In that event she has to decide whether to date the boys that she can and choose girl friends who would approve, or she must resign herself to not dating."

Since the class system, or gradient of dating desirability on the campus, is clearly recognized and adjusted to by the students themselves, there are interesting accommodations and rationalizations which appear as a result of inferior status. Although members of Class A may be clearly in the ascendant as regards prestige, certain groups of Class B may contest the position with them and may insist upon a measuring stick which will give them a favorable position. Rationalizations which enable Class D men and women to accept one another are probably never completely effective.

The accommodations and rationalizations worked out by one group of girls who were toward the bottom of the scale of campus desirability are typical. Four of these girls were organized in one tightly compact "bunch." All four lived off campus, and worked for their room and board. They had little money to spend for clothes, so there was extensive borrowing of dresses. Members of the group co-operated in getting dates for one another. All of them accepted eleventh hour invitations, and probably realized that some stigma of inferiority was attached to such ready availability, but they managed to save their faces by seeming very reluctant to accept such engagements, and at length doing so as a result of the persuasion of another member of the bunch. The men apparently saw through these devices, and put these girls down as last minute dates, so that they rarely received any other invitations. The bunch went through "dating cycles" with several fraternities in the course of a year, starting when one of the girls got a date with one member of the fraternity, and ending, apparently, when all the girls had lost their desirability in that fraternity.

Partly as a result of the unbalanced sex ratio, the boys of the group which we are discussing have a widespread feeling of antagonism toward the coeds. This antagonism is apparently based upon the fact that most of the male students are unable to date with coeds, at least not on terms acceptable to themselves. As a result of this, boys take great pride in the "imports" whom they bring in for house parties, and it is regarded as slightly disgraceful in some groups to date a coed for one of the major parties. Other men in the dateless group take on the role of misogynists—and read Schopenhauer.

During the winter term the preponderance of men assures to every coed a relatively high bargaining power. Every summer witnesses a surprising reversal of this situation. Hundreds of women school teachers flock to this school for the summer term, and men are very scarce; smooth, unmarried boys of college age are particularly scarce. The schoolteachers are older than the boys; they have usually lost some of their earlier attractiveness; they have been living for some months or years within the school-teacher role. They are man-hungry, and they have a little money. As a result, there is a great proliferation of highly commercialized relations. The women lend their cars to their men friends, but continue to pay for repairs and gasoline; they take the boys out to dinner, treat them to drinks, and buy expensive presents for them. And many who do not go so far are available for sex relations on terms which demand no more than a transitory sort of commitment from the man.

The rating and dating complex varies enormously from one school to another. In one small, coeducational school, the older coeds instruct the younger that it is all right for them to shop around early in the year, but by November they should settle down and date someone steadily. As a result, a boy who dates a girl once is said to "have a fence around her," and the competition which we have described is considerably hampered in its operation. In other schools, where the sex ratio is about equal, and particularly in the smaller institutions, "going steady" is probably a great deal more common than on the campus described. It should be pointed out that the frustrations and traumas imposed upon unsuccessful candidates by the practice of "going steady" (monopolistic competition) are a great deal easier to bear than those which arise from pure competition. In one school the girls are uniformly of a higher class origin than the boys, so that there is relatively little association between them; the girls go with older men not in college, the boys with high school girls and other "townies." In the school which is not coeducational, the dating customs are vastly different, although, for the women at least, dating is still probably a determinant of prestige.

True courtship sometimes emerges from the dating process, in spite of all the forces which are opposed to it. The analysis of the interaction process involved seems to be quite revealing. We may suppose that in our collegiate culture one begins to fall in love with a certain unwillingness, at least with an ambivalent sort of willingness. Both persons become emotionally involved as a result of a summatory process in which each step powerfully influences the next step and the whole process displays a directional trend toward the culmination of marriage; the mores of dating break down and the behavior of the individuals is governed by the older mores of progressive commitment. In the fairly typical case, we may suppose the interaction to be about as follows: The affair begins with the lightest sort of involvement, each individual being interested in the other but assuming no obligations as to the continuation of the affair. There are some tentatives of exploitation at the beginning; "the line" is a conventionalized attempt on the part of the young man to convince the young woman that he has already at this early stage fallen seriously in love with her—a sort of exaggeration, sometimes a burlesque, of coquetry—it may be that each person, by a pretence of great involvement, invites the other to rapid sentiment-formation—each encourages the other to fall in love by pretending that he has already done so. If either rises to the bait, a special type of interaction ensues; it may be that the relation becomes exploitative in some degree and it is likely that the relationship becomes one in which control follows the principle of least interest, i.e., that person controls who is less interested in the continuation of the affair. Or it may be that the complete involvement of the one person constellates the other in the same pattern, but this is less likely to happen in college than in the normal community processes of courtship.

If both persons stand firm at this early juncture, there may ensue a series of periodic crises which successively redefine the relationship on deeper levels of involvement. One form which the interaction process may assume is that of "lover's quarrels," with which the novelists have familiarized us. A and B begin an affair on the level of light involvement. A becomes somewhat involved, but believes that B has not experienced a corresponding growth of feeling, and hides his involvement from B, who is, however, in exactly the same situation. The conventionalized "line" facilitates this sort of "pluralistic ignorance," because it renders meaningless the very words by means of which this state of mind could be disclosed. Tension grows between A and B, and is resolved by a crisis, such as a quarrel, in which the true feelings of the two are revealed. The affair, perhaps, proceeds through a number of such crises until it reaches the culmination of marriage. Naturally, there are other kinds of crises which usher in the new definition of the situation.

Such affairs, in contrast to "dating," have a marked directional trend; they may be arrested on any level, or they may be broken off at any point, but they may not ordinarily be turned back to a lesser degree of involvement; in this sense they are irreversible. As this interaction process goes on, the process of idealization is re-enforced by the interaction of personalities. A idealizes B, and presents to her that side of his personality which is consistent with his idealized conception of her; B idealizes A, and governs her behavior toward him in accordance with her false notions of his nature; the process of idealization is mutually re-enforced in such a way that it must necessarily lead to an increasing divorce from reality. As serious sentimental involvement develops, the individual comes to be increasingly occupied, on the conscious level at least, with the positive aspects of the relationship; increasingly he loses his ability to think objectively about the other person, to safeguard himself or to deal with the relationship in a rational way; we may say, indeed, that one falls in love when he reaches the point where sentiment-formation overcomes objectivity.

The love relationship in its crescendo phase attracts an ever larger proportion of the conative trends of the personality; for a time it may seem to absorb all of the will of the individual and to dominate his imagination completely; the individual seems to become a machine specially designed for just one purpose; in consequence, the persons are almost wholly absorbed in themselves and their affair; they have an *égoïsme à deux* which verges upon *folie à deux*. All of these processes within the pair-relationship are accentuated by the changes in the attitude of others, who tend to treat the pair as a social unity, so far as their association is recognized and approved.

Sexual Codes in Teen-Age Culture

IRA L. REISS

Teen-age sexual codes reflect quite clearly the bold outlines of adult sexual codes. The high degree of conformity in teen-age culture increases the observability of teen-age beliefs and adds to our understanding of adult beliefs. The teen-ager exists in a world somewhere between youthful idealism and adult realism, and his sexual codes reflect this state of being. In a very real sense, he is a marginal man with one foot in the world of the child and the other foot in the world of the adult.[1]

The teen-ager is at the stage at which it is vitally important for him to learn how to exist in society independent of his parents. For this reason, he transfers his dependence to his peers and strives to learn from them the secrets of entrance into the adult world. One would think that this vaguely defined status of "almost adult" would lead to confusion and weak statements of belief. To a large extent, this is the case, but, nevertheless, it is equally true that it leads to dogmatic statements of belief and a search for conviction through conformity. Teen-agers translate and adapt the sexual codes of adults to fit their particular circumstance and state of mind.[2]

GOING STEADY

When unchaperoned dating gained prevalence in the early part of this century, it involved a much more rapid change

Reprinted by permission of the author and of the editor from *The Annals of the American Academy of Political and Social Science*, Vol. 338 (November, 1961), 53–62.

of dating partners than occurs today. Nevertheless, by the time of World War II, going steady had taken root, and, today, it seems that slightly more than half of the high school students have some going-steady experience. Even among the early teen-agers, possibly one quarter go steady.[3]

Class differences are important in examining the going-steady complex. It seems that those high school people who go steady and plan to go to college are not likely to marry their high school steadies, and those who are from lower economic classes and who do not plan to go to college are much more likely to marry their high school steadies.[4] Thus, in looking at the custom of going steady, one must realize that there are different subtypes and that the consequences differ for each type.

Although a psychologist may point to the security of going steady as its chief reason for being, as a sociologist, I would point out how Western society has, for centuries, been developing an association of sexual behavior with mutual affection. This association is hard to achieve in casual dating; but, in steady dating, sex and affection can quite easily be combined, and, in this way, a potential strain in the social system is reduced. Another area of strain which is reduced by going steady is the conflict a girl may feel between her desire for sexual experience and her desire to maintain her reputation. For many, sexual behavior is made respectable by going steady.[5] In these ways, one may say that no other dating custom is quite as central to the understanding of teen-age sexual codes as going steady.

GIRLS' SEXUAL CODES

One of the most popular sexual codes among teen-age girls is petting-with-affection. This code is a modern day subtype of our formal abstinence standard. This subtype of abstinence seems extremely popular among high school couples who are going steady. Such couples feel it is proper to engage in heavy petting if they are going steady, the justification being that they are in love or at least extremely fond of each other. The petting-with-affection sex code probably grew along with the going-steady custom; they both illustrate adaptations of our dating institution to the newer unchaperoned dating circumstances.

What evidence do we have for such petting behavior among teen-agers? Though surely not perfect, the most extensive study of sexual behavior is that done by the Institute for Sex Research, formerly headed by Alfred C. Kinsey and now run by Paul H. Gebhard. It should be noted that the Kinsey studies are most valid for urban, white, northeastern, college-educated people, and, thus, great care must be taken when applying the results to other groups. The reader should keep in mind the tenuousness of any such generalizations made in this paper.

Kinsey's data show that, of the females who were twenty years old or older when interviewed, about one fifth to one fourth admitted they had petted to orgasm while still in their teens. Most of this behavior occurred between the ages of sixteen and twenty. About three-quarters of all the girls twenty years old or more admitted being aroused by some form of petting or kissing in their teens, and approximately 90 per cent stated they had at least been kissed during their teens.[6]

Those girls who marry in their teens start their petting and kissing behavior earlier than those who marry later. In general, the few years previous to marriage are by far the most sexually active for girls. Lower class females marry earlier, and, thus, they are more active in their teens and are more likely to marry their teen-age steadies.

The above rates are averages for Kinsey's entire sample of several thousand females; were we to take only the females born in more recent decades, the rates would be considerably higher. For example, of those females born before 1900, only 10 per cent ever petted to orgasm in their teens, whereas, of those girls born in the 1920's, almost 30 per cent, or three times the proportion, petted to orgasm by age 20.[7]

It seems clear that we have developed not only new dating forms such as going steady but also, as we have seen, new sexual codes to go with them. These new codes allow females much more freedom in heavy petting, provided affection is involved. Of course, other girls, particularly in the early teens, adhere to standards which only permit kissing, and a few others adhere to standards which allow full sexual relations, but, by and large, petting-with-affection seems the increasingly popular sex code for high school girls.

The most recent evidence of the nature of teen-age sex codes also supports these contentions. This evidence comes from research which the author is engaged in at present.[8] Some preliminary reports on this study were made in the author's book *Premarital Sexual Standards in America*. The study involves 1,000 high school and college students, most of whom are teen-agers. Although final analysis of the study has not been completed, it is clear that petting-with-affection is an extremely popular code with teen-age girls, particularly with the teen-agers who are high school juniors and seniors.

Finally, one should note that, in my own study and in the Kinsey study, religion was another key factor affecting girls' sexual beliefs and behaviors. Those girls who were devout in their religion were much more conservative in their sexual behavior and belief. Religion was not as strong a factor for boys and did not control their behavior as much. As we shall see, amount of education was the key determinant for male sexual behavior.

BOYS' SEXUAL CODES

Among the teen-age boys, we find a quite different code dominant. Abstinence is given some form of lip service, particularly among the more highly educated classes, but, by and large, it is not an operational code; it is not adhered to in the behavior of the majority of the teen-age boys. Even among the males destined for college, about 40 per cent have coitus in their teens; among those who stop their education in high school, about three-quarters have coitus in their teens, and, among those whose education stops before high school, about eight-tenths have coitus in their teens. Thus, it is clear that the majority of all males, in this sample of Kinsey's, at least, experienced full sexual relations before reaching twenty years of age.[9]

For teen-age girls, the rate of nonvirginity appears to be considerably lower. Kinsey reports approximately 20 per cent nonvirginity for females by age twenty. Of course, the greater liberality of the boys does not involve a single standard; that is, they are predominantly adherents of the double standard which allows boys to have coitus but condemns girls for the same thing. This is an ancient standard reaching back many thousands of years in Western culture. It is by no means a universal standard, however, for we do find many cultures where the sexes are treated equally.[10]

Although in recent generations, due to our greater equalitarianism and the evolving nature of the dating institution, the double standard seems to have been weakened sharply, it is still quite dominant among teen-age boys. The greater freedom allowed the male child in almost all areas of life constantly buttresses this standard and makes it seem obvious to teen-agers. Teen-agers are not sufficiently objective or sophisticated to be bothered by the contradictions in this or any other sexual code. For example, if all women abided fully by the double standard, then no men could, for the men would have no partners! Thus, this code operates only to the extent that someone violates it.

Some of these double standard teen-age boys will condemn a girl who accepts petting-with-affection, for they believe heavy petting is improper for girls. However, my own data indicate that most of these teen-age males will accept heavy petting in a going-steady relationship. They, of course, allow themselves to go further and may try to have coitus with a steady in order to see if she is a "good" girl. It is not unusual to find a relationship either broken up or its affectionate nature altered if a girl gives in to her double standard steady. Such condemnatory behavior on the part of double standard males keeps many girls from going as far sexually as they might want to. Thus, the double standard male eliminates many potential sex partners because of the attitude he takes toward such sex partners.

Teen-age double standard males are often stricter than their older brothers who accept coitus for a girl when she is in love and/or engaged. These teen-age males are supported in this rigidity by the conformity of their peer group. Double standard males typically view the act of coitus as a conquest, as a source of peer group prestige. Thus, they are quite prone to tell their friends all of the details of any affair. This characteristic tends further to discourage females from yielding to double standard males. Instead, the girl is encouraged to be, in part at least, a tease, that is, to show just enough sexual activity to keep the male interested but not enough to arouse his condemnation. Sexual behavior in this sense involves a great deal of the aspect of a game. Sex comes to be used as a power leverage to control the relationship. Under such circumstances, sexual desire is developed so sharply in the male and so differently in the female that the male wants the female to be both sexually active and sexually pure Under such conditions, sexual behavior can only with great difficulty relate directly to feelings of affection.[11] This is particularly true for the act of coitus. In fact, one finds very often an inverse relation, in that boys prefer to have coitus with girls they do not care for, because they regard the girls they do care for as "too good" for such behavior. Girls, too, may control their sexual reactions, particularly with someone they care for, until they are sure they will not be condemned for their sexual response.

Thus, in the area of coitus among teen-agers, the double standard does seem to block the association of sex and affection. However, one should quickly add that, on the level of petting, sex and affection can more easily be combined, for this behavior is much more likely to be accepted for both sexes by both males and females.

MINOR STANDARDS

There are minor teen-age standards which are more permissive than petting-with-affection or the double standard. For the older teen-ager, the most popular minor standard is what I shall call permissiveness-with-affection.[12] This standard accepts full sexual intercourse for both boys and girls, provided they are involved in a stable, affectionate relationship. The degree of stability and affection required varies among adherents from feeling strong affection to being in love and engaged. Some teen-age couples who are going steady have coitus in accord with this standard. The situation here is quite different from that of the double standard boy and his girl friend, for, in permissiveness-with-affection, both the boy and girl accept for each other what they are doing. They combine sex with affection and use affection as one of the key justifications of the sexual act.

There is a class difference in sexual standards among boys. My evidence indicates that the lower classes are more likely to be strong supporters of the double standard, while the upper classes, though still mostly double standard, contain a large proportion of boys who are not so dogmatic in their beliefs and a minority who accept permissiveness-with-affection. In general, the upper classes seem to stress equality of the sexes and the importance of affection more than the lower classes. A permissiveness-without-affection code seems more widespread at the lower levels.

Age is a crucial factor among teen-agers. Teen-agers under sixteen are much more likely to accept only kissing than are older teen-agers, who may accept petting or coitus. As noted earlier, religion does not restrict sexual behavior as much among boys as it does among girls. Education is a more important factor, with the more highly educated groups being the most conservative.

PROMISCUITY

The newspapers from time to time pick up stories of high school "sex clubs" and other forms of promiscuous teen-age sexual behavior.[13] The available evidence indicates that promiscuous coitus is common predominantly for double standard males and a few females. Promiscuous coitus is not common on an equalitarian basis, that is, where both male and female accept the behavior as right for each other. Our culture has stressed the association of sex-with-affection to such an extent that it is difficult, at least for many females, to violate this association in coitus. In the case of petting, one finds more likelihood of violation of this norm by both men and women, but, in the case of coitus, it is much more often violated by males. Ehrmann's study of 1,000 college students supports this difference between male and female sexual activity and attitudes.[14] Females, in addition to associating love with sexual behavior more than males, also have more nonsexual motives for sexual behavior, such as the desire to please the boy or to cement a relationship.[15]

During the teens, the sexual outlets of boys and girls differ considerably. The chief outlet for girls seems to be masturbation and petting, whereas for boys the chief outlets include coitus at the fore. In Kinsey's sample, about one third of the girls masturbated to orgasm in their teens, while over 90 per cent of the boys have so masturbated in their teens.[16] Despite their high rate of masturbation, males also have a high rate of coitus. The lower class boys rely less on masturbation and petting and more on coitus for their sexual outlets than do those boys who go to college.

The teen-age girl today is still typically the much more

conservative partner and the guardian of sexual limits. However, she appears increasingly to be a half-willing guardian who more and more seeks her self-satisfaction and strives to achieve sexual equality.[17]

There is a general trend in American society toward more equalitarian and more permissive sexual codes in all areas.[18] This is true for teen-age sexual codes, too. The growth within abstinence of petting-with-affection is one sign of this increasing equalitarian and permissive force. Also, within the double standard, one finds increased willingness by males to accept some coitus on the part of females, especially if it occurs when the girl is in love and/or engaged. Finally, in the minor standard of permissiveness-with-affection, one sees this trend in the increased strength of this standard among teen-agers, particularly among older, college teen-agers. And these trends toward equalitarianism and permissiveness seem even stronger among older dating couples in their twenties. The teen-agers are relatively new at sexual behavior, and they, at first, grab the basic outlines of the older couples' codes. With the passage of time, they come to behave in a somewhat more equalitarian and permissive manner.

In my current research, there is evidence that the real change-over in a teen-ager's sexual code is more one of integrating attitudes and changing overt behavior than of changing basic attitudes. In short, it seems that a person holds his basic sexual attitudes in rudimentary form in his teens, but he is not fully ready to act upon them and has not fully learned how to combine these values into a coherent code of living. As he learns to do this, his behavior changes and so does his awareness of his beliefs and their unity, but his basic beliefs may well remain the same. This entire area of how our sexual beliefs are formed and how they change is in need of more careful study. My own research is aimed at probing some aspects of this problem.

Parents are prone to be most aware of what they consider excessive sexual behavior, for they are concerned about the consequences of such behavior as they may affect their children. Thus, parents complain about sexual acts of which they become aware, and they often believe teen-agers are sexually promiscuous. Actually, according to our best estimates, the real increases in teen-age sexual behavior over the last generation are not in the area of sexual intercourse but rather in the area of petting and in the public nature of some petting behavior.[19] Thus, these parents of today have probably had similar rates of coitus but perhaps lower rates of petting. In addition, one should note that the petting behavior today very often is not promiscuous but occurs in a stable affectionate relationship.

YOUTH CULTURE: TAME OR WILD?

About twenty years ago, Kingsley Davis and Talcott Parsons wrote of a youth culture and of a parent-youth conflict and, in doing so, implied in part that youth culture was largely irresponsible, impulsive, and antiadult.[20] Many people have come to share this view and to expect rather extreme sexual behavior from teen-agers. I myself formerly accepted this view of the teen-ager as valid. However, after examining the evidence in the key areas of teen-age sexual behavior, I must admit that I can no longer accept such a conception of youth culture without serious modification and qualification. I would submit that the vast majority of our approximately twenty million teen-agers are not only not extreme but are quite conservative and restrained in the area of premarital sexual codes and behavior when we compare them to their older brothers and sisters.

There is evidence to show that teen-agers are unsure of how far to go sexually, that they feel ill at ease on dates, and that they are concerned with such "tame" issues as whether one should kiss good night on a first date.[21] A recent study showed that teen-agers rate themselves lower in comparison to adults than adults rate them. Teen-agers in this study rated adults considerably higher than themselves on most all "good" qualities.[22] These are hardly the attitudes of an arrogant or antiadult youth. They seem more those of a group desirous of becoming like adults and striving toward that goal.

Further, when we look at the rates of female petting to orgasm in the Kinsey studies, we find considerably more cf this behavior among girls in their twenties than among girls in their teens. The coitus rate for females doubles between the ages of twenty and twenty-five. Masturbation rates also increase considerably after the teens.[23] In all these ways, the teen-agers seem more conservative than those individuals who are in their twenties.

August Hollingshead's excellent study of a midwest community also gives evidence on the conservatism of youth. He found a very close correspondence between social class of parents and social class of teen-agers' dating partners. In this study, too, we are given a picture of youth culture that is very much like adult culture in its status consciousness. Hollingshead and others have also noted the fact that a large proportion of the teen-age population is virtually not involved in any dating. A good estimate for the high school age group would be that about one third of the boys and one fifth of the girls are not involved in dating.[24]

VENEREAL DISEASE AND PREGNANCY

Let us now examine two key indices, venereal disease and pregnancy, which should give us additional insights into the behavior of teen-agers. Teen-agers do have significant rates of venereal disease and illegitimacy. However, the press has largely exaggerated such rates. The teen-age rate of venereal disease for ages fifteen to nineteen is only about a third of the rate for the twenty to twenty-four age group and is also lower than that of the twenty-five to twenty-nine age group.[25]

There has been a slight rise in the number of teen-age venereal disease cases in recent years, and this has received much publicity. It is quite likely that the actual rates for teen-agers are not higher and that this slight increase is due to the greater number of teen-agers today. More than 80 per cent of the venereal disease reported is from older groups of people. Finally, the rate of venereal disease among teen-agers is not evenly distributed in the teen-age group. As far as we can tell from reported cases, it is highly concentrated in the lower social classes.[26]

When one examines the national figures for unwed mothers, one finds that 40 per cent are teen-agers. Here, too, several qualifications are needed. First, most of these reported cases are Negro, and class status in general is low. The upper classes, according to Paul Gebhard's recent study, are much more willing to resort to abortion.[27] The upper classes, also, have a greater ability to stay out of public statistics and may, thus, show lower rates. According to Clark Vincent's study, when upper class females become pregnant before marriage, it is more likely to be the result of a love affair, whereas, when lower class females become pregnant, it is more likely to be a result of a casual affair.[28] Thus, there are important class differences here, too.

When we compare teen-age unwed motherhood with that for girls in their twenties, we find that the older girls have about the same proportion of the illegitimate children. We also find that the teen-age rates are not increasing as much as the rates for older groups. For example, in 1940 teen-age mothers were 46 per cent of the total; in 1957 they were 40 per cent.

Thus, from the evidence of national figures, it seems reasonable to conclude that it is a small and specific segment of the teen-age population that becomes involved with venereal disease or premarital pregnancy. Furthermore, the people in their twenties seem somewhat more likely to be involved in such circumstances. Also, these older couples are much more involved in adult culture in terms of their occupations and their nearness to marriage, and yet their sexual behavior is less conservative.

A warning must be added at this point concerning the venereal disease rates and unwed motherhood rates. They are far from perfect indices and, as mentioned, many higher class people manage to be excluded from them because they can afford more private means of coping with their problems. However, to the extent that we use these rates, we fail to find support for the charges made about teen-agers. It is no doubt true that teen-agers are irresponsible in the sense that they seek "to have a good time," but I would suggest that, in the area of sexual codes and behavior, the evidence shows more conservatism and responsibility than one might otherwise suspect. It may be well to avoid the over-all impressions given by a general use of the term "youth culture" as described by Parsons. Here, as elsewhere, qualification and specific research is a step toward better theoretical formulation and better understanding.

A FINAL OVERVIEW

What has occurred in teen-age sexual codes in recent generations is a working out of sexual practices acceptable to teen-agers. Many of these practices are at the level of petting. In short, as unchaperoned dating came into vogue and as adolescence became more prolonged due to our specialized industrial culture, young people worked out additional sexual codes to supplement and modify the older codes of abstinence and the double standard. There always were people who engaged in coitus; today there are more, but, for girls in their teens, it is still a minor activity. When we look at petting, we note something different, for here we see a much more continuous and current change among teen-agers—it is here in this middle ground that teen-agers have come to accept a petting-with-affection standard. The equalitarian and permissive aspects of this standard in many cases lead at later ages to acceptance of the more radical permissiveness-with-affection standard. However, during the teens, petting-with-affection is probably the major standard involved in stable affectionate relationships at middle and upper class levels.

At the present time, it is impossible to predict precise changes in sexual codes. This is especially true because, as we have seen, there are differences according to social class, religion, educational level, and so forth. But one can say that all the signs indicate a continued trend toward equalitarian and permissive codes. The trend seems to be toward that which now obtains in the Scandinavian countries, with the inclusion of sex education in the schools and with permissive attitudes on the formal as well as covert levels. This does not forebode the end of the double standard, for the double standard is still deeply rooted in our male dominant culture, but it does mean a continued weakening of the double standard and more qualifications of its mandates.

Teen-agers are a paradoxical group. They are not as wild as their parents or they themselves sometimes think. Teen-agers do want independence. But, judging by their sexual codes, they want independence from their parents, not from the total adult culture.

PART II

Socioeconomic Status and Juvenile Delinquency

INTRODUCTION

Irrespective of social class, perhaps all boys break the law at one time or other. But official statistics seldom reflect this fact. We know that boys from the lower class are arrested more often relative to the frequency with which they commit offenses. Our research ought not to rely on these sources alone, but must attempt to establish the extent of delinquency among children who go undetected. When Nye, Short, and Olson studied the self-reported delinquencies of high school students, they found no special relationship between delinquent conduct and socioeconomic status.

In his research of the Marion County Juvenile Court records, Roland Chilton finds that children from low-income areas are over-represented for gainful offenses, victimizing crimes, and other potentially threatening behavior. Children from high-income sectors come into court more often for nongainful delinquencies such as traffic and liquor offenses, curfew violations, incorrigibility, and car theft. Chilton suggests that economic factors may be important in accounting for these differences in gainful delinquency, and calls for the increased use of specific offense data in our study of middle-class delinquency.

Much of our behavior is designed to find favor with others, especially those of whom we think well. Our manner of acting and the behavioral stance that we present others are associated closely with the images that we carry around of ourself. The social roles that we occupy are strongly influential in the formation of these self-conceptions. Equally important is the self-conception associated with our sex status. Whether a youth defines himself as a "tough guy," a "sissy," or "sophisticated" makes a difference in his daily conduct. Leon Fannin and Marshall Clinard present findings on the self-conception of training school boys from the lower and middle classes. Boys from each class think of themselves in somewhat distinct terms, and their self-conceptions are related to specific kinds of behavior.

Socioeconomic Status and Delinquent Behavior

F. IVAN NYE, JAMES F. SHORT, JR., AND VIRGIL J. OLSON

Delinquency is commonly described in the literature as primarily a phenomenon of the lower economic strata.[1] Such studies, dealing with the relationship between juvenile delinquency and socioeconomic level, have used court records, police files, and other official records of delinquency. These bases are adequate, within certain limitations, for an examination of "official delinquency," but they are unreliable as an index of "delinquent behavior" in the general population.[2] Estimates of the extent of delinquent behavior in the general population indicate that such behavior may be more evenly distributed in the various socioeconomic strata than official records lead one to believe. Porterfield, for instance, found that college students committed many more delinquent acts than is commonly known and that these delinquent acts were as serious as those which brought other young people, less fortunate economically, into court.[3] Research by Murphy, based on the case histories of adolescents, yielded similar results.[4] Wallerstein and Wyle found that, in a group of upper-income individuals, 99 per cent answered affirmatively to one or more offenses.[5] Short's research on criminal behavior in selected groups likewise bears testimony to the fact that delinquent and criminal behavior are by no means limited to the lower economic groups.[6]

Despite the abundance of criticism that has been leveled

Reprinted from *The American Journal of Sociology*, Vol. 63, No. 4 (January, 1958), 381–389, by permission of The University of Chicago Press.

against the use of official records as an index of delinquent behavior in the various socioeconomic levels, recent studies continue either to confuse "official delinquency" with "delinquent behavior" or to equate the two phenomena. An example of the former is provided by Dirksen, who presents one of the more extreme positions in assessing the role of the economic variable in juvenile delinquency.[7] His study may indicate the class differential in alleged or official delinquency, but generalizations to delinquent behavior in the general population cannot be made from these results.

TABLE 1. Percentage Distribution of Boys in Western High Schools and State Training School Samples by Socioeconomic Level

Socioeconomic Level	Western High Schools		State Training Schools	
	No.	Per Cent	No.	Per Cent
(High) 4	114	13.6	6	4.1
3	282	33.5	19	13.0
2	333	39.6	48	32.9
(Low) 1	112	13.3	73	50.0
Total	841	100.0	146	100.0

$\chi^2 = 117.01 \quad P < .001 \quad \bar{C} = .45$

Other recent studies utilize such data as obtained from court files and other official records as an index of delinquency.[8]

Cohen, in one of the most recent treatments of juvenile delinquency, has said concerning the disparity between official delinquency rates and delinquent behavior rates in the general population: "If many delinquencies of upper-class children fail to find their way into the police and court records, the same is apparently true also of many delinquencies of working-class children, and conceivably even more true."[9] Although Cohen indicates that the best *available* evidence supports the traditional and popular conception of the distribution of juvenile delinquency in the class structure, he calls for research that will make known the extent of delinquent behavior in the population not judged "delinquent."[10]

The present analysis (Table 1) shows that, in one of the

states from which a sample was drawn, the relationship between socioeconomic status and commitment to the state "training school" is similar to that shown by the studies quoted above. A disproportionate number of the official delinquents come from the lower socioeconomic categories.

After an examination of this literature, it is the opinion of the writers that the use of a measure of reported delinquent behavior rather than official records of delinquency will yield results somewhat different from those supporting the traditional conceptions of the status distribution of delinquency. We are not here concerned with etiology but with this question: Does delinquent behavior occur differentially by socioeconomic status?

The present study tests the null hypothesis that there is no significant difference in delinquent behavior of boys and girls in different socioeconomic strata.

THE RESPONDENTS

The Sample

In this study there are two principal sources of data—selected high-school groups in western and midwestern communities. In the western sample, data were gathered by questionnaire from 2,350 boys and girls in Grades IX through XII in the high schools of three western cities. These cities ranged in size from 10,000 to 25,000. They are thus clearly urban but not metropolitan.

The three western communities sampled in this study differ from the state in which they are located in two significant characteristics. They experienced a much higher growth from 1940 to 1950, and the average income level was higher. (See Table 2.) Related to the higher growth rate is the lower average age and the smaller proportion of old people in these communities. From a state-wide sample drawn in another study[11] it was found, as would be expected, that horizontal mobility was greater in the present sample than for the state and is presumably greater than that for the country as a whole.

The midwestern data were gathered by a questionnaire soliciting comparable data from 250 boys and 265 girls in

TABLE 2. Selected Population Characteristics for Western Communities from Which Sample Is Drawn, Compared with Those Characteristics for Western State and the United States[a]

Selected Population Characteristics	Communities from Which Sample Is Drawn	Western State	United States
Median years of school (twenty-five years old or over):			
Male	11.1	11.3	10.0
Female	11.1	12.1	10.3
Median age	27.5	31.8	31.6
Per cent 65 and over	3.0	9.3	8.2
Per cent over fourteen years of age in labor force:			
Male	89.1	77.9	79.3
Female	32.1	31.6	33.2
Median income—families	$4,515.00	$3,755.00	$3,431.00

[a] *United States Census* (1950). Urban statistics are used for western state and the United States. Comparable data are not available for midwestern communities.

Grades IX through XII in the high schools of three midwestern communities. One of the high schools is located in a suburban residential town with a population of less than 2,500. The second is a rural town of less than 2,500 population. The third is a consolidated high school in a rural township. The population of these three communities has remained fairly stable since 1940.

No samples from large cities or from large non-Caucasian groups are included, and generalizations to such populations must await further research.

MEASURE OF DELINQUENT BEHAVIOR

Delinquent behavior in the present study was measured by means of an anonymous delinquency check list administered to adolescents who are not adjudged delinquent[12] and by a delinquency scale constructed from it. The list is designed to include a broad sampling of juvenile misconduct, though it does not include several of the more serious types of delinquency (e.g., rape, breaking and entering, and armed robbery).

MEASURE OF SOCIOECONOMIC LEVEL

The occupation of the father was utilized as an index of socioeconomic level of the respondent. A combination of the North-Hatt and Mapheus Smith scales was employed. These scales were combined and applied to data gathered from a sample of Washington State high-school students by Empey in a study of occupational aspiration and anticipation.[13]

Research in social stratification lends support to the use of occupation as a measure of socioeconomic status.[14] It has the following advantages: (1) Occupation correlates highly with other criteria of class and status position, such as subjective class affiliation, income, educational level, subjective class ratings, and others. (2) Occupation is related not only to income but to values, attitudes, and goals; to a certain extent it determines the social relations among societal members. (3) The use of occupation as a criterion of socioeconomic status makes it possible to correlate a child's delinquent behavior with the socioeconomic level of his immediate family rather than with the demographic area in which he lives. (4) In addition, data on the occupation of the father are generally obtained more accurately from adolescents than income, years of schooling of the parents, value of the home, rental, and other items with which the adolescent may not be familiar.

Comparison of the percentage distribution by major occupational groups for the western sample and the midwestern sample indicated that the differences between the proportions of each sample falling in the several socioeconomic levels were not significant. The two samples are not significantly different as to range or distribution of occupations. The combined occupational prestige scale contains ten categories of occupations, each representing a range of occupations within the total scale. In the present study these ten categories were combined into four status groupings which include the following types of occupations: (1) unskilled and semiskilled labor (e.g., migratory worker to restaurant cook); (2) skilled labor and craftsmen (e.g., house-painter to linotype operator); (3) white collar and small business (e.g., newspaper columnist to owner-operator of a mine); and (4) professional and large business (e.g., interior decorator to United States Supreme Court justice). No attempt was made to classify adolescents who live in families in which there was no adult male. Elimination of this small group (108 out of a total of approximately 2,350 cases) does not seriously influence the findings of the study. Separate analysis of this group indicates that its members tend to be more delinquent than all others; but, when status is held constant by two independent measures (education of mother and comparison of income with that of "others"), no significant relationship between status and delinquency is found.

FINDINGS

The data were subjected to five tests in an attempt to locate significant differences in delinquent behavior by socioeconomic status. First, four-by-four tables were constructed in which social status was categorized as described above. Delinquent behavior on each item was divided into four categories. Typically these were: (1) did not commit the act; (2) committed the act once or twice; (3) committed the act several times; (4) committed the act very often. The distribution of each delinquent act by social status was tested separately by the chi-square test. Tests were computed separately for boys' and girls' samples, followed by tests in which the boys' and girls' samples were combined for twenty-one delinquency items. This was done separately for the western and midwestern samples. In all, 126 chi-square tests were made with the western and midwestern data.

In the western samples two significant differences were found. Since 63 chi-squares were computed from the western data, three differences significant above the 5 per cent level might be expected to occur by chance.[15] These two differences did not follow any consistent pattern. "Heterosexual relations" were committed most frequently by lower-class boys, but "purposely damaged or destroyed property" was committed most frequently by upper-class boys and girls. In the midwestern samples three significant differences were found. Since 63 chi-squares were computed from the midwestern data, three differences significant above the 5 per cent level might be expected to occur by chance. Furthermore, the three do not follow any consistent pattern. "Taking a car without permission" was committed most frequently by lower-class boys; "running away from home," most frequently by upper-class girls. It was concluded, therefore, on the basis of the chi-square test of the four-by-four tables that there is no reason to reject the null hypothesis.

However, it was possible that the differences in delinquent behavior might be cumulative and that a simple dichotomy of "committed" or "did not commit" the act might reveal differences not apparent in the more detailed analysis.[16] Thus a second test was made in which all delinquent behavior items were dichotomized and in which the relationship of delinquent behavior to socioeconomic status was again tested by the use of chi square. For the western sample seven items were found to differ significantly by socioeconomic status. "Skipped school" and "taken a car for a ride" were most frequently admitted in the lowest socioeconomic category, both in the boys' and in the combined boys' and girls' samples. "Purposely damaged or destroyed property" was most frequently admitted in the highest socioeconomic category, both in the girls' and in the combined boys' and girls' samples. "Heterosexual relations" were most frequently admitted by the boys in the lowest socioeconomic category. In all, 63 chi-square tests were made of the dichotomized delinquency items—21 for girls, 21 for boys, and 21 for the combined western samples (boys and girls). Seven significant differences are somewhat in excess of the number expected by chance, but not all are consistent. Similarly, in the midwestern sample 63 tests were made with none significant at the 5 per cent level. Of the 126 tests made in the two samples, 7 are significant, which is little if any in excess of the number that might occur by chance.

The possibility still remained that there were significant differences between some of the socioeconomic categories in their degree of delinquent involvement. A third test was therefore made. Percentages were computed from the dichotomized delinquency items, and significance of differences between proportions was computed.[17] Since with four socioeconomic categories, six comparisons are possible, for each item the total number of comparisons is 6×21, or 126 in each sample.

In the western boys' sample, of the 126 tests of significance of differences between proportions, 6 were found significant. For three delinquency items the offense was committed most frequently by the lowest socioeconomic category; for three, by the middle category. For the western girls' sample, five significant differences were found. Four of these delinquencies were committed most frequently by upper socioeconomic girls and one by lower socioeconomic girls. In the combined (boys' and girls') western sample, eight significant differences were found. Four were committed most frequently by upper and four by lower socioeconomic categories. For the western samples, 378 tests were possible, of which 19 (or 5 per cent) proved significant. At the 5 per cent level of significance this is about the percentage of differences that should appear significant by chance.

Since one category of the midwestern sample is very small, the analysis by significance of differences between categories was completed for the combined sample only. This test of 126 comparisons found two significant differences, one offense being committed most frequently by the lower and one by a middle category.

The third test involved a total of 504 possible tests of significance, of which 21 were found to be significant. At the 5 per cent level of significance this number might be expected to occur by chance. Furthermore, in only one-third of the cases was the act most frequently committed by the lowest socioeconomic status category. On the basis of this third test it must again be concluded that the evidence does not permit rejection of the null hypothesis.

Some patterning of significant differences did occur. In all the tests made for the individual items, a total of 33 significant differences were found, as can be seen from Table 3. These differences were concentrated chiefly in the lower- and upper-class groups, and 26 of the 33 differences concerned five offenses. These offenses and the class groups reporting their higher incidence were: truancy (lower-class children); heterosexual relations (lower-class boys); car theft (lower-class boys); destroying property (upper-class boys); and gang fights (upper-class children). It seems likely that some of these differences are also spurious.

In addition to the tests of individual delinquent behavior items, the distribution of delinquency scale types by socioeconomic status was tested for significant differences.[18] Ten tests were made of distribution of scale types by socioeconomic status. Four samples were tested in both the western and the midwestern high-school populations: girls fifteen and younger, girls sixteen and older, boys fifteen and younger, and boys sixteen and older. One test was made in the boys' and girls' training schools of students sixteen and

TABLE 3. Summary of Tests of Significance Between Socioeconomic Status and Delinquent Behavior of Boys, Girls, and Combined Samples of Three Western and Three Midwestern Towns

Sample and Test	No. of Possible Differences	No. of Differences Significant	Socioeconomic Status in Which Highest Proportion Committed Delinquent Act[a]: Lower	Middle Two	Upper
4–4 Table χ^2					
Midwestern boys	21	2	1	0	1
Midwestern girls	21	1	0	0	1
Midwestern combined	21	0	0	0	0
Western boys	21	1	1	0	0
Western girls	21	0	0	0	0
Western combined	21	1	0	0	1
2–4 Table χ^2					
Midwestern boys, girls, and combined	63	0	0	0	0
Western boys	21	3	3	0	0
Western girls	21	1	0	0	1
Western combined	21	3	2	0	1
Significance of difference between proportions (t score):					
Western boys	126	6	3	3	0
Western girls	126	5	1	0	4
Western combined	126	8	4	0	4
Midwestern combined	126	2	1	1	0
Total	756	33	16	4	13

[a] Act that was significantly different by socioeconomic category.

older. Of these 10 tests, 9 proved non-significant, with $P > .20$ in each case. (See Table 4.) The tenth test (western boys sixteen and over) was significant at the 5 per cent level.

TABLE 4. Distribution of Delinquent Behavior Scale Types for Western Boys Twelve to Fifteen Years Old by Socioeconomic Status

Socioeconomic Level	Scale Types: Low[a] *N*	Low[a] Per Cent	Intermediate[b] *N*	Intermediate[b] Per Cent	High[c] *N*	High[c] Per Cent
(High) 4	25	18	7	7	16	16
3	48	34	35	35	28	27
2	54	39	42	42	40	39
(Low) 1	13	9	16	16	18	18
Total	140	100	100	100	102	100

$\chi^2 = 9.99 \quad P < .20$

[a] Scale Type No. 1 = no admitted offense.
Scale Type No. 2 = admitted driving without driver's license.
[b] Scale Type No. 3 = admitted the above items plus defied parents' authority openly.
Scale Type No. 4 = both the above plus petty larceny.
Scale Type No. 5 = all the above plus taking automobile without permission.
[c] Scale Type No. 6 = all the above plus drank alcoholic beverages.
Scale Type No. 7 = all the above plus heterosexual relations.
Scale Types No. 8–15 = all the above plus some or all more than once or twice.

SELECTIVE FACTORS

Not all adolescents are in school. Since the "drop-outs" may be more delinquent than those in school and may be disproportionately recruited from the lower socioeconomic strata, a further test was considered necessary. In the western communities children are required to attend school until sixteen years of age. A check of census data in these towns shows that, in 1950, 97.5 per cent of children aged fourteen and fifteen were attending school. Of those not attending, there were a number with extreme physical and mental handicaps presumably unrelated to the present analysis. "Drop-outs" were, therefore, so few proportionately that they could not affect (considerably) the findings in these age categories. The relationship of socioeconomic status to delinquent behavior was tested within this younger age group separately, and six significant differences were found. Two acts were committed less frequently by the upper-status group, three by the lowest, and one by the middle groups.

THE NON-CLASSIFIED CATEGORY

Not all respondents could be classified in terms of socioeconomic level (28 per cent of boys were "non-classifiable"). For example, "works on a newspaper" was deemed insufficient information for assignment to a particular category. These cases were necessarily omitted from the above analysis. It was considered desirable to know whether this non-classifiable group differed markedly from the group analyzed. A second measure of socioeconomic status—the education level of the father—was employed. Differences in education level of the father in the classified and non-classified groups were tested and found not significant. The two groups were then compared by delinquent behavior scale types, and again differences were found to be not significant. It was concluded, therefore, that the findings were not biased by the exclusion of the non-classified group.

SUMMARY

The null hypothesis was tested that there is no significant difference in delinquent behavior of boys and girls in different socioeconomic strata. The study was conducted in three western communities and three midwestern communities. The population included all pupils in Grades IX through XII. Delinquent behavior was measured by means of a delinquency check list and a delinquent behavior scale. Data were gathered anonymously by questionnaire under classroom conditions. Socioeconomic status was determined by the father's occupation, using a combination of the North-Hatt and Mapheus Smith occupational prestige scale.

The data were put to five tests: (1) The chi-square test was applied to the data in four-by-four tables for boys and girls separately and combined. (2) Delinquent behavior categories were dichotomized, and the chi-square test was applied to the data in two-by-four tables. (3) A test of significance of difference between proportions was applied to subgroups showing marked differences for the two-by-four tables. (4) A test was made of the distribution of delinquency scale types by socioeconomic status. (5) A separate test was made with adolescents of fourteen and fifteen years of age to minimize the effect of school "drop-outs." The tests employed failed to uncover enough significant differences to reject the null hypothesis.

This study does not attempt to explain the etiology of delinquent behavior, but the findings have implications for those etiological studies which rely upon the assumed class differential in delinquent behavior as a basis for a delinquency theory. Our data suggest that several *single* measures of socioeconomic status and delinquency are not highly correlated in rural areas and in small towns and cities.

Although present findings are negative, attention is called to the seemingly non-random distribution of significant differences in Table 3. The two middle socioeconomic categories are highest on delinquent behavior on only 4 tests in contrast to 29 for the highest and lowest categories combined. These seemingly non-random differences may be caused by underreporting of delinquent behavior by the middle classes or by slightly more effective social control and socialization by middle-class parents.

Middle-Class Delinquency and Specific Offense Analysis

ROLAND J. CHILTON

Systematic examinations of juvenile delinquency often ignore the well-known fact that juvenile delinquency does not describe a homogeneous phenomenon, but is a term used to

Written especially for this volume.

describe a wide variety of conduct. Most investigators, of course, realize that delinquency includes a wide range of behavior such as theft, aggressive and assaultive acts, and relatively minor infractions of local ordinances. Yet many of them continue the practice of combining all types of offense information in their attempts to understand the general problem of delinquency. This procedure may be particularly inappropriate in the investigation of middle-class delinquency since the total number of infractions committed by middle-class children may overdramatize the extent and importance of middle-class delinquency.

For an accurate assessment of the importance of middle-class delinquency, it is necessary to know something about the frequency, variety, and seriousness of specific kinds of delinquent conduct committed by middle-class children. If children from more advantaged homes engage in less delinquency than lower-class children, and if the acts they commit are less serious in terms of injury to persons and damage to property, then the conduct of these children cannot, with any confidence, be viewed as an indication of an increasingly serious delinquency problem. If this is true, economic factors may still be important for an understanding of the differences between lower- and middle-class delinquency.

Our analysis assumes that a comparison of the specific kinds of delinquency committed by middle- and lower-class children is more promising than an examination of some overall count of delinquent acts by middle-class youths. Earlier studies have suggested that children from economically advantaged families are more likely to commit certain kinds of delinquent acts than are children from poorer families. Following this lead, there is reason to believe that the examination of specific offense information will indicate that middle-class children engage more frequently in some types of delinquency than in others.

An example of a study that suggests this is Wattenberg and Balistrieri's analysis of police reports on 230 boys charged with automobile theft in Detroit.[1] Their investigation focused on specific offense information by comparing factors related to automobile theft with factors related to all other delinquent acts combined. Of particular importance for our discussion is their conclusion that automobile theft was a "favored-group delinquency" because the children involved were more likely to come from neighborhoods rated "above average" by the police investigators, and less likely to come from overcrowded homes. Also, there was a "tendency" for these boys to live in all-white neighborhoods, to live in single family homes not in need of repair, and to have only one parent working. These areas might quite accurately be referred to as middle-class neighborhoods.

Wattenberg and Balistrieri also noted that the arrests of Negro delinquents for car theft were disproportionately low compared with the Negro-white ratio of arrests of juveniles for all other offenses combined. For all offenses combined police contacted approximately twice as many white as Negro children, but three times as many white children were arrested for automobile theft.

Wattenberg and Balistrieri accepted the explanation of some Detroit policemen that the danger and difficulty involved in car theft accounted for the under-representation of Negro children arrested for automobile theft. But our analysis assumes that this Negro-white difference in automobile-theft referrals probably reflects a difference in the kinds of delinquency in which Negro and white children are likely to engage. Negro children, for example, may be more likely to engage in profitable or gainful delinquent activity. Since automobile theft is not generally financially profitable, and since it usually does not lead to permanent gain because the vehicles are seldom retained and are rarely sold illegally by juveniles, such an explanation might account for the difference in Negro-white automobile-theft referrals.

If this explanation is correct, Negroes ought also to be under-represented in arrests for other nongainful offenses such as traffic and liquor law violations. It seems plausible also that children, irrespective of color, in poor economic situations will also be attracted to gainful types of delinquency. In an analysis of specific offense data, we should expect to find that offenses involving economic gain will more frequently involve children from low income areas, and that car theft and other nongainful offenses will occur with a higher frequency in high income areas.

DATA

The information used in the following analysis was taken from the records of the Marion County Juvenile Court (Indianapolis) for 1958 through 1960, and from the 1960 U.S. Census of Population and Housing. The name, address, sex, race, and offense of each child referred to, and accepted by, the court during this period were recorded as were all offenses with which the child had been charged in earlier referrals. The addresses were used to determine the census tract in which each child lived at the time of his last referral, and this information was used to make counts of several specific offenses for each census tract. The census report provided much additional information for each tract, but only the figures showing median family income and the number of Negro residents in each tract are used in this analysis.

Median income information was used to sort tracts into five categories. Twenty-one tracts with the lowest median income were grouped as low income tracts, 21 tracts with the highest median income were grouped as high income tracts, and the remaining tracts were grouped into three additional sets each including 21 tracts classified by median income. This provided a crude basis for viewing the tracts with the highest median income as middle-class areas.

Table 1 presents the results of our analysis of 105 Indianapolis census tracts. Almost all (96 of 99) tracts located entirely within the Indianapolis city limits were used. Nine of 44 tracts situated around the edge of the city were also used. Those tracts that were not used contained very small populations or information about them was insufficient.

Examination of Table 1 reveals that children from high income tracts come into contact with the juvenile court much less frequently than would be expected by the number of children eligible for referral, i.e., of juvenile court age. Combining columns 4 and 5 (42 tracts) we find that eligible children from high income tracts constitute 40 percent of all such children, but they account for only 17 percent of all court referrals. Children living in the 21 lowest income tracts make up 20 percent of the population of children of juvenile court age, yet 42 percent of all juvenile offenses are committed by these children. Combining columns 1 and 2 reveals that 37 percent of the children of juvenile court age live in the 42 tracts with the lowest median incomes, but these children commit 65 percent of all offenses.

Not only are children from high income tracts generally under-represented in juvenile court referrals, but for certain

TABLE 1. Specific Offense Information for Tracts Grouped by Median Income

	1 Low $3,210–4,552	2 $4,613–5,527	3 Medium $5,530–6,067	4 $6,103–7,000	5 High $7,030–10,281	
Larceny	474(48.9)+[a]	206(21.2)	157(16.2)	91(9.4)	42(4.3)—	970
Robbery	48(62.3)+	13(16.9)	13(16.9)	2(2.6)	1(1.3)—	77
Receiving	25(55.6)+	10(22.2)	4(8.9)	2(4.4)	4(8.9)+	45
Assault	114(47.7)+	67(28.0)	26(10.9)	17(7.1)	15(6.3)—	239
Weapons	21(48.8)+	13(30.2)	4(9.3)	3(7.0)	2(4.7)—	43
Loitering	26(56.5)+	12(26.1)	4(8.7)	4(8.7)	0(0.0)—	46
Truancy	170(50.0)+	74(21.8)	62(18.2)	25(7.4)	9(2.6)—	340
Disorderly	136(40.2)—	84(24.9)	60(17.8)	36(10.7)	22(6.5)—	338
Auto Theft	183(31.4)—	137(23.5)	129(22.2)	75(12.9)	58(10.0)+	582
Vandalism	16(36.4)—	9(20.5)	10(22.7)	5(11.4)	4(9.1)+	44
Trespass	106(33.2)—	92(28.8)	60(18.8)	36(11.3)	25(7.8)+	319
Burglary	239(42.5)+	124(22.1)	101(18.0)	65(11.6)	33(5.9)—	562
Runaway	156(36.1)—	107(24.8)	108(25.0)	42(9.7)	19(4.4)—	432
Incorrigible	112(40.1)—	45(16.1)	70(25.1)	25(9.0)	27(9.7)+	279
Traffic	11(25.6)—	9(20.9)	9(20.9)	6(14.0)	8(18.6)+	43
Liquor	67(34.2)—	55(28.1)	31(15.8)	21(10.7)	22(11.2)+	196
Curfew	208(41.3)—	102(20.2)	85(16.9)	58(11.5)	51(10.1)+	504
Other	208(45.1)+	89(19.9)	81(18.8)	38(8.5)	32(7.1)+	448
Combined	2,320(42.1)	1,248(22.7)	1,014(18.4)	551(10.0)	374(6.8)	5,507
Eligible	10,758(20.0)	9,088(16.9)	12,289(22.9)	9,755(18.1)	11,867(22.1)	53,757

[a] Plus marks indicate a proportion higher than the proportion of all offenses combined found in a given category. Minus signs indicate a smaller than expected proportion.

offenses they are greatly under-represented. They are seldom referred to the court for robbery, loitering, truancy, larceny, and running away. On the other hand, if we compare the percentage of all traffic violations committed by these children with the percentage of all offenses charged against them, we may say that they are over-represented for traffic offenses. The same may be said of them for liquor violations, curfew violations, incorrigibility, car theft, and vandalism.

When specific offenses are grouped according to the harm usually incurred, an interesting pattern emerges. Offenses involving property damage but no permanent material gain, such as vehicle taking, trespassing, and vandalism, are more frequently committed than would be expected by children from high income tracts. On the other hand, property offenses involving permanent material gain, such as larceny, robbery, and acts involving injury to people, such as assault, are committed more frequently than would be expected by children from low income tracts.

Violation of local ordinances, where neither property damage nor injury to people occurs, also presents an interesting pattern. Infractions where it is the condition or situation of the child which constitutes the offense (such as loitering or carrying a concealed weapon) are committed more frequently than expected by children from low income areas. In these offenses it is not something which the child does that makes him delinquent. It is the threat that he presents. He is actually injuring no one at the time of his arrest, and he is neither taking nor destroying property. He is simply "hanging around" or has a weapon in his possession. Traffic violations and liquor law violations which are more "active" violations of local ordinances—but less threatening to police and other citizens—are committed more frequently by children from high income areas.

The overall pattern suggests that children from low income areas are over-represented for offenses involving permanent gain, personal injury to others, or what the police believe to be the threat of injury to property or people. Children from high income areas are more likely to come into court for property offenses that do not lead to personal gain, or for the violation of rules intended to control the driving, drinking, and late hours of teen-agers. Approximately 52 percent of all offenses involving children from high income areas fall into this last category. Only 30 percent of the offenses of children from low income areas fit this description.

This analysis raises an old and important question concerning the appropriateness of using information (median income) about an area to arrive at conclusions concerning individuals in the area. Children living in an area characterized by a low median income may be members of families in the area with relatively high incomes, or the reverse may be true.[2] Thus, it would be desirable to have knowledge of the individual family income for each child coming to the attention of the juvenile court. In the present case such information was not available, a situation which made the use of area information a logical alternative.

There is ample reason to believe that any distortion introduced by this procedure works to understate the relationship between income and specific offenses when comparing low- and middle-class delinquency. This proposition is supported, in part, by the homogeneous nature of the populations in most areas of American cities. The fact that there is a wide discrepancy in median incomes between low and high income areas also supports this notion. Further evidence is provided in this study by an analysis of specific offenses, using race as a variable for which there is both area information and individual information.

RACE AND SPECIFIC OFFENSES

As we have indicated, Wattenberg and Balistrieri found that approximately twice as many white as Negro children were contacted by the police for offenses other than car theft, but three times as many white children were arrested for automobile theft. Our analysis of the Indianapolis data produced similar results.

Census reports of the Negro population in each tract were used to order the tracts by the proportion of Negro residents, and to divide them into five equal sets. Table 2 reveals a pattern similar to that observed in Table 1, where income was used to classify tracts. These results suggest that children from tracts with large Negro populations are proportionately less frequently involved in car theft relative to other offenses. But these children appear over-represented when specific offenses such as, robbery, assault, disorderly

TABLE 2. Specific Offense Information for Tracts Grouped by the Percentage of Negro Residents[a]

	Percent Negro				
	1	2	3	4	
	45–99	10–44	.5–9	Under .5	
Larceny	333(34.3)+[b]	284(29.3)	182(18.8)	171(17.6)—	970
Robbery	43(55.8)+	18(23.4)	10(13.0)	6(7.8)—	77
Receiving	19(42.2)+	10(22.2)	7(15.6)	9(20.0)—	45
Assault	117(49.0)+	53(22.2)	29(12.1)	40(16.7)—	239
Weapons	22(51.2)+	12(27.9)	5(11.6)	4(9.3)—	43
Loitering	30(65.2)+	12(26.1)	0(0.0)	4(8.7)—	46
Truancy	87(25.6)—	111(32.6)	89(26.2)	53(15.6)—	340
Disorderly	164(48.5)+	73(21.6)	35(10.4)	66(19.5)—	338
Auto Theft	148(25.4)—	149(25.6)	123(21.1)	162(27.8)+	582
Vandalism	9(20.5)—	18(40.9)	5(11.4)	12(27.3)+	44
Trespass	79(24.8)—	91(28.5)	57(17.9)	92(28.8)+	319
Burglary	173(30.1)—	133(23.7)	127(22.6)	127(22.6)+	562
Runaway	93(21.5)—	117(27.1)	125(28.9)	97(22.5)+	432
Incorrigible	85(30.5)—	71(25.4)	43(15.4)	80(28.7)+	279
Traffic	8(18.6)—	10(23.3)	8(18.6)	17(39.5)+	43
Liquor	40(20.4)—	49(25.0)	47(24.0)	60(30.6)+	196
Curfew	130(25.8)—	150(29.8)	116(23.0)	108(24.4)+	504
Other	169(37.7)+	137(30.6)	68(15.1)	74(16.5)—	448
Combined	1,749(31.8)	1,498(27.2)	1,076(19.5)	1,157(21.0)	5,507
Eligible	11,229(20.9)	9,983(18.6)	11,016(20.5)	21,529(40.1)	53,757

[a] Information for the 21 tracts in which Negroes comprised from 0 to .05 percent of the population is combined in this table with information for the 21 tracts in which Negroes made up .06 to .49 percent of the population. Over 40 percent of the tracts in Indianapolis have almost no Negro residents.

[b] Plus and minus symbols have the same meaning as those in Table 1.

conduct, and carrying concealed weapons are examined. The similarity between Tables 1 and 2 reflects the fact that all tracts with large Negro populations are low income areas, but not all low income areas are heavily populated by Negroes.

If we overlook, momentarily, the distinction between area information and characteristics of individuals we may infer from Table 2 that Negro children are less likely than white children to be charged with automobile theft, running away, trespassing, truancy, vandalism, curfew violations, liquor and traffic violations, but more apt to be charged with larceny, robbery, loitering, and carrying a concealed weapon. Although our results are consistent with the Wattenberg and Balistrieri study, the proportion of white car theft offenders to overall delinquency activity is not as great. This result is altered, however, when data for individuals are considered. With area information, we can never be certain that the large number of children arrested for larceny in areas with large Negro populations are, in fact, Negro offenders. However, our

TABLE 3. Frequency of Specific Offenses Committed by Negro and White Children

	Negro	White	
Larceny	402(41.4)+[a]	568(58.6)−	970
Robbery	53(68.8)+	24(31.2)−	77
Receiving	24(52.3)+	21(47.7)−	45
Assault	131(54.7)+	108(45.3)−	239
Weapons	28(66.0)+	15(34.0)−	43
Loitering	37(80.9)+	9(19.1)−	46
Disorderly	184(54.5)+	154(45.5)−	338
Auto Theft	132(22.6)−	450(77.4)+	582
Traffic	8(17.6)−	35(82.4)+	43
Liquor	29(14.6)−	167(85.4)+	196
Runaway	93(21.6)−	339(78.4)+	432
Incorrigible	75(26.9)−	204(73.1)+	279
Truancy	77(22.6)−	263(77.4)+	340
Curfew	136(26.9)−	368(73.1)+	504
Vandalism	11(24.3)−	33(75.7)+	44
Trespass	101(31.6)−	218(68.4)+	319
Burglary	172(30.6)−	390(69.4)+	562
Other	198(44.1)	250(55.9)	448
Combined	1,891(33.9)	3,616(66.1)	5,507

[a] Plus and minus signs have the same meaning as those in Table 1.

strong suspicion that the area analysis accurately reflects the activities of the individuals, and perhaps understates them, is borne out by our analysis of offenses by race based on individual data.

Table 3 indicates that Negro children are greatly over-represented in arrests for robbery, loitering, and carrying a concealed weapon, and greatly under-represented in arrests for liquor violations, traffic violations, running away, truancy, and auto theft. Those offenses for which white children are proportionately more often brought into court include such nongainful offenses as vandalism, curfew violation, truancy, incorrigibility, liquor and traffic violations, running away, and car theft. These results reinforce our findings based on our analysis of area information and suggest that the "area information—individual data" distinction may be overemphasized in problems of this kind.

DISCUSSION AND CONCLUSIONS

This examination of specific offense information for arbitrarily drawn income categories illustrates the importance of such information for our understanding of the nature and extent of middle-class delinquency. It suggests that the analysis of middle-class delinquency does not necessarily lead to conclusions that minimize the importance of economic factors. On the contrary, specific offense analyses may show that for some offenses economic factors are more important than was previously anticipated.

The results of this study support those critics of delinquency area research who have questioned the use of combined delinquency information.[3] More important, the findings concerning the relationship of income to specific offenses suggest that an important aspect of delinquency may be consistently overlooked as a result of the widespread use of the term "juvenile delinquency" in a general sense. If children in comfortable economic circumstances are less likely to be involved in gainful offenses, and more likely to be involved in drinking parties, traffic violations, and joyriding, it would be a mistake to regard an increase in this kind of "middle-class delinquency" as evidence against the possible importance of economic factors. Also, it seems entirely possible that many of the conflicting conclusions concerning the nature of middle-class delinquency stem from our loose and conflicting definitions of delinquency. Consistent use of more specific offense information in delinquency research might resolve some of the conflicting interpretations and explanations of juvenile misconduct.

Differences in the Conception of Self as a Male Among Lower and Middle Class Delinquents

LEON F. FANNIN AND
MARSHALL B. CLINARD

This study investigated differences between lower and lower-middle class white delinquents in conception of self as a male, and behavioral correlates of such differences.

Despite the theoretical importance of self-conception from the symbolic interactionist viewpoint, attempts by sociologists to exploit it in empirical research have been comparatively limited.[1] Probable reasons for this include the theoretical complexity of the concept and the consequent difficulty in formulating operational procedures.[2] Thus, conception of self is difficult to utilize partly because an individual has many self-conceptions, not simply one, which undergo modifications through time. A person conceives of himself, for example, as a male, with certain descriptive traits attached to this conception, but also as a son, an engineer, attractive, criminal, likable, and so on.

Some self-conceptions may have greater importance than

Reprinted by permission of the authors and of the editor from *Social Problems*, Vol. 13, No. 2 (Fall, 1965), 205–214.

others because they are more generalized and thus function in a wider variety of social actions. Self-conceptions related to many occupational roles, such as those ascribed to the military elite, high level business executives, or confidence men, would appear to be of this nature.[3]

Another such generalized self-conception, and the subject of this study, is that attached to sex status. Indeed, of all self-conceptions this may be one of the most decisive, as there are relatively few actions in which the participants conceive of themselves as sexless, or are so conceived by others. A "proper" sex self-conception may thus sharply limit approved behavioral alternatives.

The present study focused upon possible differences in the degree to which certain "masculine" traits were held by delinquents from the lower and middle classes. That male self-conceptions may vary by social strata, and be related to behavioral differences, is suggested by a number of studies, particularly those of Miller, Cohen, and Wolfgang, despite some contradictory results.[4] It seemed reasonable to hypothesize that: (1) lower class males would conceive of themselves as tougher, harder, more powerful, and dangerous, and place greater value upon physical prowess and aggression than middle class males; consequently, (2) they probably would be involved more often in physically violent offenses, and define and act with less verbal sophistication and dexterity, but more physical aggression, in dating and sexual behavior.

RESEARCH PROCEDURES

Characteristics of the Samples

Data to test these hypotheses were collected from random samples of lower and lower-middle class white delinquents committed to a training school in a mid-western state. All boys present at the school during the summer of 1962 who were 16 or 17 years old, and who had resided in urban areas of at least 300,000 population, were given a class rank on the basis of their fathers' or guardians' levels of occupation and education. The distribution of these ranks was then differentiated into lower, working, and lower-middle class levels.

Delinquents from the working class were eliminated to obtain class levels as disparate as possible. Class levels higher than the lower-middle[5] were desired but only one boy represented a higher level. The lower and middle classes were treated as separate statistical populations, and 25 cases were randomly selected from each; the sampling fractions were 23.4% and 75.8%, respectively. The limitations in using institutionalized cases and small samples were fully recognized.

Data Collection

Depth interviewing and self-conception scales elicited the most crucial information, with official records used to determine class affiliation and reported delinquent histories. The interviews were structured, although the respondents were unaware of it, and it was believed a high degree of rapport was attained with most of the boys.

Operationally, self-conception as a male was defined by the relative intensity of specific traits which the delinquents felt characterized them when they were placed, verbally, in varying situations that made them explicitly aware of their sex status. Their responses to these situations were then elicited through intensive probing by open-ended questions and by forced-choice scales.

These scales were constructed on the basis of a technique developed by Bennett,[6] whereby the respondent selects traits, three at a time from a list of 15 until none remain, which are ranked "most" or "least" descriptive of himself, or of others, or of situations, and so on. The trait lists provided by Bennett were not used as such because they would not have elicited enough of the type of information desired; rather, four new lists were developed (see Tables 1 and 2 below). Lists I and II contained a majority of traits believed to be positively evaluated by American males while Lists III and IV contained a majority of traits negatively evaluated.

Each list of 15 traits was administered three times, with the situation under which the respondents selected traits varied each time. They were asked to rank the traits contained in each list according to: (1) how they felt the traits *actually* described them as males (actual, or perceived, self); (2) how they *would like* to be as males (ideal self); and (3) how they felt *other people in general* believed them to be as males (generalized looking-glass self). These selections were scored from zero to four points for each trait, so that

TABLE 1. Social Class Comparison of Item Means from Trait Lists I and II for Actual, Ideal, and Generalized Looking-Glass Selves

Trait Lists	Actual Self		Ideal Self		Generalized Looking-Glass Self	
	Lower Class	Middle Class	Lower Class	Middle Class	Lower Class	Middle Class
List I						
Fearless	1.89[a]	1.52[a]	1.37	1.81	1.74	2.00
Loyal	3.05[a]	3.71[a]	2.63[a]	3.71[a]	2.21[a]	3.16[a]
Brave	2.58	2.49	2.79	2.76	3.00	3.00
Strong	2.26	2.33	2.47	2.62	2.37	2.21
Active	2.79	3.29	2.64	2.71	2.16	2.89
Tough	1.88[a]	1.45[a]	1.63[a]	.91[a]	1.74	1.79
Athletic	2.47	2.52	3.05	2.90	2.18	2.42
Hard	1.42	1.29	1.47[a]	1.05[a]	1.88[a]	1.42[a]
Reckless	1.11	1.00	.84	.71	1.00	1.05
Courageous	2.59	2.90	3.05	3.19	2.89	3.05
Loud	1.40	1.24	1.16	1.00	1.68[a]	.89[a]
Powerful	2.04[a]	1.50[a]	1.90	1.91	2.42[a]	1.63[a]
Rough	1.68	1.14	1.05	1.24	1.21	1.60
Smart	1.89[a]	2.86[a]	3.00	3.19	2.20	2.42
Violent	.95	.76	.95[a]	.29[a]	1.32[a]	.47[a]
List II						
Clever	1.95[a]	2.95[a]	3.00	2.38	2.53	2.89
Cruel	1.21	.95	.89	1.05	1.42[a]	.63[a]
Lucky	2.32	2.05	2.89[a]	3.62[a]	2.47	2.63
Fierce	2.58[a]	1.05[a]	1.95	1.67	1.47	1.42
Bad	1.14[a]	1.57[a]	.84	1.05	1.32[a]	1.74[a]
Wild	1.05	1.19	1.16	.81	1.53	1.21
Proud	3.11	3.71	3.47[a]	3.06[a]	2.74[a]	3.21[a]
Dangerous	1.11[a]	.57[a]	.95	.67	.54[a]	1.00[a]
Bold	2.21	2.24	2.21	2.14	2.37[a]	1.74[a]
Firm	2.16	2.52	2.79[a]	3.14[a]	2.42	2.78
Shrewd	2.11	2.05	1.42	1.76	1.88[a]	1.69[a]
Cunning	2.79	2.14	1.95	1.90	2.00	1.74
Stern	2.32	2.81	2.74	2.71	2.68	2.26
Smooth	2.26[a]	2.72[a]	2.53	2.71	2.79	2.63
Fighter	1.68	1.48	1.21	1.33	1.84[a]	2.53[a]

[a] Differences between means for lower and middle classes are significant at the .05 level (Student's test). The range for any mean is 0 to 4.

those which the boys felt described them most closely had the highest values.

TABLE 2. Social Class Comparison of Item Means from Trait Lists III and IV for Actual, Ideal, and Generalized Looking-Glass Selves

	Actual Self		Ideal Self		Generalized Looking-Glass Self	
Trait Lists	Lower Class	Middle Class	Lower Class	Middle Class	Lower Class	Middle Class
List III						
Proper	1.63	1.33	1.69	1.48	1.42	1.32
Loving	2.26	2.43	2.74	3.00	1.75[a]	2.63[a]
Graceful	1.58	1.24	2.00	1.95	1.92	1.42
Modest	1.58	1.57	1.89[a]	.95[a]	1.69	1.47
Respectable	2.63	2.43	3.00[a]	3.62[a]	2.63	2.37
Shy	1.74	2.10	.53	.19	1.42	1.16
Sympathetic	1.53[a]	2.57[a]	1.32	1.81	1.79	2.21
Gentle	1.95	1.86	2.68[a]	2.02[a]	2.11	2.26
Courteous	2.26	2.10	2.05	2.33	2.42	2.32
Peaceful	2.68	2.43	2.58	2.51	2.37	2.58
Friendly	2.84[a]	3.52[a]	3.05	3.10	3.16	3.68
Soft	.96	.86	1.05	.67	1.21	.74
Neat	2.78[a]	2.14[a]	2.57[a]	3.05[a]	2.68	2.89
Affectionate	2.05	2.14	1.53[a]	2.05[a]	1.69	1.95
Tender	1.53	1.28	1.32	1.27	1.74[a]	1.00[a]
List IV						
False	.95	.71	.79	.71	1.32[a]	.68[a]
Kind	2.89[a]	3.33[a]	3.21	3.29	3.32	3.37
Sweet	1.79	1.88	2.53	2.68	2.32	2.78
Upright	2.32	2.71	2.78	2.95	2.21	2.37
Sensitive	2.74	2.62	2.37	2.52	2.11[a]	2.78[a]
Feeble	.63	.62	.37[a]	.85[a]	1.11[a]	.47[a]
Delicate	1.84	1.52	1.84	1.95	1.85	1.53
Helpless	1.17	1.14	.89	.76	1.44[a]	.89[a]
Safe	2.89	2.81	2.68	3.05	2.68	3.07
Timid	1.89	1.95	1.79	1.62	1.89	1.58
Afraid	1.37	1.71	1.11	1.14	.95	1.32
Fearful	1.84	1.62	2.11[a]	1.23[a]	2.32	2.21
Quiet	3.68	3.10	3.21	2.97	3.11	2.84
Loved	2.58[a]	3.33[a]	3.74	3.66	2.32[a]	3.11[a]
Weak	1.42[a]	.95[a]	.58	.62	1.05	1.00

[a] Differences between means for lower and middle classes are significant at the .05 level (Student's test). The range for any mean is 0 to 4.

SELF-CONCEPTIONS AND SOCIAL CLASS

The findings indicate that while the male self-conception is very similar across class lines, there are a few crucial differences which apparently are related to a diverse range of behavior patterns.

A partial test of the first hypothesis, stating in the null form that *there is no significant difference in the conception of self as a male held by lower and middle class delinquents*, is provided by analysis of the delinquents' responses to the Trait Lists (see Tables 1 and 2). Almost one-third (32.2%) of the means calculated from Lists I and II and over one-fifth (22.2%) of the means from Lists III and IV are significantly different by class ($p < .05$), and since these differences are largely in the expected direction, the null hypothesis is tentatively rejected.

Tough Guys and Loyal Comrades

Lower class boys felt themselves to be (actual self) tougher, more powerful, fierce, fearless, and dangerous than middle class boys. It was unexpected, however, that they did not feel themselves to be significantly more violent, hard, and pugilistic. Middle class delinquents, on the other hand, conceived of themselves as being more loyal, clever, smart, smooth, and bad. This greater stress upon loyalty by the middle class is surprising,[7] even though the lower class also ranked it very high.

When responses depicting the ideal self and the generalized looking-glass self are studied, essentially the same traits separate the class levels, with some interesting exceptions. The lower class would like to be (ideal self) tougher, harder, and more violent than the middle class, while the latter would like to be more loyal, lucky, and firm. When their interpretations of how other people in general view them are analyzed (generalized looking-glass self), approximately the same findings hold, except that the middle class felt others believed them to be more dangerous, bad, and pugilistic. It would seem to be quite clear that the norms from which these delinquents believed others evaluated them were sharply different, because the lower class had been actually involved in more assaults, robberies, fights, and other delinquencies (see below) than the middle class and yet the latter felt others believed them to be more "dangerous" and "bad."

The more negatively connoted traits used in Lists III and IV were far less discriminatory except for a sharp difference in responses to "love" and related traits. Middle class boys felt they were loved to a significantly greater degree and felt others also believed them to be more loving. In addition, they conceived of themselves as being more friendly, sympathetic, and kind.

These differences were strongly supported and supplemented by the results gained from informal interviewing. While discussing the type of "reputation" desired among their closest male friends, and among females and police, lower class boys stressed their ability and willingness to fight, their physical power over others, and their fear of nothing. These traits appear to be similar to those ascribed by Sykes to prison inmates who attempt to prove their masculinity to others and to themselves, in a one-sexed community, by over-emphasizing such "masculine" traits.[8] Middle class boys, on the other hand, stressed loyalty to friends above all, their desire to be clever and smooth, and also to be daring.

An additional trait which appeared to more adequately characterize the lower class boys was a greater degree of callousness in their relations with others, particularly in regard to "enemies" (which may reflect a relative lack of propathic role taking). This trait was perhaps clearer in their relations with homosexuals and adolescent females.

While exciting exploits and incredulous adventures were highly evaluated by members of both class levels, it appeared that middle class boys conceived of themselves as more daring. They liked to take risks and regàle others with their fascinating tales. Some of the adventures they told during the interviews were injected with much the same drama they had probably seen in movies and on television, particularly when they viewed themselves as "desperate heroes."

From an over-all perspective, then, it would appear these classes differ chiefly in that significantly more lower class delinquents feel themselves to be "tough guys," while more middle class delinquents feel themselves to be "loyal and daring comrades."

These class differences cannot be explained by differential membership in gangs, where a stress upon toughness would be expected, as an almost identical proportion participated in gangs, namely 84% of the lower and 80% of the middle class ($p > .70$).

The degree to which these boys conceived of themselves as tough guys, however, varied within the class levels. Briefly, the range of such conceptions appeared to run typologically from the "bruising marauder" to the "fearful warrior." The former is a boy who is constantly proving his toughness by fighting unrelentingly at the slightest provocation, or who initiates brawls because he "likes to fight." His perception of ridicule, or the merest hint of disbelief about his masculinity, is extremely acute and he will settle the matter immediately by force. He is looked upon with respectful apprehension by his peers as a "nut," "crazy bastard," "a real goner," and as "dangerous" because he is always stirring up trouble; he is, in short, a disliked deviant.

The fearful or reluctant warrior is a "brittle tough guy" who does not like fighting or physical violence but considers himself at least minimally "tough." This self-conception is to a large extent defensive[9] and could probably be changed comparatively easily if he were placed in social situations other than the tough world in which he lives.

SELF-CONCEPTIONS RELATED TO BEHAVIOR

It had been hypothesized that if these differences in self-conceptions by class had meaning, this would probably be reflected in behavioral differences, such as frequency of physical violence, occupational aspiration, and attitudes toward sexuality. To a large extent these expectations were fulfilled. Six statistical tests were made and five allowed rejection of the null hypothesis.

Physical Violence

One of the more important of the tests was a comparison of the frequency with which reported and unreported robberies and assaults were committed by members of the two class levels. The vast majority of all lower class delinquents, 84%, had committed at least one such offense compared to 28% of the middle class ($p < .01$); 28% of the lower and

8% of the middle class had committed 10 or more violent offenses.

Class level was also related to the frequency of fighting with other boys. Lower class delinquents fought singly and in groups significantly more often ($p < .05$) than middle class delinquents, with 20% of them averaging five or more fights per month compared to 4.0%. The possibly greater lack of propathic role taking characteristic of lower class boys also appeared in their techniques of fighting. More of them used weapons, and more advocated "stomping" (kicking a fallen opponent, particularly in the face). As one very "tough guy" answered when questioned about the frequency and circumstances under which stomping should be used: "Always! You're a sucker if you don't because the other guy would sure as hell do it to you. I always try to kick the guy's teeth out myself, but anywhere's good."

Lower class boys also regularly carried weapons on their persons significantly more often than middle class boys ($p < .02$); 80% usually carried a knife, gun, or "knuckles," compared to 48% of the middle class. The most frequent reason given for having a weapon close at hand was self protection.

One factor which ran counter to expectations was the similarity in the frequency of forcible rape committed by boys of both classes ($p > .05$); the proportions having done this were 12% in the lower and 16% in the middle classes, but differences in class definitions of "rape" may have been an important obscuring variable.

Occupational Aspirations

While occupational aspirations are influenced by a wide variety of factors, it was anticipated that one which might help to explain the different aspirations of the lower class would be their orientation toward certain categories of work as related to their male self-conceptions.

Eighty per cent of the lower class boys wanted a type of adult occupation in which they could work with their hands, while only 36% of the middle class desired this ($p < .01$). Some of the reasons given for these lower aspirations were that it was a "real man's" type of work while a desk job was somewhat effeminate; it was "better" for a man to work with his hands; you had to "have something on the ball" to work with machines while anyone could work at a desk job; and white collar work was in some sense "cheating" because it was *not really work.* Finally, an occupational role of greater attraction for lower class boys was that of the combat infantryman, or even better, the "fighting marine."

Sexuality

Masculinity was also expressed differently by members of the two class levels in their orientation and behavior toward adolescent females.[10] Toughness, callousness, and physical prowess appeared to be dominant for the lower class, while sophistication, dexterity, and verbal manipulation seemed prominent for the middle class.

Dating was viewed by the lower class, for example, primarily as the *means* to an end (sexual intercourse) while the middle class stressed dating as an *end* in itself (the fun element in going out). Sixty-eight per cent of the lower class boys believed intercourse was the normal goal in dating a girl, while 40% of the middle class felt this way ($p < .05$).

For the lower class boy, sexual intercourse was to be achieved by the raw force of his masculinity; he would not "seduce" his date so much as he would "conquer" her. The aura of his maleness should be enough for the girl, without stooping to demean himself by clever, witty, and manipulative verbal "propaganda." The female should surrender herself to this image of the "all man" rather than be converted to willingness by gentle and smoothly coined phrases. The latter approach to the lower class is sissified. In short, when attempting to gain sexual intercourse, the lower class boy more often viewed himself as a "rough and manly conqueror" while the middle class boy thought of himself more often as a "slick seducer."

Similarly, the "teaser" as a female type was evaluated differently by members of the two class levels.[11] To lower class boys, she more often represented unmitigated and unforgivable viciousness and deserved "anything her date would do to her," including a beating. To middle class boys she was scorned and considered indecent for "leading a guy on like that" but should not be "slapped around." At most she probably should be "dumped out of the car and made to walk home."

DISCUSSION

A number of implications emerged from this study's findings, although the small size of the samples and the relative primitiveness of the procedures used to elicit self-conception data must be kept in mind. The data suggest that a significant proportion of offenses involving physical violence may be committed by delinquents who stress certain "masculine" traits in their self-conceptions as males, which help channel and legitimize such violence. Self-conception may act as a closure factor,[12] restricting the possibilities of behavior to a narrowed universe. In terms of rehabilitating violent offenders, consequently, it would seem feasible that a highly selective program directed toward the limited ends of changing this aspect of the self-conception might prove more helpful than a global effort at pervasive personality change, or other current techniques. It cannot be inferred, obviously, that all deviant aggression by males can be explained by this type of self-conception,[13] as the latter may result from behavior, but it may help to explain a portion of it.

Another implication of the findings is that this tough guy self-conception may be related to a wide range of other types of behavior, deviant and nondeviant, including drinking patterns, leisure habits, divorce and desertion, illegitimacy, and so on. This needs intensive investigation, as do other types of self-conceptions.

Finally, empirically oriented analyses of the components of social interaction may help to better understand deviant and nondeviant behavior; this refers not only to further studies of the types and interrelation of self-conceptions, but also to analyses of the various aspects of role taking, the relationship between role taking and role playing, the internalization of significant and generalized others and their specific influence upon behavior, and the complex interrelationships of these factors within the "social self."

SUMMARY

The conception of self as a male held by lower and lower-middle class delinquents was probed by informal depth interviewing and by forced-choice scales. While self-conceptions were found to be quite similar, lower class boys did conceive of themselves as being tougher, more fearless, powerful, fierce, and dangerous, while middle class boys felt they were more clever, smart, smooth, bad, and loyal. Descriptively, these were labeled as "tough guy" and "loyal and daring comrade" self-conceptions.

These self-conceptions were then found to be related to specific types of behavior. The "tough guys" significantly more often committed violent offenses, fought more often and with harsher means, carried weapons, had lower occupational aspirations, and stressed toughness and related traits in the reputation they desired and in sexual behavior.

Rehabilitative and preventive efforts to decrease violent offenses might be more profitable if focused upon this aspect of the offender's social self. The possible relation of the tough guy self-conception, and other types of self-conceptions, to varying types of behavior was also pointed out.

PART III

Patterns of Middle-Class Delinquency

INTRODUCTION

Zip-guns, flick-knives, and violent gangs are largely foreign to the world of middle-class youths. This is not to deny their occasional outburst of aggression, nor the versatility and seriousness of their delinquencies. Surely all children lie and steal and middle-class youths are no exception. Some drink liquor and get drunk, others gamble for money, damage property, and drive cars without a license. There are boys who steal cars, have fist fights, and engage in sexual intercourse. A few experiment with drugs. In these and other activities they resemble city boys from the lower classes.

Yet delinquency among middle-class boys looks different when compared with delinquency in the lower class. It takes on a different "look"—a middle-class style. There is a newspaper report of a teen-age gambling casino operated by three teen-age youths in the basement of a suburban home. The 17-year-old host dressed in a white dinner jacket and black tie, and a limousine service provided transportation for the teen-age "guests." From most accounts, violence occupies little part of the daily routine of middle-class boys. Strong-arm tactics, weapon-carrying, and fearlessness are not typical of these youths. This is evident in the report on middle-class "gangs" by Howard and Barbara Myerhoff, although Harrison Salisbury reports incidents of violence occurring in the suburbs. The behavioral front of middle-class youths, the objects of their delinquencies, and their vocabulary of motives coincide with, and are expressive more of, the role of the socially sophisticated teen-ager. In part, this relates to differences in self-conception, role models, and in the values and attitudes that circumscribe the role of adolescent in the lower and middle classes.

But data are scarce. To what extent do respectable roles among middle-class youths include expectations of delinquency? For example, does the role of high school athlete require engaging in the occasional drinking bout? What kinds of delinquency confer status among middle-class youths? To what degree are certain types of delinquency institutionalized within the middle-class youth culture? What is the social role of "juvenile delinquent" among middle-class adolescents? Research designed to answer these questions and to capture the quality—precise descriptive accounts—of the daily delinquent activities of these youths is needed urgently.

In this section, the Myerhoffs describe their observations of "gangs" of middle-class youths. William Wattenberg and James Balistrieri report that automobile theft is correlated with boys from socially advantaged homes. George Maddox and Bevode McCall report their findings and discuss the drinking and abstinence patterns among adolescents. The present writer suggests that certain kinds of delinquency in the middle class are related to the social roles of boys and to their differential participation in legitimate teen-age activities. In a recent study of middle-class youths, Nancy Barton Wise reports similarities in delinquency among boys and girls. Finally, in Harrison Salisbury's account of delinquency in the suburbs, vandalism, violence, and aggression are not uncommon among some middle-class youths.

Field Observations of Middle Class "Gangs"

HOWARD L. MYERHOFF AND
BARBARA G. MYERHOFF

The sociological literature about gangs contains at least two sharply conflicting descriptions of the extent of gang structure and the nature of their values. In the most prevalent view, the gang is seen as a kind of primary group, highly structured, relatively permanent and autonomous, possessing a well developed delinquent subculture which is transmitted to new members. The gang is interpreted as meeting strongly felt needs of its members and as providing a collectively derived solution to common problems of adjustment. Different writers who hold this view have stressed different problems, but nearly all have agreed that one of the most important functions of the gang is to establish close bonds of loyalty and solidarity between members of a tightly knit peer group.

Cohen[1] has identified the primary needs met by the gang as those of resolving status frustration for lower class boys, and providing an expression of masculine identification for middle class boys. Parsons[2] has also emphasized the achievement of sexual identity as a problem dealt with by delinquent behavior. Cloward and Ohlin,[3] following Merton's conception, have specified the discrepancy between aspirations toward success goals and opportunities for achieving them as the problem giving rise to gang behavior. Kvaraceus and Miller[4] have stressed the inherent conflict between lower and middle class values and the delinquent's predisposition to the former

Reprinted by permission of the authors and of the editor from *Social Forces*, Vol. 42, No. 3 (March, 1964), 328–336.

in explaining gang behavior. Eisenstadt,[5] and Bloch and Niederhoffer[6] have pointed to the gang as a collective response to the adolescent's striving toward the attainment of adulthood and the frustrations attendant on the transition from one age status to another. These authors identify different components of the gang subculture according to their interpretation of its function, but implicit or explicit in all these positions is the view of the gang as an integrated and relatively cohesive group.

A strikingly different interpretation of the structure of gangs describes them as informal, short lived, secondary groups without a clear cut, stable delinquent structure. Lewis Yablonsky[7] has suggested a conceptualization of the gang as a "near-group," specifying the following definitive characteristics: diffuse role definitions, limited cohesion, impermanence, minimal consensus on norms, shifting membership, emotionally disturbed leaders, and limited definition of membership expectations. On a continuum of the extent of social organization, Yablonsky locates the gang midway between the mob at one end and the group at the other. The gang is seen as in a state of equilibrium, moving sometimes closer to one end of the continuum and sometimes the other, but never actually becoming completely disorganized like a mob or completely organized like a group. He contends that detached worker programs, by treating the gang as a true group, may actually make it one. When a detached worker acknowledges a gang's leaders, recognizes its territory, membership, name, and purpose, he crystallizes its organization, lending it a structure which it did not previously have. This Yablonsky calls the "group-fulfilling prophecy."

The gangs he has observed are, in actuality, quite different from groups. They are "near-groups" which have a diffuse and malleable structure that enables them to meet the varied and individual needs of the members. For many gang members who are unable to meet the demands and responsibilities of more structured social organizations, it is the gang's very lack of organization and absence of expectations which constitute its primary sources of satisfaction. Youths affiliate with a gang not for a feeling of belonging and solidarity but because it is an organization within which they can relate to others in spite of their limited social abilities. The flexibility of gang organization means that it can meet diverse, momentary needs of the members who, accordingly, participate in it with varying intensity. Yablonsky suggests that in a gang there are a few core members, surrounded by a large number of peripheral members to whom the gang is much less important and who are more loosely attached to it.

James F. Short, Jr., objects to Yablonsky's description of the gang as a near-group on the grounds that he has overstated the case,[8] but agrees, nevertheless that gangs do not have "the stability of membership, the tightly knit organization and rigid hierarchical structure which is sometimes attributed to them."[9] Most of the groups he has observed have the kind of shifting membership which Yablonsky described.

The supervisor of a large, long lived detached worker program in Los Angeles with many years of gang experience there and in Harlem has given a description much like that of Yablonsky.[10] He observed that delinquent gangs seldom act as a corporate group and that most of their anti-social activities are committed in groups of two's or three's, or by a single person. He found communication between members to be meagre and sporadic, reflecting the same limitations in social abilities that Yablonsky identified. In fact, one of the goals of his detached worker program is the structuring of gangs into social groups, encouraging cooperation and communication between members and a gradual assumption of social responsibilities. When successful, a detached worker is able to form a gang into a club which elects officers, collects dues, arranges activities, and eventually establishes non-delinquent norms and role expectations. Thus by substituting the satisfactions of membership in an organized social group for delinquent activities, the program provides an aspect of socialization which gang members have not previously experienced. The program is able, in this way, to prepare gang members to meet the requirements and responsibilities of conventional, adult social life. The technique is apparently the self-conscious application of what Yablonsky has called "the group-fulfilling prophecy," and seems to be quite a successful one.

The field observations presented here are based on the experiences of a participant-observer who spent two weeks among several groups of deviant and non-deviant middle class youths in a suburb of Los Angeles. These observations are particularly pertinent to the prevailing conflicting interpretations of the extent of gang structure. The middle class youngsters described here were located through lists of "hangouts" provided by local police, school authorities, and probation officers. The observer "hung around" these places and when asked who he was, which was seldom, explained that he was a writer doing a series of articles on teenagers. The youngsters talked freely in front of and to the observer, and after a short time included him in many of their activities, such as house and beach parties, drag races, car club meetings, bull sessions, and bowling. Altogether, about eighty youngsters ranging in age between fifteen and eighteen were observed. All were Caucasian, most in high school, Protestant, and in appearance and manner readily distinguishable from the lower class boys and girls who occasionally mixed with them.

Impressions, activities, and conversations were recorded by the observer in a daily journal, and roughly classified into the following categories: values and peer interactions, deviant activities, and group organization.[11] It should be kept in mind that these comments are observations, not findings. Many authors have lamented the dearth of speculation about as well as empirical observations of gangs, in both the middle and lower classes. Cohen and Short recently said about middle class delinquent subcultures: "The saddest commentary, however, is that we are faced with a poverty of speculation, without which there can be no meaningful research, without which, in turn, there can be no conclusions that are more than speculation."[12] These observations and comments lead to some of the speculation which must precede meaningful empirical research, and their greatest value may prove to be heuristic.

VALUES AND PEER INTERACTIONS

The youngsters observed, like most groups of teenagers, were rather uniform in dress and demeanor. Their self-possession and poise, along with elaborate grooming and expensive, well tended clothes combined to give an impression of urbanity and sophistication beyond what would normally be expected of this age group. For most events, the girls wore tight capris, blouses or cashmere sweaters, silver fingernail and toenail polish, towering intricate coiffures, brush applied iridescent lipstick, and heavy eye make-up. The boys, like the girls, were uniformly clean, and like them preferred their pants as tight as possible; levis were rarely seen. Usually an Ivy League shirt was worn outside the pants and over this a nylon windbreaker. At beaches both boys and girls wore bikinis and apparently no one without a deep and even tan ever dared appear. The overall impression fostered was one of careful, elegant casualness sustained in manner as well as appearance. The complete absence of the social and physical awkwardness usually associated with adolescence was indeed striking.

The content of conversation among these groups did not differ appreciably from what one would expect to find among most teenagers; it concerned clothes, dates, sex, school classes and activities, bridge, sports, and so forth. But no subject dominated the conversation as much as the car, which seemed an object of undying, one might say morbid, fascination. The majority of girls and boys owned their own cars and virtually all had access to a car, usually a late model American or foreign sports car. "Custom jobs" were not rare and cars were often "shaved," "chopped," "channeled," and "pinstriped." All were scrupulously clean and highly polished. The argot concerning the car was as elaborate and subtle as one might expect in view of its importance; such matters as "dual quads," "turning seven grand," "slicks," "3:7 trans ratio" were frequently discussed with great intensity. Driving skill and mechanical expertise were prized far above mere ownership of a desirable car.

The car, in fact, permeated every aspect of these youngsters' social life. The size of groups which gathered was usually limited by the number a single car could hold, and when several cars congregated, at drive-ins for example, youngsters demonstrated a distinct unwillingness to leave the car. Radios in cars were never off and all activities took place against a background of popular music. The car also affected the places frequented, with drive-in movies and restaurants preferred. After school and on weekends, many of these youngsters could be seen slowly cruising in their cars, up and down the neighborhood streets, greeting acquaintances, chatting, taking friends for short rides, all with an air of easy sociability. These cruises in manner and purpose were reminiscent of the Spanish late afternoon *Paseo,* in which young people stroll casually up and down streets closed off for that purpose. The cars were the location for nearly all social events engaged in by these youngsters. They were the site of bull sessions, drinking bouts, and necking parties. In all, the car provided a mobile parlor, clubhouse, dining room, and bedroom; it was at once the setting and symbol of much of adolescent deviant and non-deviant sociability and sexuality.

Several writers have emphasized the dominant role of the car in patterns of middle class deviance. Wattenberg and Balistrieri[13] found auto theft to be characteristic of "favored groups," older white boys who had better relations with peers and came from more desirable neighborhoods than did boys charged with other types of offenses. T. C. N. Gibbens[14] studied adolescent car thieves in London and also found them to be a "favored group," not because they lived in better neighborhoods but because they came from homes which were intact and affectionate. All these findings and impressions may be interpreted as supporting the contention of Parsons[15] and Cohen[16] that the primary middle class problem to which delinquency is a response is the establishment of masculine identity. Indeed, the sexual significance of the car has been widely recognized. Gibbens comments that: "In the simplest cases joy-riding is of the common 'proving' type, in which an overprotected lad from a 'good' home commits an offense to prove his masculinity. . . . The daring act represents a bid for independence, and the car provides a feeling of power in which he feels so lacking. . . ."[17] Certainly, this view is corroborated by the observations of middle class youths offered here, among whom the car, if not a sufficient cause of masculinity, is at least a necessary condition for it.

In view of the importance of the car, it was not surprising to find that the only formal social organizations to which many of these youngsters belonged were car clubs, whose membership often transcended the class and age affiliations typical of the more informal gatherings. These clubs usually consist of about fifteen members and are devoted to the building and legal and illegal racing of cars. In order to be admitted, youngsters' cars must undergo rigorous police safety inspections and members may be expelled or excluded for too many traffic tickets. In marked contrast to the informal groups, these clubs are highly structured. Meetings are regular and frequent, membership is stable, leaders are elected for specified terms, and the clubs have names, plaques and jackets. The meetings are conducted strictly according to Robert's Rules of Order, fines are levied for infractions of rules, dues are collected, and events are planned in detail and in advance. A well developed pattern of mutual aid and extension cooperation has been established and it is not unusual for members to pool money, skills, and time to build a car which is entered in races and rallies by the entire group. It is obviously no accident that the only object around which spontaneous, unsupervised yet structured groups form is the car.

DEVIANT ACTIVITIES

The deviant behavior of the groups observed varied greatly in seriousness. Some of their activities may be considered deviant only because technically illegal, such as curfew violation and beer drinking, while more serious infractions such as theft and narcotics are less common. The more serious deviant activities seemed to involve the least number of people at one time; youngsters were alone or with a friend or two on these occasions. The less serious infractions were not usually the purpose of a gathering but were rather incidental to another activity. These included spontaneous drag racing, drinking, and much sexual activity.

Of the more serious violations, theft was certainly the most common. Many boys spoke of frequent and regular stealing, often from employers. Ready access rather than need or desire seemed to determine the choice of stolen objects. These items were seldom traded or converted into cash. Great pride was evidenced in the cleverness with which the thefts were executed and a good performance seemed more important than the acquisition of goods. Several boys boasted about never having been caught although they had been engaging in this activity for years. The stolen goods were by no means small, inexpensive, or easily portable, but included such items as tires, car radios, phonographs, tape recorders, and television sets. Great care was taken in order to ensure that stolen goods were not missed. Thefts were timed so as to coincide with events such as inventories, and the filling of orders.

It is not possible on the basis of these observations to estimate the frequency of these thefts but one can say with certainty that they were by no means uncommon. This phenomenon appears to be very similar to "white collar crime" and as such raises questions as to the generalizability of theories of delinquency causation based solely on socio-economic variables. As Wattenberg and Balistrieri have pointed out: "The point of impact of the concept of [white collar crime] lies in its assumption that the form of anti-social or illegal conduct rather than its frequency varies from . . . class to class in our society."[18] It may well be that the "white collar delinquent" engages in as many anti-social activities as do lower class youngsters but a combination of factors, particularly the form of delinquency, interact to prevent these activities from coming to the attention of the authorities, or if apprehended, prevent the middle class youngsters from being officially handled and recorded. Indeed, there is already much evidence to suggest this is the case.[19]

The same discretion, judgment, and self-possession which characterized thefts was observed in the homosexual, and to a lesser degree, the heterosexual gatherings. These events were held in private homes and occasionally included slightly older boys from nearby colleges. They were not events which were likely to attract the attention of police or even parents. The homosexual youngsters often met one another at small cabarets, coffee houses, and bars in which few lower class teenagers or adults were to be seen. They also met in several private clubs whose members were primarily upper and middle class teenage homosexuals. These youngsters were typically inconspicuous and did not indulge in egregious displays of homosexuality either in dress or manner. While in the clubs, many were openly solicitous and flirtatious, but upon leaving, their more conventional manners were resumed. The same caution was apparent among those who purchased and used narcotics, usually marijuana. It was smoked at small, quiet parties, rarely while driving or in public places. It was not unusual to hear these poised, well dressed youngsters speak of stealing, using narcotics, and the advantages and disadvantages of their respective college choices in the same tone of voice and conversation.

The middle class group anti-social activities which *do* come to the attention of the authorities are of a rather different nature than those just described. Several examples of these were provided by a local probation officer assigned to the neighborhood. On one occasion, he recalled, a group of about ten boys went back and forth across a busy intersection between 5:30 and 6:30 in the evening, effectively bringing traffic to a complete standstill until dispersed by the police. Another time, a car full of boys drove slowly down a main shopping street spraying the well dressed shoppers with the contents of a fire extinguisher. One incident involved a group of boys who stole an old car and took it to a vacant lot and while one boy drove the car around in circles, the others threw stones at it, until it was nothing but a battered corpse.

There is a mischievous, often amusing overtone to all these incidents; they are not the kind likely to be thought malicious or violent. Rather, they are spontaneous and gratuitous, proving nothing but providing "kicks." This behavior is not the kind which is likely to seriously alarm parents or police and has none of the grim overtones usually associated, correctly or not, with the activities of lower class gangs. In general, the non-violent nature of the deviant activities of these youngsters is salient, and personal aggression rare. The anti-social activities observed among these groups rarely took the form of open defiance of authority; manipulation rather than rebellion appeared to be the preferred technique for handling trouble with authorities. Cohen and Short have postulated just such a difference between lower and middle class delinquency:

> "*. . . we are persuaded that further research will reveal subtle but important differences between working class and middle class patterns of delinquency. It seems probable that the qualities of malice, bellicosity, and violence will be underplayed in the middle class subcultures and that these subcultures will emphasize more the deliberate courting of danger . . . and a sophisticated, irresponsible, 'playboy' approach to activities symbolic in our culture, of adult roles and centering largely around sex, liquor, and automobiles.*"[20]

How closely that description fits the middle class groups observed is readily apparent.

Interestingly enough, even while engaging in flagrant, frequent infractions of the law, these youngsters sustained the opinion that their activities would in no way interfere with their future plans. They did not define themselves as delinquents or even trouble makers and did not expect others to do so. More likely than not, upon graduating from high school and entering college, as most planned to do, these youngsters will leave their deviant activities behind without a trace in the form of official records, self-definition, or residues of unpleasant experiences with authorities. The police seemed to share this expectation. An incident was observed in which a boy was picked up for drinking and curfew violation. In the patrol car he expressed his concern lest the occasion jeopardize his chances for entering college. The officer, who had until that point been rather surly, hastened to reassure the boy that such a possibility was quite unlikely, and implied that nothing would come of the visit to the station.

The same expectations were shared by the people who worked at the places where these youngsters congregated—waitresses, life guards, theater managers—who did not feel that even as a group they constituted a serious nuisance. Their tolerance is no doubt increased by middle class youngsters' liberal spending habits which make it worth their while to put up with an occasional annoyance. But in addition their attitudes are affected by the usually pleasant relations they have with these boys and girls, whose interpersonal experiences with adults and peers are more harmonious and extensive than those observed among the more socially inadequate lower class gangs observed by Yablonsky and the supervisor of the detached worker program in Los Angeles. This difference in social ability is hardly surprising in view of the middle classes' traditional specialization in entrepreneurial activities. The techniques of smooth social relations are the bread and butter of the middle classes, and middle class teenagers, deviant and non-deviant alike, demonstrate remarkable agility in the manipulation of social situations. Their interpersonal skills enable them to control their social environment to a much greater degree than possible for lower class teenagers who have not had the opportunity to acquire and perfect these techniques.

GROUP ORGANIZATION

It can be seen that the groups observed, with the exception of disturbed leadership, precisely conform to Yablonsky's description of a near-group. Certainly, they do not qualify for the term "gang" as it is usually used, nor do they have well developed delinquent values. On the contrary, the similarity between these youngsters' values and those of the adult, dominant society is conspicuous. Such a continuity has been suggested by Matza and Sykes[21] in a recent article in which they contend that the values underlying much juvenile delinquency are far less deviant than commonly portrayed, due to a prevailing oversimplification of middle class values. The authors argue that existing alongside the official, dominant values in society is another conflicting set which they call subterranean. These are values which are frequently relegated by adults to leisure time pursuits and are not ordinarily allowed to interfere with the regular course of a conventional life. Matza and Sykes point out that the content of these subterranean values has been described by Veblen in his portrayal of the "gentleman of leisure"—disdain for work, identification of masculinity with tough, aggressive behavior, and the search for thrills and adventures. The authors feel that the delinquent emphasizes a society's subterranean values but instead of relegating them to after-hours activities, he makes them a way of life, a code of behavior. The delinquent, then, has not evolved an original set of values but has only taken over one aspect of those held by most people along with their publicly proclaimed, respectable middle class values.

J. A. Pitt-Rivers[22] has suggested the concept "infra-structure" to describe what Matza and Sykes have referred to as subterranean values. The infra-structure is a set of values which exists alongside and in opposition to the official beliefs and behavior required by the formal systems of authority. It is not merely a set of separate beliefs held by one segment of the community but is that part of the social structure consisting of the personal, internalized version of officially endorsed values. The two systems are seen by Pitt-Rivers as interdependent, representing the private and public morals held simultaneously by everyone in the social system. The opposition of the value systems creates a structural tension or ambivalence which, though never really sharp enough to seriously endanger the social order, nevertheless provides a predisposition to deviance from officially prescribed behavior. The relation between the two systems is continuous and while certain people or groups are more influenced by one system than the other, both affect all behavior to some degree.

In the light of the observations presented here, one may postulate that just as certain individuals and social groups are closer to one set of these values than the other, so are different age groups. Adolescence may be understood as a period in the life span of the individual when he is closer to deviant or subterranean values than he will be as an adult or has been as a child. Several authors have conceptualized adolescence as a period of license, a time for social and sexual exploration. Benedict[23] has pointed out the expectation that the adolescent will be irresponsible, though as an adult a few years later he can no longer be, and Erikson[24] has described adolescence as a psycho-social moratorium, set aside for experimentation in establishing an identity prior to the assumption of adult roles. One implication which can be drawn from these interpretations is that a teenager's "deviant behavior" may be in actuality a phase in his history when he is allowed and even expected to behave in accord with a set of subterranean values which do not disappear when he becomes an adult but instead are acted upon only on more appropriate occasions.

The adolescent in our culture, it is suggested, may be viewed as an aristocrat, a gentleman of leisure who, for a time, is not required to work but is allowed to play, explore, test limits, indulge his pleasures, and little else besides. This description of the delinquent as a kind of aristocrat closely resembles Finestone's characterization of the Negro teenage narcotic addict.[25] The "cat" is an individual who has developed an elaborate repertoire of manipulative techniques for dealing with the world, eschewing violence in favor of persuasion and charm. "He seeks through a harmonious combination of charm, ingratiating speech, dress, music, the proper dedication to his 'kick' and unrestrained generosity to make of his day to day life itself a gracious work of art."[26] The similarity between this depiction of the "cat" and the youngsters described here is indeed remarkable, especially in light of the differences between them in race, class, and circumstance.

There is, then, much reason to think that Matza and Sykes are justified in urging that delinquency might be better understood as an extension of the adult conforming world rather than as discontinuous with it. One advantage of this interpretation is that it allows for a single explanation of lower and middle class delinquency and thus avoids the inconsistency inherent in theories which specify the influence of socioeconomic factors in the etiology of lower class delinquency and psychological factors in the etiology of middle class delinquency. It is likely that much may be gained by exploring the similarity between the delinquent and the rest of society rather than his deviance from it. Certainly these observations suggest that middle class deviants may differ from lower class delinquents not in the frequency of their anti-social activities, but only in the form which they take and the sophistication, social intelligence, judgment, and skill with which they are executed.

SUMMARY

These observations have raised several important issues concerning the structure and values of delinquent groups. It may be that the extent of gang structure is frequently exaggerated and that such groups may not be as cohesive, structured, and stable as they are commonly depicted. The groups described here manifested all but one of the characteristics (disturbed leadership) described by Yablonsky as those of a near-group. There is a coincidence of opinion based on three sets of observations (Yablonsky's, the supervisor of a detached worker program in Los Angeles, and those reported in this paper) suggesting that the common conception of the gang as a highly organized primary group is not always accurate and may be the result of the gross exaggerations made possible by the dearth of empirical observations of gangs. Exaggeration may also have taken place in the extent of the differences between delinquent values and those of the dominant society. The observations reported in this paper are in accord with the suggestions of Matza and Sykes that the delinquent subculture is an extension of values held by most members of the society but indulged in less openly and less often. Certainly the behavior and beliefs of the middle class youngsters observed are not dramatically different from those of most conventional teenagers or adults.

In view of these three sets of observations, the following questions may be asked: (1) How often and to what extent are gangs primary groups with elaborate delinquent subcultures, and how prevalent are such groups when compared with the loosely structured, secondary, impermanent collectivities with little or no delinquent subculture such as those described here? (2) In view of the conflicting characterizations of the extent of gang structure and the nature of gang values, would not there be more scientific value in describing gangs in terms of at least these two variables rather than primarily on the basis of the content of their deviant activities? (3) To what extent, if any, does adult recognition, particularly in the form of the assignment of detached workers to gangs, legitimize and formalize these groups, lending them a cohesion and solidarity which they previously might not have had? (4) Has the emphasis on the deviant activities of these groups obscured their similarity to conventional teenagers and adults, thereby exaggerating the differences between delinquents and non-delinquents? And (5) would it not be more fruitful to examine the extent and nature of the similarities rather than differences between deviant and non-deviant teenagers and adults?

The action implications of these questions are far-reaching. If, as Yablonsky suggests, the gang meets different needs for different members, a uniform approach on a gang basis is inappropriate. More suitable would be an attempt to help individual members develop the interpersonal skills which would enable them to participate in structured, socially accepted groups. Or, by deliberately applying techniques such as Yablonsky's "group-fulfilling prophecy," gangs might be made into non-deviant clubs. And, if delinquent values are but a continuation of one aspect of the accepted value system subscribed to by most law abiding people, a program designed to integrate these values into a more appropriate place in deviant youngsters' lives (for example, by providing socially acceptable means of expressing aggression and seeking adventure) would be more honest and effective than attempts to eliminate them altogether.

At this stage, only one firm conclusion is justified. The variables in terms of which gangs can best be understood have not yet been identified and are not likely to be until widespread and systematic empirical observation is conducted. The impressions reported here suggest just how valuable and unsettling such observation may prove.

Juvenile Delinquency in the Middle-Class Youth Culture

EDMUND W. VAZ

A youth culture of middle-class adolescents is not endemic to a society. Adolescents have not always been as freely available to one another as they are today. Their community of interests, consensus of opinion, and the uniformities of action that spotlight the contemporary scene constitute a relatively new phenomenon in society, one not easily envisaged in the past. Seventy-five years ago the social structure of society, the organization of family life, educational standards, rights and obligations of the student role, and the routine activities among middle-class youth tended to handicap the emergence of a middle-class youth culture.

Few are the middle-class children today who are reared in an atmosphere of Puritan severity. No longer must children be seen and not heard, kept indoors, and off the streets. Patterns of hard work and hard saving are apt to be a thing of the past. No longer is it enough for a boy to enjoy the right to the opportunity of an education; there exists the felt right to a high school diploma, and a college degree is becoming more a matter of perseverence than of burning the midnight oil. Relaxed parental control in today's middle-class family, and the general freedom enjoyed by adolescents have been used traditionally to explain lower-class adolescent behavior. Use of the now popular term "street-corner society"

Part of this article is taken from "Middle-Class Adolescents: Self-Reported Delinquency and Youth Culture Activities," ***The Canadian Review of Sociology and Anthropology*****, Vol. 2, No. 1 (February, 1965), 52–70. Reprinted by permission of the editor.**

is no longer warranted to describe the joint activities of lower-class boys only. The corner drug store, the drive-in, and the coffee bar are as much a precinct of the middle-class teen-ager as of his lower-class brother.

The world of middle-class boys is largely peer oriented, conspicuously non-intellectual, and is outstanding for its concern with status and the pursuit of "fun and games." Notwithstanding the diversity and size of groups among these boys, they possess a relatively common system of values, norms, and practices, and their collective behavior patterns are distinguishable. Their tacit ratification of norms, and conformity to existing practices, foster the flow of teen-age behavior and reflect its legitimacy within the culture. This has helped strengthen the role of adolescent in the middle class, given it newly won status, and has contributed to the stability of the youth culture.

The content of the middle-class youth culture is neither delinquent nor rebellious, and seldom does it antagonize middle-class sentiments. Usually it reflects adult expectations, values, and institutions, and adult groups have encouraged development of the youth culture, advertised its prominence, and utilized its resources which has strengthened its position within the larger system. The proliferation of "extracurricular" activities has received widespread parental approval and mirrors the proclaimed educational value of the "life adjustment" and "social maturity" of the child. This congruence of attitudes between parents and educators lends structural support to the youth culture. Not only do parents encourage youth participation in social events, they also organize opportunities for regular teen-age activities. The respectability and popularity of these activities help convince parents (and adolescents) of their value, and the variety of programs testifies to widespread adult concern for adolescent participation. This tends to strengthen adolescent relationships and helps build mutual respect between adolescents and adults in the community.

Similarly, communal support of high school athletics has kept pace with the rapid growth of college and professional sports. High schools serve as preparatory training grounds for professional talent, and organized sports (e.g., Little League Baseball) has contributed widely to the general popularity of sports in the high school and community. Successful high school teams enhance community status and the reputation of families of participating athletes. Communal moral support and financial subsidization contribute to the development of athletic talent for schools, and spotlight its value for the community. The convergence of common purpose and action between community and schools reaffirms common values. Continued interest and participation by students comply with adult expectations, and promote the general reputation of schools, coaches, and of athletes in the youth culture, which helps consolidate the youth culture within the larger institutional network.

Full "membership" in the adolescent system is contingent largely upon the exercise of one's role, which requires active participation in youth culture activities and relationships. Learning the skills and nuances of a role often occurs through trial and error, but it also requires instruction from others. Middle-class youngsters are tutored early in the conduct required for future social success. Participation in age-restricted, sometimes adult-supervised social events, introduces youngsters to incipient forms of heterosexual relations and teen-age games. Older boys and the mass media are also valuable sources of instruction in the details and marginal maneuvers used in "handling" the opposite sex.

The significance of "socializing" for the middle-class adolescent cannot be overemphasized. Both teachers and parents expect the child to be a "joiner," and, to perform his role adequately, active participation in teen-age events is mandatory. Boys who pursue academic interests only are noticeably disapproved. Yet the student who excels both academically and socially is fully acceptable and mirrors the success of the educational system.

The pursuit of status is intense among middle-class adolescents, and often it is to his peers that the adolescent looks for respect. Peer-group membership and conformity to role expectations confer social approbation and tend to publicize (through frequency of interaction) collective teen-age solidarity. In a newly developing culture where norms are not fully institutionalized, where structural stability and internal coherence are only partially realized, and where traditional role expectations are obscure, conformity as a moral imperative is especially helpful and desirable.

COMPETITION

Competition pervades all parts of a boy's life in the middle-class youth culture. It influences his choice of clothes, his preference in music and girls, his necking techniques, and the manipulation of his car. Peer-group standards are often the critical criteria by which a boy forms his opinions and gauges his behavior. Throughout his daily activities competition prevails, and peers stand alert to criticize, to pass judgment, and to offer approval. Ultimately, competition with "everyman" becomes "internalized" and the "generalized other" becomes an ubiquitous audience always keeping score. The absence of others, or the fact that only strangers are present, fails to deter a boy's struggle for attention. Continuously on parade, even when he is alone, the adolescent "guns" his engine, "drags" the streets, squeals the tires of his automobile ("lays a patch"), coercing attention, seeking approval.

Were competition uncontrolled in the youth culture, it might corrode friendships and damage group relationships. The conditions under which current teen-age activities occur tend to preserve social ties and strengthen group cohesion. Typically, adolescent activity occurs under a veneer of non-competitive good-fellowship and fun. This unserious quality to their joint activity fosters their belief in the impression that they create. And the rhetoric in terms of which they describe their behavior, "It's all in fun," "It's just for kicks," or "We were just having a few laughs," enables them to escape opprobrium should they be accused of more deliberate competitiveness. Increasing use of this vocabulary of motives obscures underlying competition, and tends to prevent them from making clear-cut distinctions among their everyday practices and games. Thus, "heavy" necking, "hooliganism," "playing chicken" at 100 m.p.h., drinking bouts, and sexual escapades are often described as merely "having fun."

MARGINAL DIFFERENTIATION

Throughout the daily legitimate activities (dating, dances, riding about with friends, "hanging" about the drug store, playing sports, etc.) of middle-class boys, veiled competition for status stimulates their experimentation in behavior.

These "operating inventions"[1] attract others, win approval and nourish competition, and take the form of behavioral nuances, sufficiently novel to distinguish them from existing patterns and competing efforts of peers. Although all behavior is, perhaps, partly exploratory, stabs at marginal differentiation are likely to be guarded, tentative, ambiguous, and to transpire in a situation characterized by "joint exploration and elaboration" of behavior.[2] Yet extreme conduct of any kind is apt to be strongly disapproved among "sophisticated" youths, and there exist strong motivations to conform to prevailing norms and patterns. But the boundaries of legitimacy are not impregnable, and it is during these legitimate fun-ridden activities, where boys are encouraged to join in, that unobtrusive acts lead gradually to unanticipated elaboration beyond the precincts of legitimacy. Since adolescent activities occur in a spirit of good will, creative efforts are applauded, encouraged, and behavioral novelty is seldom considered delinquent. However, innovation is tolerated only within the limits of acceptable adolescent interests. In this way behavioral differentiation does little injury to existing norms and values, and group status is not undermined. As newly developing practices gain approval, they acquire their own morality, and each move becomes circumscribed by game rules. In this setting delinquency needs not emerge from anti-social motives. Delinquent acts, rooted in anti-social impulses, are apt to transgress acceptable conduct, violate middle-class norms, and be disapproved altogether. The motives for much middle-class delinquency are learned through sustained participation in everyday respectable, adolescent activities. In this manner delinquency becomes gradually routine in the middle-class youth culture.

To help substantiate some of the ideas in this paper, evidence is presented from a larger study of middle-class delinquency. Data on the self-reported delinquency of 850 middle-class boys are offered and interpreted according to their social roles in the youth culture. Evidence is presented on the relationship between differential delinquency involvement and (a) the active participation of boys in legitimate teen-age activities, and (b) their peer orientation. Data are included on the relationship between the seriousness with which boys perceive engaging in delinquent acts and their differential participation in legitimate teen-age activities. To emphasize the delinquent content of the middle-class youth culture, the relationship between differential delinquency involvement and the seriousness with which boys define engaging in delinquent acts is investigated.

RESEARCH

During the spring of 1963 questionnaires were administered to 1,639 white high school boys in grades 9 through 13 in five coeducational high schools located in four Canadian communities. Appropriate techniques were used to minimize collusion and maximize anonymity of subjects. The communities differ in size and are urban or semi-urban in character, and the high schools are located in middle-class socioeconomic areas.

Delinquency was measured by a check list of 21 items of behavior. The items are violations of the law or are offenses on the basis of which juveniles can be adjudicated as delinquent. Both serious and minor offenses are included, such as driving a car beyond the speed limit, breaking and entering, intoxication, and the use of drugs for kicks. Offenses such as gang fights, armed robbery, and rape were not included. The boys were asked how often they had committed each offense; response categories included very often, quite often, several times, once or twice, never.

To establish the socioeconomic position of subjects, three indicators were used in the following order: (a) father's occupation, (b) father's level of education, and (c) size of organization in which father works. Using father's occupation, subjects were first classified according to the Blishen Occupational Class Scale.[3] Questionnaires initially difficult to classify, or that included only father's level of education, were reviewed and grouped according to the second indicator. Subjects whose fathers had "completed high school" or completed "some college" were classified into Group III, and those who had "finished college" or higher were sorted into Group II. A small number of remaining questionnaires, with ambiguously reported job titles only, were categorized with the help of the third indicator according to the writer's judgment. All subjects classified into Groups II ($n = 337$) and III ($n = 513$) were combined and hereafter are termed "middle class."

Table 1 reveals sharp differences in the responses of

younger and older boys. Important considerations in interpreting the data are the social roles of middle-class boys and the rights and obligations—varying sets of role criteria—by which boys may claim status to their roles. To the extent that a boy conforms to these criteria his peers will judge and reward him accordingly.

TABLE 1. Self-Reported Delinquent Behavior of Middle-Class Boys by Age Group

Type of Offense[a]	Percent Admitting Commission of Offense Age 13–14	15–19	Percent Admitting Commission of Offense More than Once or Twice Age 13–14	15–19
Driven a car without a driver's license	28.6	62.3	9.1	27.9
Taken little things that did not belong to you	61.0	67.2	10.4	16.7
Skipped school without a legitimate excuse	23.6	40.8	3.9	13.6
Driven beyond the speed limit	5.8	51.2	1.3	39.7
Participated in drag-races along the highway with your friends	6.5	31.1	2.0	16.3
Engaged in a fist fight with another boy	45.8	56.0	7.1	8.7
Been feeling "high" from drinking beer, wine or liquor	11.7	39.0	2.6	17.9
Gambled for money at cards, dice, or some other game	42.2	66.0	16.9	37.4
Remained out all night without parents' permission	19.5	25.8	5.2	9.5
Taken a car without owner's knowledge	5.2	12.5	0.7	3.1
Placed on school probation or expelled from school	0.7	5.6	0.0	1.2
Destroyed or damaged public or private property of any kind	44.8	52.0	11.7	14.8
Taken little things of value (between $2 and $50) which did not belong to you	9.7	16.0	0.7	3.5
Tried to be intimate with a member of the opposite sex	18.2	37.8	7.8	17.6
Broken into or tried to break and enter a building with the intention of stealing	5.2	7.5	0.7	1.0
Sold, used or tried to use drugs of some kind	1.3	1.0	0.0	0.3

TABLE 1. Self-Reported Delinquent Behavior of Middle-Class Boys by Age Group (*Continued*)

Type of Offense[a]	Percent Admitting Commission of Offense Age 13–14	15–19	Percent Admitting Commission of Offense More than Once or Twice Age 13–14	15–19
Bought or tried to buy beer, wine, or liquor from a store or adult	3.3	24.8	0.7	11.7
Taken money of any amount from someone or place which did not belong to you	30.5	32.7	7.1	6.9
Taken a glass of beer, wine, or liquor at a party or elsewhere with your friends	32.5	64.8	8.4	35.2
$n =$	154	682[b]		

[a] Two items are omitted because they were used solely as reliability check measures.
[b] Fourteen cases of boys over 19 years are omitted.

Some of the delinquent practices are more realistically possible and readily available for older boys as relevant criteria of status. For younger boys these practices are less meaningful to their social role. To learn the rules and tricks of smoking marijuana or of purchasing liquor takes time and effort and requires the opportunity. Youngsters are apt not to claim status in terms of these practices. Nevertheless, younger and older boys share, in part, a relatively common frame of experience. In and out of school, on and off the playing field, youngsters show deference to their teen-age elders, strengthen growing identifications, and they are eager to learn and anxious to participate. Thus, drinking games, sexual intimacy with girls, and truancy are not uncommon among these boys.

As youngsters assume gradually the role of older teen-ager new attitudes and practices are required of them. New criteria become applicable in terms of which peers judge them and, depending upon their ego-involvement in their role, they evaluate themselves. Older boys care less about the practices and criteria of status that matter to younger lads. What a youngster considers serious an older boy will define as "kid stuff." Delinquent activities that are relatively popular among boys occupying different roles will depend on the alternative criteria available for status gain.

Table 1 shows that petty theft is the only offense committed by the majority of younger boys. Other popular delinquencies, among younger boys, include fist fighting, vandalism, gambling, stealing money, and drinking liquor. These offenses are popular also among older teen-agers, but in some cases the difference in responses is small. There is a difference of only 11 percentage points between younger and older boys who fist fight. Less than 7 percentage points separate younger and older boys who admit petty theft. About 45 percent of younger boys and 52 percent of older teen-agers report vandalic behavior.

Ironically, the world of younger boys is a masculine world, girls occupy little of their time. Their role in the middle class (perhaps among all social classes) is characterized by a particular image of masculinity. The values of adventure, bravado, manliness, and muscular prowess circumscribe their role, and usually they make every effort to prove that they are "all boy." Most younger lads approve of practices that enable them to display their courage, exhibit their physical strength, and thereby "improve" their self-image. To "take a dare," to engage in varying kinds of vandalism, fighting, and petty theft are practiced frequently among younger boys. Failure to participate in at least one of these types of games may deny a boy's claim to being "all boy" among his peers. The data indicate that typical of these boys are the more masculine offenses.

The older adolescent role requires increased participation in dominant youth culture activities. Parties, dances, sport events, cars, and girls occupy a larger part of a boy's time. "Sophistication" replaces masculinity, and a premium is put on the cultivation of social skills and a "social personality." The rougher habits of younger lads are taboo. Yet a change in roles and the gradual transformation of a boy's self-image take time and involve uncertainty and strain. Under such conditions boys are apt to revert, occasionally, to an earlier set of responses and standards to which they are still partly committed. Thus, older boys continue temporarily their earlier delinquencies. But once they learn their new role, feel committed to its standards, and begin to judge themselves by it, earlier practices, no longer serviceable, are seldom recruited. Petty theft, vandalism, stealing money, and aggressive behavior, concomitant with the role of the youngster, become relics of an earlier role.

If the role of older teen-ager calls for sophisticated behavior, it tends also to generate a more sophisticated brand of delinquency. Yet, theirs is no criminal world, there is no community of delinquent gangs, no body of criminal values, malicious attitudes, and predatory skills. The young hoodlum, the adolescent thug, and the gang leader are types of a nether world. It is the crew-cut and the clean look, the "nice guy," and the high school star who claim status among these boys. Drinking, drag-racing, speeding, sex practices, truancy, and gambling assume a larger part of later adolescent behavior. At age 16 a boy immediately acquires greater access to an automobile. Besides being a symbol of status the car allows the teen-ager to expand his circle of friends, makes available girls otherwise inaccessible to him, and also offers him increased opportunity to break the law. Sixty-two percent of older boys admit having driven without a permit. Over 50 percent have driven beyond the speed limit, and 31 percent admit dragging along the highway. Admittedly, the values of courage and daring underlie the practice of dragging, but its value for these boys is less to demonstrate their masculinity than it is to exhibit their driving skills and to highlight the efficiency of their cars. Since the automobile is an extension of self, these practices enable a boy to increase his popularity among peers.

Drinking practices (at parties, sport events, in cars during intermission at high school dances), sex games with girls, and gambling are symbolic of adolescent sophistication, serviceable for youth culture participation, and very likely a means for acquiring popularity. Sixty-five percent of older boys admit drinking liquor at a party; 39 percent admit having felt "high," and over 37 percent have tried to "go the limit" with a girl. And once boys begin to drink they are expected to buy their liquor.

New interests and non-academic, time-consuming activities are necessary in maintaining a boy's popularity and very likely subvert his interest in school work. Thus, truancy tends to gain popularity among older youths. Similarly, gambling very likely increases among boys who gradually obtain larger sums of money. Most of these activities are predominantly sociable forms of delinquency and, apart from the intimate stages of sexual congress, are seldom practiced in private.

They strengthen peer-group relationships, consolidate normative patterns among teen-agers, and contribute to the cohesion of the middle-class youth culture.

Table 1 shows also that sociable delinquencies such as automobile offenses, drinking, gambling, and sex violations rank highest among older boys who admit committing offenses more than once or twice.

DELINQUENCY INVOLVEMENT AMONG MIDDLE-CLASS BOYS

In order to establish the differential delinquency involvement of boys, two Guttman scales were obtained.[4] Eleven items were selected on the basis that they might measure a common dimension of middle-class delinquency and using 850 boys, aged 13–19, eight of the items scale satisfactorily. Dichotomizing each item, a reproducibility coefficient of .920 was obtained with random distribution of error. Scale items include: taken little things that did not belong to you; gambled for money at cards, dice, or other games; driven a car beyond the speed limit; skipped school without a legitimate excuse; been feeling "high" from drinking beer, wine, or liquor; bought or tried to buy beer, wine, or liquor from a store or adult; taken a glass of beer, wine, or liquor at a party or elsewhere with your friends; and tried to be intimate (go the limit) with a member of the opposite sex.

A second scale was obtained for 682 boys aged 15 to 19. Dichotomizing each item, eight items scale satisfactorily giving a reproducibility coefficient of .914. Scale items include: taken little things that did not belong to you; taken a glass of beer, wine, or liquor at a party or elsewhere with your friends; driven a car beyond the speed limit; been feeling "high" from drinking beer, wine, or liquor; driven a car without a driver's license or permit; tried to be intimate (go the limit) with a member of the opposite sex; bought or tried to buy beer, wine, or liquor; and skipped school. Each delinquency scale was trichotomized into low, medium, and high categories.

Not all boys engage actively in the social events of the middle-class youth culture, and not all delinquency is found among those who do. However, it is noteworthy that our scales highlight a non-violent component of delinquency.

Items such as drinking liquor, skipping school, speeding, purchasing liquor, and sexual intimacy are noticeably sociable practices, and are conspicuously in accord with the typical, legitimate affairs of the youth culture. This kind of conduct seems to "fit" the sophisticated self-image of the older middle-class adolescent.

Two situation-type items (each with two response categories) were used to establish the peer orientation of boys. Three items were used to measure the active participation of boys in typical teen-age activities. One item deals with the time a boy spends riding about with his friends in the evenings. The second concerns the frequency of dating girls. The third item enquires about the time a boy spends around the local "hangout" in the evenings. Each item has five weighted response categories, and cases were distributed into high, medium, and low categories.

DIFFERENTIAL DELINQUENCY INVOLVEMENT AND PEER-GROUP ORIENTATION

Ordinarily adolescents are preoccupied with those of their own kind, friends and acquaintances who hold their values, share their opinions, and talk their language. Recurrent participation in peer activities tends to increase one's status in the eyes of peers, and opportunities (dates, parties, dances, etc.) for further social activity are the cherished rewards for conformity to prevailing norms. Under these conditions, to be a "loner" is a passport to pariahdom, but from our perspective the "loner," the boy who is not peer-oriented, is less apt to engage in delinquency.

When each peer orientation item is tested against delinquent participation, results are significant ($p < .001$). In each case the majority of peer-oriented boys rates high in delinquency. Boys who favor parents rank lower in delinquency. To substantiate further these results, composite results of the peer orientation items were cross tabulated with delinquency involvement.

Table 2 indicates that over 80 percent of high peer-oriented boys aged 15 to 19 rank high or medium in delinquency. Being parent-oriented is no guarantee against delinquency, but considerably fewer parent-oriented boys are

TABLE 2. Combined Items on Peer Orientation by Differential Delinquency Involvement: Middle-Class Adolescents by Age Groups

Peer Orientation	Delinquency Involvement 15–19 Years High	Med.	Low	All Ages High	Med.	Low
High	13.2	14.1	6.2	14.0	11.8	6.0
Medium	7.9	18.5	18.0	10.0	18.2	17.4
Low	2.9	7.8	9.4	3.7	6.5	10.7
Non-responses	0.0	0.0	0.0	0.0	0.0	0.0
	$n = 682$			850		
	$\chi^2 = 58.03$, 4df, $p < .001$			$\chi^2 = 75.36$, 4df, $p < .001$		
	$C = .283$ $\bar{C} = .346$			$C = .287$ $\bar{C} = .352$		

highly delinquent. If we are correct, peer-oriented boys are more in demand in the typical carrousel of teen-age activities of which delinquency is an unanticipated result. The more a boy engages in such events the greater the likelihood of his becoming delinquent.

DIFFERENTIAL DELINQUENCY INVOLVEMENT AND YOUTH CULTURE PARTICIPATION

We have described the middle-class youth culture as predominantly social in character. We have implied that the boy who has ready access to an automobile, who dates girls, attends dances, who goes to parties, and who is regularly engaged in sports is more likely to begin drinking, drag-racing, gambling, and to become partner to sexual practices and other sophisticated forms of delinquency. The more restricted, unsociable adolescent is less apt to become so involved.

When responses to the question, "How often do you drive about with friends in the evening" were cross tabulated with delinquency involvement, results revealed that approximately 90 percent of boys, aged 15 to 19, who drive about with friends three or more times per week, rank high or medium in delinquency. Boys who drive about once a week or less, are much less likely to rank high in delinquency. The same pattern holds for boys of all ages ($p < .001$).

The majority of boys who date girls three or more times a week are highly involved in delinquency. Most boys who seldom or never date rank low in delinquency. Again the pattern holds for both age groups ($p < .001$).

The third item asked was, "How often do you spend some time about the local 'hangout' in the evenings throughout the whole week?" When responses are matched against delinquency involvement, the results are significant ($p < .001$). With an increase in the social pursuits of boys, there is an increase in their delinquent behavior. Table 3 is important because it indicates the overall youth culture participation scores of boys and their delinquency involvement. Among boys highly active in legitimate activities about 90 percent fall into the two highest delinquent categories. Among low participants about 35 percent rank high in delinquency.

TABLE 3. Combined Scores on Active Participation in Youth Culture by Differential Delinquency Involvement: Middle-Class Adolescents by Age Groups

Youth Culture Activities	Delinquency Involvement: 15–19 Years			Delinquency Involvement: All Ages		
	High	Med.	Low	High	Med.	Low
High	15.1	16.0	3.5	16.9	10.1	3.1
Medium	7.0	18.0	15.3	9.2	18.9	12.4
Low	2.0	6.9	15.7	1.9	7.9	19.4
Non-responses	0.2	0.0	0.2	0.1	0.1	0.0
	$n = 682$			850		
	$\chi^2 = 151.26$, 4df, $p < .001$			$\chi^2 = 251.67$, 4df, $p < .001$		
	$C = .426$ $\overline{C} = .522$			$C = .478$ $\overline{C} = .586$		

ACTIVE PARTICIPATION IN YOUTH CULTURE AND BOYS' PERCEPTION OF DELINQUENT ACTS AS SERIOUS CONDUCT

The adolescent who is actively engrossed in social affairs is especially susceptible to current teen-age perspectives, attitudes, and opinions. Absorbed with his peers, listening to what they say, watching their actions, engaging in their games, prevailing teen-age attitudes gradually become part of his own behavioral and motivational baggage. Delinquency in the middle-class youth culture is an unanticipated consequence of conformity to the expected patterns of respectable teen-age behavior. Seldom is it defined illegal, and these boys rarely develop an image of themselves as delinquent. Under these circumstances certain types of delinquent practices are apt not to be taken seriously by middle-class boys. Paradoxically this relatively unserious attitude towards delinquency is learned while engaging in typically non-delinquent activities.

Twelve items were used to measure the seriousness felt by boys toward selected delinquent acts, and the distribution of scores was trichotomized into low, medium, and high categories. When responses to youth culture items are matched separately against scores on the perceived seriousness of delinquent acts, Chi-square values are significant in each instance ($p < .001$). Boys who are highly active in teen-age affairs (dating, driving about with friends, etc.) define delinquent acts less seriously than do boys who participate infrequently in such pursuits. More important is the association between overall scores on both variables (see Table 4). Again Chi-square values are significant ($p < .05$) for both age groups.

TABLE 4. Separate and Combined Scores on the Relationship Between Youth Culture Activities and the Perception of Delinquent Acts as Serious: Middle-Class Adolescents by Age Group

Youth Culture Activities by Perceived Seriousness of Delinquent Acts	15–19 Years χ^2		C	$\bar{C}$	All Ages χ^2		C	$\bar{C}$
Driving about with friends in evening	77.94	S[a]	.319	.368	106.71	S	.333	.384
Takes out a girl in evening	36.72	S	.225	.275	41.11	S	.214	.262
Spends time about local "hangout"	82.80	S	.340	.380	104.13	S	.330	.369
Youth Culture Activities: Combined Scores	83.08	S	.109	.133	113.91	S	.343	.420

[a] S = Significant at .05 level.

Teen-agers who are caught in the vortex of typical social activities are especially popular and enhance their social standing among peers. This is difficult to relinquish and they are apt to persist in their quest for social rewards. Through prolonged youth culture involvement they learn the prevailing attitudes and definitions and ultimately become involved in delinquency. But since this is seldom discovered and accords with routine events, neither the behavior nor the boys are apt to be considered delinquent. The seductive appeal of the middle-class youth culture and the rewards that reside therein very likely contain the seeds of delinquency.

A difficulty in appreciating delinquency among middle-class adolescents is that the majority of their everyday activities receive the blessing of parents, which tends to inhibit the development of a socially recognized image of the middle-class delinquent. This seeming immunity from the delinquent role perhaps confirms the teen-ager in his delinquent ways. Since delinquent practices emerge so unobtrusively from non-delinquent activities, middle-class teen-agers are apt less to define them as serious practices. Yet middle-class delinquency is not a happenstance affair. It is one thing for boys to break the rules, define their acts as serious and, perhaps, feel guilty. But boys who break rules and are indifferent about their violations are certainly to be viewed in a different light. The association between delinquency involvement and the seriousness with which they define delinquent acts suggests strongly a delinquent content to the middle-class youth culture. Moreover, it lends stability to the delinquent norms developing in the culture.

TABLE 5. The Perception of Delinquent Acts as Serious Behavior by Differential Delinquency Involvement: Middle-Class Adolescents by Age Groups

Perceived Seriousness of Delinquency	Delinquency Involvement 15–19 Years			All Ages		
	High	Med.	Low	High	Med.	Low
Not Very Serious	15.4	11.7	6.3	15.8	9.9	5.4
Moderately Serious	7.2	18.0	12.2	9.5	16.9	10.4
Serious	1.8	11.0	16.1	2.8	10.1	19.1
Non-responses	0.0	0.2	0.0	0.0	0.1	0.0
	$n = 682$				850	
	$\chi^2 = 102.04$, 4df, $p < .001$			$\chi^2 = 187.58$, 4df, $p < .001$		
	$C = .360$ $\bar{C} = .441$			$C = .425$ $\bar{C} = .521$		

Table 5 reveals that the definition of engaging in delinquency as serious behavior tends to correspond with the differential involvement in delinquency. These results subvert the idea that delinquency among middle-class boys is an occasional phenomenon.

Because behavior is illegal does not exempt it from having objective consequences for the adjustment of boys and for the middle-class youth culture. In the first place, as long as delinquency remains relatively faithful to middle-class values, it tends to reaffirm the social standing of the adolescent. Drinking games, dragging a car, "scoring" with a girl, or getting mildly drunk at a party are apt to be normative practices among these boys and are congruent with the dominant social orientation of the middle-class youth culture. Since these kinds of conduct emerge from societally endorsed activities, and once they do not get "out of hand," they are likely perceived by parents as signs of maturity. This will prevent a boy from developing a delinquent self-conception, confirm his image of himself as an "average boy," and legitimize his claim to the adolescent role.

In addition, conformity to legitimate teen-age norms serves to sustain existing delinquent patterns. Until middle-class delinquency openly violates middle-class values and sentiments it is not likely to arouse collective parental concern over the teen-age culture. The fact that periodic outbursts among these boys are blamed on a few "troublemakers"—whose behavior is attributed typically to personality pathology—prevents delinquency from being considered normative within the culture. Since the recreational programs of middle-class youngsters coincide with current educational programs and reflect strongly felt values of adults, this helps deflect attention from the youth culture, and its relationship to the larger social structure, as a major source of juvenile delinquency among middle-class youth.

Automobile Theft: A "Favored-Group" Delinquency

WILLIAM W. WATTENBERG
AND JAMES BALISTRIERI

The purpose of this paper is to explore certain implications of "white-collar criminality." That concept, based largely on evidence dealing with adults, challenges the adequacy of some generalizations concerning crime and its causation. The point of impact of the concept lies in its assumption that the form of antisocial or illegal conduct rather than its frequency varies from social class to class in our society. If this is so, then there is need to search for factors common to the causation of delinquency or similar misconduct at all social levels rather than to accept without reservation the vast mass of research linking juvenile misconduct with neighborhood situations which in turn reflect the economic status of the adult population.

In general, the ecological findings are that delinquency rates are highest in those sections of a city where, among other things, rentals are low and the occupations are typically unskilled or semiskilled labor. The relative poverty of the population is associated with high transiency rates, substandard housing, and a breakdown of family and other controls. Often youth is also exposed to a conflict of cultures. This constellation of influences is assumed to give rise to a neighborhood subculture of which delinquency patterns are

Reprinted from *The American Journal of Sociology*, Vol. 57, No. 6 (May, 1952), 575–579, by permission of The University of Chicago Press.

one aspect. This subculture transmits to youth a readiness to embark upon delinquent behavior.

Challenging all this is the contention that crime is culturally defined rather than culturally determined and that it is not the fact of criminality but the form of it which varies with socioeconomic level. Thus, we have burglars and embezzlers, holdup men and black-marketeers, prostitutes and fashionable mistresses. The antisocial conduct of the "lower classes" affronts the middle-class legal norms and so leads to prison terms and criminal records. The antisocial deeds of "respectable" folk are likely to draw much milder treatment. All this casts doubt on many research data by implying that we have not been measuring the extent of crime or of delinquency but only of the varieties we do not like. By such reasoning, no theory of delinquency or criminality can be adequate unless it explains the "white-collar" offenses as well as the more obvious forms of theft and violence. It is assumed that, if this were done, the present emphasis on relationship of socioeconomic variables to crime might have to be discarded.

For the field of juvenile delinquency, the existence of "white-collar" offenses is difficult to establish. We have fairly good figures on assaults, burglary, truancy, and similar offenses. However, the early manifestations of patterns which could develop into bribery, bucket-shop operations, and price-control evasions are not likely to draw police attention. Certainly, statistical evidence would be hard to get. Apparently the best we could do would be to assume that among juveniles there was much hidden misconduct analogous to adult "white-collar" crime.

An alternative would be to search for some class of offense which departed from the usual high correlation with socioeconomic or ecological variables. Then, by exploring the similarities and differences between the offenders thus identified and a run-of-the-mill group, we might find more clues as to causal factors common to antisocial character formation in privileged as well as underprivileged groups. To be most helpful, in this respect the offense must be sufficiently common and widespread so that it is not peculiar to a single neighborhood. Also, to avoid argument as to antisocial quality, the offense should be clearly illegal and generally condemned. Otherwise, as in the case of the recent debate between Hartung and Burgess,[1] we would be bogged down in claims and counterclaims as to whether or not the offenders were real delinquents.

Evidence of the existence of such an offense was turned up in connection with another investigation.[2] In a study of

TABLE 1. Relationship between Automobile Theft and Race of All Boys Interviewed on Complaint by Detroit Police, 1948[a]

Race	Total	Number: Involved in Automobile Theft	Number: All Others	Per Cent: Involved in Automobile Theft	Per Cent: All Others
White	2,774	230	2,544	88.5	70.5
Nonwhite	1,096	30	1,066	11.5	29.5
Total	3,870	260	3,610	100.0	100.0

[a] $\chi^2 = 38.29$; $n = 1$; $P < 0.01$.

the complete police records of 1,170 boys all of whom had passed their seventeenth birthdays it was found that during the period when they had been ten to sixteen years old automobile thefts were proportionately three times as frequent among white boys as among Negroes. (The general ratio of delinquencies was two to one; automobile theft approached seven to one; results were significant well beyond the 1 per cent level of confidence.) The same offense was proportionately heavier among boys of West European parentage. Again, results were statistically reliable. This is significant because the largest recent foreign immigration to Detroit's transitional areas was from Eastern Europe.

The police explanation of the small proportion of Negroes involved in automobile theft was one of danger and difficulty. Veteran police officials said that colored youngsters were almost sure to be challenged by parking-lot attendants and thus were barred from some opportunity to take cars. Also, it was widely believed that squad-car crews were prone to investigate credentials of Negro young people driving automobiles. However, these explanations, even if accurate, did not account for the nationality differentials among white boys. Therefore, it was decided to dig deeper.

All investigations made by Detroit police of boys aged ten to sixteen inclusive for 1948 were secured and analyzed.

These reports included some fifty items of information obtained by interview with the boys and their parents on such matters as housing, neighborhood conditions, family relationships, peer-group activities, and recreation. In all, data were available for 3,870 boys, of whom 2,774 were white. These records were carefully sorted, and all records involving any form of automobile theft were segregated. There were 260 such records. As shown in Table 1, the previously discovered tendency for automobile theft to be a "white" offense was thoroughly verified.

In order to avoid various possible distorting influences, such as the correlations between race and such variables as housing, employment discriminations and the like, it was decided to confine the remainder of the study to comparisons among white boys only. The 230 involved in automobile theft were compared on every available recorded item of information with the 2,544 charged with other offenses. In all cases the chi-square computation was employed to establish the degree of statistical reliability with which the null hypothesis could be rejected. A total of fifty tables was prepared and tested. Of these, nine proved significant at the 1 per cent level of confidence; five more, at the 5 per cent level. Thus, the number of tables showing statistical significance was more than five times chance expectation. For convenience, the statistically significant factors will be discussed below in terms of the clusters into which they fell.

SOCIOECONOMIC LEVEL

The automobile-theft group again met the requirements of the category denoted by the title of this article. As compared with the other boys in trouble, they were reliably more likely to come from neighborhoods rated "above average" by the police and less likely to come from neighborhoods rated as "slums." This was borne out by the more objective evidence of the ratio between the number of rooms in the dwelling unit and the number of persons occupying the unit. The proportion of boys from dwellings with less than one room per person was significantly smaller than for all other boys contacted by the police. There were other tables of inconclusive reliability which supported this general picture. In these the tendency was for the automobile-theft group to come from racially homogeneous neighborhoods, to live in single-family homes, to come from homes not showing need of repairs, and to have only one parent employed.

On one socioeconomic item no relationship with automobile theft was found. When police were asked to classify the family income as either "adequate" or "inadequate," both the automobile-theft group and all other boys came from the same percentage of homes classed as having "adequate" income. However, fewer boys involved in automobile thefts had parents both of whom had to work to secure that level of income.

AGE

As might be expected, automobile theft was largely confined to the older boys; it was relatively rare below the age of fourteen. Accordingly, a number of items in which chronological age was a factor were significantly related to the offense. These included reliable tendencies for the boys involved in automobile theft to be better developed physically, to have completed sex development, to be in the junior high school grades in school, to have records of previous offenses, to have laboring jobs, and to use some of their earnings to purchase their own clothing.

PEER-GROUP RELATIONSHIPS

This group also showed evidence of socializing well with other young people. The statistically reliable tables showed they were less likely to be classed by the investigating officers as social "lone wolves" and were more likely to be members of definite gangs with a reputation of either being rambunctious or engaging in organized theft. Although the statistical reliability was inconclusive, it seemed likely that they also got along well with their classmates in school.

MISCELLANEOUS

There were three statistically reliable tables that do not fit into any of the three clusters described above. When police officers rated the attitude of the boys toward themselves, they were more likely to class it as "responsive." Also, in disposing of the cases, the police were more likely to be stern and either file an official complaint or otherwise refer the case to the juvenile court. This, of course, was an indication of the seriousness of the offense in the eyes of the police, even though they were not required to file delinquency petitions in such cases. The third significant table dealt with the degree of the parents' participation in their sons' recreation; for the automobile-theft group this was more likely to be ranked in the medium level of "occasional," as contrasted to "regular," on the one hand, or "seldom," on the other. Interestingly, this was the only item involving family relationships where statistical significance appeared.

More consequential for the purpose of this article were the similarities between the automobile-theft group and the less privileged other white boys involved in all other offenses. In the list below we give only those items not previously mentioned which failed of significance in the present series of comparisons but were found reliably linked to repeating among all boys interviewed by Detroit police in 1948.[3]

1. *Number and sex of siblings*
2. *Boys' expressed attitude toward home*
3. *Boys' expressed attitude toward parents*
4. *Boys' feeling of being "picked on"*
5. *Boys' appearance*
6. *Estimated intelligence*
7. *Hobby and sports interests*
8. *Membership in organized youth groups*
9. *Church attendance*
10. *Attitude toward school*
11. *Attitude toward teachers*
12. *School grades*
13. *Chores around home*
14. *Method by which parents gave boys money*
15. *Comparability of boys' recreational equipment with playmates*
16. *Attitude toward adult neighbors*
17. *Distance of home from nearest recreational facility*
18. *Parents' attitude toward boys*
19. *Parents' attitude toward police*
20. *Marital status of parents*

21. *Degree of quarreling between parents*
22. *Family ownership of a car*

In summary of the chi-square-tested comparisons, then, we get the following general picture of white juveniles involved in automobile theft: they were more likely to come from relatively favored neighborhoods, to be older, and to have good social relationships with their peers. On indexes of family relationships, school adjustment, and religious training they were like a cross-section of all other white boys interviewed on complaint by the Detroit police.

DISCUSSION

To some extent the above findings buttress the implied contentions of the writers on "white-collar" criminality. That is to say, there is here shown to exist at least one type of offense which is relatively less correlated with low socioeconomic level and neighborhood disintegration than the general run of juvenile offenses. This being the case, it is fair to argue that we need to look for formulations of causal influences beyond the customary "bad" neighborhood factors. We have reason to assume that there may be other varieties of antisocial conduct which would not so swiftly be indicated by police or court statistics and which are sufficiently prevalent in good neighborhoods and among high socioeconomic folk to rule out their being dismissed as exceptions.

Interestingly, in the case of automobile theft, we are dealing with a group that is well socialized as far as primary-group relationships are concerned. These boys are not isolated, peculiar individuals. In the rubrics of the Hewitt and Jenkins[4] study of clinic cases they are neither the quarrelsome, "unsocialized aggressives" nor the pathetically neurotic "overinhibited" children. Rather, they are similar to the "socialized delinquents" in all respects save residence in deteriorated neighborhoods.

There may be a possible systematic explanation in the general picture of this last-mentioned "type." On the basis of a very elaborate statistical analysis, Hewitt and Jenkins described this group as characterized by good ability to relate to people and by a conscience partially formed in the sense that it did not include the prohibitions of the wider society.

The value systems of such individuals were quite responsive to the immediately present code of interpersonal relations pertaining to their friends but only weakly responsive to the more abstract rules codified in statutes and ordinances. Thus, if a boy's friends got pleasure from riding in automobiles, he would oblige in carefree fashion by borrowing a car. Similarly, if an adult with a similar value system found he could get along well in business by violating price controls or by bribing public officials, he would be untroubled by compunctions. However, if his immediate associates would react hostilely to such crude or dangerous crimes as burglary or physical assault, he would shun such behavior. Of course, in a "bad" neighborhood where such out-and-out criminality was tolerated, that might enter into his conduct. Much would depend upon the limits prevalent among his associates.

The common element in all this is a rather general type of personality structure. If such is indeed the case, the causes of all varieties of antisocial conduct having this quality are to be found in how that personality structure is formed. Hewitt and Jenkins believe they could trace it to a lax kind of family in which children are not rejected but rather have weak affectional relationships with their parents, who exercise little supervision over them. It is easy to see that such a pattern might be relatively prevalent where parents are bedeviled by a struggle for existence and are bewildered by the culture conflict found in slums. However, with some variation, it also could be found in better neighborhoods where parents are forever "on the go" or even where children are reared by a succession of servants.

Using methods very different from Hewitt and Jenkins, the studies conducted by the Committee on Human Development of the University of Chicago in "Prairie City" led to a description of a very similar type of personality. In their reports it is called "the adaptive person."[5] This "type" is described as having high "social intelligence" and as conforming easily to the expectations of whatever group in which it is found. Their case studies led them to believe that the family relationships were the important factor in its development. The relationships in the home were characterized as easygoing and the parents as having "broad and tolerant" moral views and as setting few restrictions on the social activities of the children.

Whether we accept the formulation of Hewitt and Jenkins

or that of Havighurst and Taba, the principal point would be that a variety of permissive upbringing produces a personality "type" with little moral courage and a potentiality for engaging in antisocial behavior finding support among associates. Obviously, this is only a hypothesis, to be tested by carefully designed studies. In all probability, as our storehouse of scientifically verified knowledge grows, such a hypothesis would undoubtedly have to be modified. At best it would apply to only one of a number of patterns leading to delinquency and crime. It would hardly cover adequately all types of misconduct, delinquency, crime, and fraud.

It should be pointed out that even the admittedly incomplete hypothesis now being advanced hardly negates the theories built on statistics showing high correlations between delinquency rates and socioeconomic variables. Rather, it would offer an explanation of how some cases contributing to such correlations might arise. The tensions induced by relative poverty, culture conflict, and social pressures might interfere with the parents' supervision over their children or otherwise lead parents to be lax in a fashion which would produce in slum areas a relatively high proportion of young people prone to engage lightheartedly in the theft, violence, and immorality tolerated by the neighborhood's culture.

SUMMARY

In this study 230 white boys charged with automobile theft were compared with 2,544 others in trouble with the Detroit police in 1948. They had good peer-group relationships, came from relatively more favored neighborhoods, but were otherwise similar to juvenile offenders in general. It was suggested that the common factor accounting for one general class of antisocial behavior regardless of socioeconomic factors was a personality structure which readily accepted the values of immediate associates but responded weakly to the enactments of larger social entities.

Patterns of Drinking and Abstinence

GEORGE L. MADDOX
AND BEVODE C. McCALL

The principal concern of this chapter is to describe patterns of drinking behavior and abstinence among eleventh and twelfth grade students in the high schools of a midwestern city. *Pattern of drinking behavior* as it is used here refers to events and circumstances which are regularly associated with the act of drinking, including the specific uses of alcohol as they occur in time and space, whether and how the use of alcohol is considered a part of the self-image of the user, and the location of users within one or another social group.[1] Consideration is given, correspondingly, to the *pattern of abstinence*.

In the chapters that follow a teen-ager is considered to be a *user* of alcohol if he reports that his exposure to alcohol has not been confined to isolated tastes or drinks but is recurrent, however infrequent this may be. The student who reports no recurrent use of beverage alcohol is designated a *nonuser*.

The students were also asked whether they preferred to think of themselves and to be thought of as *drinkers* or *nondrinkers*. This question was designed to explore the relationship between the use of alcohol and the inclusion of this act as part of the self-image of the user. Everyone develops through time a portrait of himself, a perception of his own person both as a discrete entity and as one who stands in

Reprinted by permission of the authors and of the publisher from *Drinking Among Teen-Agers*, New Jersey, Rutgers Center of Alcohol Studies, 1964. Excerpts are taken from pp. 25–57. Some tables are omitted.

relation to other persons or selves.[2] For the adolescent the development of a sense of individual identity is a crucial problem. Erik H. Erikson considers this the crucial problem of the adolescent who is building a bridge between what he was as a child and what he is about to be as an adult. Whether or not the young people in this study preferred to think of themselves or be thought of as drinkers or as nondrinkers is not considered *the* crucial piece of information which totally defines their emerging conception of self or sense of personal identity. Their choice in this regard is considered an important piece of information about how they relate themselves to a commonly used social object, alcohol, and a commonly observed social act among adults, drinking. In the analysis which follows, attention is given to the matter of self-identification with alcohol use as something to be explained, just as the act of using or not using alcohol is to be explained.

In the chapters that follow then, *users* will sometimes be subdivided into those who designated themselves as *drinkers* and those who designated themselves as *nondrinkers*. The *nonusers* constitute the third major category among the adolescents in this study. After a description of the various responses to alcohol by these selected teen-agers, they will be located within the community in which they live by patterns of use or abstinence.

A DESCRIPTION OF RESPONSES TO ALCOHOL

Prevalence of Drinking and Drinkers

Determination of the prevalence of teen-age drinking must be distinguished from determination of the prevalence of self-designated drinkers. When the 1,962 high-school students in the study (903 boys and 1,059 girls) were asked, "Do you consider yourself to be a drinker?" only 177 (about 9%), of whom 48 were girls, responded affirmatively. All of these students were found to be actually users. An additional 279 (14.2%) students, of whom 107 were girls, designated themselves nondrinkers but reported recurrent use of alcohol. Thus, 456 (23.2%) of the students in the study were found to be users: 301 boys and 155 girls.

Among the nonusers 13% of the boys and 15% of the girls reported that they had never tasted alcohol. At the other extreme, 13.6% of the 177 drinkers and only 2 nondrinkers reported that they drink "often" or "very often." Students who reported extensive drinking, therefore, constitute only slightly more than 1% of all the teen-agers studied and about 6% of the users.

Depending on the criteria chosen, the prevalence of drinking and self-designated drinkers among these students may be described in several different ways:

1. 92% of the teen-agers studied had drunk or tasted alcohol at some time;
2. 23% reported that they are not abstainers and that they drink some alcoholic beverage at least occasionally;
3. 9% designated themselves as drinkers;
4. 8% indicated that they had never tasted alcohol;
5. about 6% of the users reported frequent consumption of alcohol.

The possible significance of this reluctance of some users to designate themselves as drinkers in spite of the fact that they reported drinking on some occasions is suggested in the interview data. The students made definite distinctions between "tasters," "social drinkers," and the "drinker–drunkard–alcoholic." One student described succinctly the frequently encountered objection to the designation of oneself as a "drinker":

"If you asked me if I were a drinker, I would think you were asking me if I go out every night and I'd tell you no, because I don't drink often. But if you ask me if I drink rarely, I'd say yes, because I do. I consider myself a person who drinks but not a drinker."

"Social drinking" for these teen-agers implies "going out on the town, all fixed up and maybe talking to someone," or "being with the crowd." As for distinctions among drinkers, drunkards, and alcoholics, there was less clarity although they were clearly distinguishable from social drinkers. The drinker–drunkard was typically described as a person "who spends most of his time drinking." Emphasis was placed on the extent of, motivation for, and degree of dependence on drinking, although none of these points was developed by students with much precision. Major emphasis was placed by them on distinguishing the drinker–drunkard–alcoholic from the social drinker. While the former was sometimes described as a person "drowning his sorrow" with alcohol or one who "just can't stay away from it," the latter was never referred to in these terms. This suggests that for the self-designated drinker this label was the equivalent of social drinker. The drinking self-designated nondrinker, on the other hand, appears to have attached a different and unacceptable meaning to the same label.

At least two other explanations of the reluctance of some users to identify themselves as drinkers may be suggested here in anticipation of subsequent discussion. The drinking nondrinker may reflect the adolescent who is experimenting with the use of alcohol but has not yet integrated its use with his conception of self. Or, this apparently contradictory behavior may reflect ambivalence on the part of some adolescents who drink but find this behavior morally unacceptable. More will be said about this later.

What and How Much Do Teen-Age Students Drink?

Beer is the most frequently used beverage of boy users (Table 1).[3] Slightly more than half report drinking one or more bottles of beer in an average week and one in eight of them reported drinking six or more bottles. Although one in four of the girl drinkers indicates the consumption of one or more bottles of beer during an average week, the reported amount of their drinking is much less than that indicated by the boys.

The self-designated nondrinkers among the users did not report using any alcoholic beverage very frequently and no particular beverage was singled out by them. Eleven per cent of the boys and 6% of the girls in this category reported drinking at least one bottle of beer in the average week. Wine, the second most frequently reported beverage of drinkers, is used by approximately the same percentage of boys and girls. About one in three of the drinkers drank one or more glasses of wine during an average week. Among the nondrinkers, boys and girls exhibited the same pattern of use they reported for beer.

Whisky and mixed drinks are the beverages least frequently drunk by the users. About one in four of the boy drinkers indicated that they drink one or more "shot" glasses

TABLE 1. Estimates of Personal Consumption of Beer, Wine, Whisky and Mixed Drinks in an Average Week Among Users, By Sex and Self-Designation, in Per Cent

Average Weekly Consumption	Nondrinkers		Drinkers	
	Boys	Girls	Boys	Girls
Beer				
Rarely or never use	89	94	44	73
Between 1 and 3 bottles	5	6	22	15
Between 3 and 6 bottles	5	0	19	8
More than 6 bottles	1	0	13	2
No answer[a]	0	0	2	2
Totals	100	100	100	100
Wine				
Rarely or never use	82	91	60	61
Between 1 and 3 wine glasses	8	5	18	25
Between 3 and 6 wine glasses	0	0	5	0
More than 6 wine glasses	2	0	3	4
No answer[a]	8	4	14	10
Totals	100	100	100	100
Whisky				
Rarely or never use	86	90	64	69
Between 1 and 3 shot glasses	4	3	16	17
Between 3 and 6 shot glasses	2	1	5	4
More than 6 shot glasses	[b]	0	6	2
No answer[a]	8	6	9	8
Totals	100	100	100	100
Mixed Drinks				
Rarely or never use	79	84	63	69
Between 1 and 3 mixed drinks	7	8	9	19
Between 3 and 6 mixed drinks	2	0	4	2
More than 6 mixed drinks	0	0	3	2
No answer[a]	12	8	21	8
Totals	100	100	100	100
N	172	107	129	48

[a] "No answer" is probably most adequately interpreted as "never use."

[b] Less than 1%.

(jiggers, probably about 1 oz.) of whisky or highballs during an average week. Only a slightly smaller number of the girls in this category drank this amount. As in the case of wine, the boys were more likely than the girls to consume larger amounts.

One in six of the boy drinkers had one or more mixed

drinks in an average week while almost one in four of the girls in this category reported this amount.

No distinctive pattern of use appears in the reports of nondrinkers about their consumption of whisky and mixed drinks. Only a small number of these reported regular use of these beverages. It should be noted, however, that a larger percentage of girl nondrinkers (8%) reported using mixed drinks than any other alcoholic beverages. In brief, about one in two boy drinkers reported the consumption of beer one or more times a week and about one in four of these indicated that they use wine, whisky, mixed drinks or a combination of them one or more times in the average week. About one in four girl drinkers revealed a pattern of drinking one or more of these beverages on the average of at least once a week.

On the basis of interview data the differences in patterns of usage are at least partially explained by three considerations: (1) the students indicated an awareness that whisky is "more powerful" than beer or wine; (2) beer, and to some extent wine, is a common beverage in many homes, is on sale in most grocery stores and is, therefore, most accessible to to them; (3) there is a slight but identifiable association on the part of the students between masculinity and the use of beer and whisky, and between femininity and the use of wine and mixed drinks.

Attention should be called to the large number of users who never, or rarely, drink beer during an average week, in spite of the fact that beer is the most commonly used beverage. This underscores the observation earlier that among teen-agers who drink, those who drink frequently and extensively are a small minority.

Occasions for Drinking

All the students, regardless of sex, use, or self-designation as drinker and nondrinker, essentially agreed that the most likely occasion for teen-age drinking is at a party, particularly a "wild," "beer" or "unsupervised" party (Table 2). This association between drinking and the "wild" party is especially pronounced among girls. Drinking among the teen-agers is not closely associated by those students with entertaining in the home, with school activities, or with occasions on which adults or relatives are drinking. Rather,

TABLE 2. Responses to, "What Are the Three Most Likely Occasions for Drinking Among Teen-Agers in High School?" By Use, Self-Designation and Sex, in Per Cent[a]

Occasions	Nonusers		Users			
			Nondrinkers		Drinkers	
	Boys	Girls	Boys	Girls	Boys	Girls
Party or dance	18	12	11	17	11	5
"Wild," "unsupervised," "beer," etc., party	45	59	45	45	38	60
Social visits among kinsmen or friends	14	10	3	8	6	5
Weddings, holidays	8	11	7	8	6	6
Other	15	8	34	22	39	24
Totals	100	100	100	100	100	100

[a] The total number of times a type of occasion was mentioned as one of the three responses is expressed as a percentage of the total of responses to the question.

the most likely drinking occasion is found at a party attended only by teen-agers.

The most commonly reported occasions on which students are most likely to drink are when with a group of age peers at a party where others are drinking, or in connection with special events or holidays (Table 3). While drinking with

TABLE 3. Responses of Users to, "Which of the Following Best Describe(s) the Situation in Which You Drink?" By Self-Designation and Sex, in Per Cent[a]

Situations	Nondrinkers		Drinkers	
	Boys	Girls	Boys	Girls
With a gang of friends	22	10	23	21
At parties where others drink	24	32	23	17
With parents or relatives	16	20	18	33
Special events or holidays	25	33	21	20
Fishing or hunting trips	10	2	8	2
Weekend recreation	0	3	7	6
Anywhere, anytime	3	0	[b]	1
Totals	100	100	100	100

[a] Multiple responses are included in these distributions. The total number of times a type of situation was mentioned is expressed as a percentage of the total number of responses to the question.

[b] Less than 1%.

age peers is prominently reported, specific or implicit inclusion of parents or other adult figures in situations in which the teen-ager drinks should be noted. Girls, moreover, were more likely than boys to describe the presence of parents or relatives who were drinking as occasions for their own drinking. Boys, on the other hand, were more likely than girls to report fishing or hunting trips as occasions. These reflect aspects of distinctly different patterns of drinking reported by boy and girl teen-agers.

Among nonusers, both boys (56%) and girls (67%) were more likely to have "tasted" alcohol on occasions when adults or relatives were drinking than at any other time. The next most frequent response by boys in this category was "with a group of friends" (18%), and by girls, at "special events" (20%). As on the reported occasions for drinking by boy and girl users, girl nonusers were more likely than boys to report the drinking of parents and relatives and less likely to indicate peer group situations as occasions for their "tasting."

These teen-age users, therefore, were more likely than nonusers to indicate peer group situations as occasions for their drinking. Conversely, they were less likely to indicate situations in which parents or relatives are present as occasions for their own drinking, although adults were reportedly present in a number of instances. In each of these categories, distinct male and female patterns of drinking are identifiable. In each case the girls were more likely to report situations in which parents or adult relatives are present as the most likely drinking or "tasting" occasion for themselves. Boys were more likely to report peer group situations.

Places for Teen-Age Drinking

There was essential agreement among both users and nonusers that teen-agers are most likely to drink at places removed from adult supervision and control. The "unsupervised party," "in secret where others will not know," "in automobiles" and "on back roads" illustrate the most frequently indicated places. Although students in the interviews also consistently mentioned having their first drinking or "tasting" experiences in the home and in the presence of parents, they emphasized that the most likely places for teen-age drinking are those where adults are absent. The inconsistency is only apparent. Materials from the interviews suggest that it may be resolved, at least in part, by recognizing that (1) drinking—or as students typically said, "tasting"—alcohol at home with parents does not necessarily authorize drinking in peer group situations or indicate approval of teen-age drinking on the part of parents; (2) parents, if they allow their children to drink in their presence, typically allow children to use alcohol only as "tasters"; (3) the purchase of alcoholic beverages is illegal for persons under 21 years of age in the state of Michigan; and (4) unsupervised drinking is socially defined by parents as inappropriate behavior for adolescents. Thus, teen-agers were not in doubt about general parental disapproval of unsupervised teen-age drinking. Therefore, if the teen-ager drinks with peers, he typically must do so in situations not controlled by adults. He may, however, "taste" alcohol in the presence of adults.

COMMUNITY SOCIAL STRUCTURE, DRINKING AND ABSTINENCE

Social interaction among individuals is not ordinarily a matter of chance. Individuals usually participate in and are members of social groups whose standardized symbols of communication allow them to place themselves in relation to others and to anticipate what is likely to happen in any given social situation. Group life is structured and organized to facilitate the accomplishment of those tasks and the achievement of those goals or values which are considered important by members of a group. The shared rules of behavior (social norms) which come to order the common ways of interaction within groups provide a basis for shared expectations about appropriate behavior.

Individuals may be placed or place themselves (1) formally in a group (e.g., doctor, father), (2) in terms of an informally defined interpersonal relationship (e.g., friend, one of the gang), (3) in terms of some particular value or disvalue (e.g., patriot, drinker), or in a combination of categories. Some of the factors involved in this positioning are ascribed at birth (e.g., race and sex) or are closely related to the biological development of the individual (e.g., age), while others are primarily achieved (e.g., occupation, education). The joining of a position with a definition of appropriate and expected behavior in given social situations is conveniently designated by the concepts *status* and *role*.

How one comes to recognize and identify oneself and others with various roles is fundamentally a matter of learning. One learns the traditional expectations about behavior characteristic of the groups which are relevant for him as these expectations are interpreted by both the statements and the behavior of others. One learns, for example, that all individuals do not play identical roles, and that the playing of some roles by certain individuals is sometimes required or encouraged, and at other times, discouraged or prohibited. But even persons who are presumably playing the same roles do not necessarily interpret the expectations identically; they also may sometimes presume to play certain roles in spite of discouragement or prohibition from other members of the group. The teen-age adolescent, for example, typically is not permitted to play some roles reserved for adults but may only "play at" them. This obviously does not mean, however, that no teen-agers prematurely claim the right to play or actually play some adult roles. Some teen-agers do. Drinking is a case in point.

The drinking behavior or abstinence of the adolescent cannot be understood without recognition of the position which he occupies in relevant social groups and how he conceives the roles associated with that position. The discussion which follows in the remainder of this chapter will consider specifically how three important aspects related to the positioning of an individual—sex, age, and socioeconomic status—are related to patterns of teen-age drinking and abstinence.

The starting point for age–sex differentiations and the practical justifications for them lie in the differing social potentialities of men and women at every age level. Social definitions of what it means to be male or female are involved in addition to biological differences. Some sex and age categories are recognized in all societies; for example, infant boy or girl, adult man or woman, old man or woman. Moreover, definitions of appropriate behavior of the young man and woman characteristically anticipate cultural definitions of appropriate adult behavior of men and women which adults share.

In addition to prescribing certain occupational and behavioral expectations, assignment to and membership in a particular age–sex group provide an individual with patterns for the proper behavior in his relationships with members of other age–sex groups. Consequently, the following paragraphs depict successively those aspects of sex and age in American social structure which have relevance for understanding the patterns of teen-age drinking and abstinence. The relationship between the patterns of drinking or abstinence and the socioeconomic status in the community, both the status of the teen-ager's family and his own status aspirations and expectations, will also be considered.

Sex Identification and Alcohol

The importance of sex differences in the pattern of response to alcohol use among teen-agers is illustrated by the relationships between sex and both the use of alcohol and choice of self-designations. Boys, for example, were much more likely to designate themselves as drinkers and to be users than were girls (Table 4). Among users, the percentage of boys is greater among drinkers than among nondrinkers. This same point may be made in another way. Forty-six per cent of the students in this study are boys, 54% girls. If the estimated sex distribution of nonusers presented in Table 4 is used, it is found that 67% of the boys are nonusers, 33% users. Among the users, 19% designated themselves as nondrinkers and 14% as drinkers. Correspondingly, 85% of the girls are nonusers, 15% users. Among the users, 10% designated themselves as nondrinkers and 5% as drinkers.

The sex differences in the pattern of teen-age drinking apparently reflect a basic distinction, of which drinking is only one aspect, between male and female roles which adults

TABLE 4. Designation of Self as "Drinker" or "Nondrinker," By Sex and Reported Use, in Per Cent

Sex	Nonusers	Users: Nondrinkers	Users: Drinkers
Male	39	62	73
Female	61	38	27
Totals	100	100	100
N	265	279	177

in our society also make. Surveys of adult drinking behavior in the United States consistently report that more women than men are abstainers and that women drinkers report drinking less.[4] Not only is drinking behavior of men and women in the United States different, it is also expected to be different. With drinking, as in other kinds of behavior, the American woman is subjected to a double standard.[5] The different cultural definitions of appropriate male and female behavior with regard to the use of alcohol observed in the larger society are reflected in what the teen-agers themselves say.

Although some teen-agers specifically rejected the "rightness" of a double standard for the drinking behavior of men and women, all of them recognized it as operative among both teen-agers and adults. One adolescent drinker said, for example:

"I think I would be embarrassed if my girl drank even if I were drinking. And the same way when they [girls] smoke. I don't think it looks right. But I think some girls expect their boy friends to smoke. I don't know why but I think that's right because boys—they expect it—oh, I don't know whether you would say rugged, go out and do things just for fun where girls—well, it just doesn't look right for her to do it."

In spite of the difficulty in articulating his feelings, this student was able to put across his point: Some behavior just "doesn't look right" for the girl and drinking is such behavior. Even a girl drinker with an equalitarian orientation who thought, "if [drinking] is good enough for a boy it is good enough for a girl," nevertheless observed, "I think a lot of people, even the police, don't think it's as bad for a boy as a girl to drink, but I don't know why that is. Maybe they feel that a girl can get carried away too far. . . ."

The two points illustrated in these excerpts from interviews were frequently echoed in the comments of other students. How basic this view is is reflected in the fact that recognition of felt differences in expectations for boys and girls were often accompanied by "I don't know why."

The students tended to circumscribe rather narrowly the situations in which drinking by girls is appropriate, if at all. As noted in the previous discussion of the places where teen-agers drink, the girl is more likely than the boy to associate drinking by girls with the home or with situations in which parents or relatives are present. Although the boy was likely to say that drinking by girls "just doesn't look right," no comparable statement was applied by girls to males in general. One explanation of the different assessments by students of the appropriateness of male and female drinking behavior is found in the association between the willingness of the girl to drink outside the home and moral laxity. "It's okay," said one boy, "if you are going to pick up girls someplace if they drink; but for the one that you really decide to marry—well, they wouldn't go." A girl nondrinker also observed, "Parents are more concerned about girls than boys because they know they expect a certain amount of devil from boys but not from girls. . . . Parents don't even like to see their girls smoke."

Definitions of appropriate male and appropriate female behavior with regard to the use of beverage alcohol are widely shared within the social groups in which these high-school students participate. The difference in expectations is reflected both in what the students do with alcohol and in what they say about the appropriateness of that behavior. The students' definitions as well as their behavior appear to be similar to and to reflect adult role definitions and role behavior involving the use of alcohol.

Age Grading and Reference Groups

Because of these different perceptions of adolescent and adult drinking behavior, a teen-ager's identification with either adolescents or adults is related both to his reaction to the use of alcohol and to his own self-conception as a drinker or a nondrinker. The propositions developed here are that (1) the older the student the more likely he is to be a user and, if a user, to identify himself as a drinker; and (2) the greater the identification and experience with adult roles and the greater the expectation of achieving adult status immediately after graduation from high school, the more likelihood that a student will be a user and, if a user, will identify himself as a drinker.

Users were found to be older than nonusers, and self-designated drinkers older than nondrinkers. Thus older teen-agers, those who were approaching an age when claims to adult status are increasingly feasible, were more likely than younger ones to indicate an acceptance of alcohol use. The association between increasing age and the probability that a student would be a user can be illustrated in another way. If an estimate of the age distribution of the boy nonusers is made, it is found that the percentage of nonusers among boys 16 years old or younger is 74%; among the 17-year-olds it is 71%; but among those 18 years old and over, the percentage of nonusers decreases to 53%. Similarly, among girls, the percentage of nonusers decreases from 91% of those 16 years old or younger, to 86% of the 17-year-olds, to 61% of those 18 and older.

Since the achievement of personal identity and the interpersonal competence necessary to maintain that identity is one of the basic tasks of the adolescent approaching young adulthood, the teen years are a time of increasing independence from adult supervision and of increasingly frequent assertions of personal autonomy. It should follow then, that teen-agers who are most advanced in the achievement of personal autonomy would not only be older but also be most likely to use adult roles as points of reference. And, insofar as the adult is perceived as likely to be a drinker, these students should also be more likely than others to be users and to identify themselves as drinkers. The data tend to support this interpretation.

Most students reported that they live with both their parents. In such situations they are likely to be defined as children, not the young adult peers of their parents. On the other hand, one might expect that, in the absence of a parent of the same sex, a child would have the occasion if not the necessity to play adult roles sooner than he might ordinarily. Among boys living in family units in which the father was present 68% were nonusers, as compared with 53% living in units in which the father was absent. Correspondingly, 87% of the girls living with their mothers were nonusers, compared with 77% of those whose mothers were absent. Whether this relationship is to be explained in terms of accelerated achievement of emotional and economic independence, of pressure to assume adult responsibility for self or others, of differences in parental control, or of a combination of these cannot be answered from these data.

Money is purchasing power and purchasing power is, to some extent, discretionary power. One facet of the individual's achievement of increasing autonomy, therefore, lies in having access to money not directly subject to parental control. One source of such money for a teen-ager is provided by earnings from work away from home. If users, as we have argued, are more likely than others to identify themselves with adult roles, then one would expect them to have greater access to financial resources which permit the autonomy in decision making associated with adulthood. This is found to be the case, although the difference between users and nonusers in this instance is minimal. For both boys and girls users are more likely than nonusers to have access to money not directly subject to parental control. Since the right to make one's own decisions and the availability of the economic resources to implement these decisions is associated with adulthood, the achievement of some measure of financial independence does make independent decisions, including decisions about drinking, increasingly a live option for the working teen-ager. It is important to note also that working outside the home, in addition to providing an independent source of income, provides the teen-ager with the opportunity to observe at close range other adults playing and interpreting adult roles.

Users and drinkers are not only more likely than others to have experience in jobs outside the home; they also are more likely to have plans for the assumption of adult-role responsibilities immediately after high school. Nonusers tend to be oriented toward college, users toward the full-time job or enlistment in the armed services, both of which are associated with adult role playing: an estimated 77% of the boys and 92% of the girls planning to attend college are nonusers, compared with 58% of the boys and 82% of the girls planning to enter the work force or armed forces.

Differences in the importance which users and nonusers attach to adolescent peer groups would also be expected if the proposition being developed here is correct. Users are, in fact, found to be less oriented than others to organized activities involving teen-age peers. This difference is reflected both in the higher proportion of users who participate in no high-school organization and in the smaller number of organizations to which those who do participate belong.

When organized nonschool activities are considered, nonusers are again less likely than users to report no participation. Among boy participants, users are generally less active than nonusers in all types of activities except group sports. Among girls, users are less likely than nonusers to participate in all types of organized nonschool activities. Moreover, the users, in spite of being less active than others, were no more inclined than the nonusers, in fact were slightly less inclined, to increase their participation.

These data suggest the need to make a basic distinction among various teen-age groups with regard to drinking. Since users, and even more so the self-designated drinkers, constitute a minority of students in the study and report participating least in organized group activity both inside and outside the school, it would not be warranted to maintain that adolescent groups in general are a source of support for drinking. On the contrary, most students perceived adolescents as abstinent, suggesting just the opposite. In a minority of cases, peer group participation may be important in the development and support of the self- and social conception of drinker. But more important, it appears that those groups in which the user participates are composed of those teen-agers who are older, have achieved some financial independence, have more immediate plans for establishing themselves occupationally, prefer adult models of behavior and are least involved in the organized teen-age activities either inside or outside the school.

In sum, the user, and particularly the self-designated drinker, appears most likely to be the teen-ager who is playing essentially adult roles and whose preferred groups are composed either of adults or of other teen-agers whose behavior identifies them with adult status. There was no indication from the responses of these students that most teen-agers or teen-age peer groups in these high schools are basically antagonistic to perceived adult definitions of the inappropriateness of drinking by adolescents. Nor was there any indication in the interviews that "storm and stress" surrounded the issue of drinking for these older adolescents. Rather, it was those students apparently most advanced in the assumption of adult roles who were most likely to drink and to designate themselves as drinkers.

Socioeconomic Status of the Family

Users were not equally distributed throughout the range of socioeconomic status as defined by the occupations of fathers. Rather, they are concentrated at the lower end of the status continuum. Teen-agers classified in the lower socioeconomic strata of a community might be expected to have neither the resources nor the status aspirations to make the postponement of a full-time job, marriage, or entrance into the armed services a feasible or desirable option.[12] The postponement of full adult status by continuing professional or technical preparation is more likely to appear both possible and desirable among teen-agers from families with higher status.

As expected, when census classifications of the father's occupations are used, the users were concentrated in the lower occupational classifications (Table 5). Among boys, 54% of the nonusers had fathers in white-collar occupations (professionals, managers, clerks or salesmen) in contrast to

TABLE 5. Father's Occupation (Census Classification), By Use, Self-Designation and Sex, in Per Cent

	Nonusers		Users			
			Nondrinkers		Drinkers	
	Boys	Girls	Boys	Girls	Boys	Girls
Professional–managerial	39	34	21	15	15	23
Clerical–sales	15	9	16	8	18	10
Craftsmen–operatives	34	50	28	35	25	25
Other	12	7	35	42	42	42
Totals	100	100	100	100	100	100
N	104	161	172	107	129	48

the users among whom 63% of the nondrinkers and 67% of the drinkers had fathers employed in blue-collar occupations (craftsmen, operatives, service workers). A similar distribution is noted among the various categories of girls. Forty-three per cent of the nonusers reported the father to have a white-collar occupation. Among the users, in contrast, 23% of the nondrinkers and 33% of the drinkers made this report. Since the distribution of occupations among the random sample of nonusers approximates the distribution among all the nonusers among the students in the study, the relationship between the status of an adolescent's family and alcohol use can be illustrated in another way. Among boys, 75% of those with a father in a white-collar occupation were nonusers; 65% of the remaining boys were. Similarly, among relatively upper-status girls, 90% were nonusers; while among others, 82% were.

The Warner Index of Status Characteristics, because it

includes education and source of income in addition to an evaluation of occupational status, is a more refined indicator of class than is the census classification of occupations alone. When students are placed in terms of social class based on the Warner Index, a modified picture of the relationship between drinking and class emerges (Table 6). Users are less clearly located in the lower range of the status structure than was the case when occupational classification of the father alone was used. The user was more likely than others to be found at the upper and lower extremes of the class structure. The nonuser, on the other hand, was most likely to be found in the middle range of status. Seventy per cent of the middle-class boys were nonusers in contrast to 63% of those in the upper class, 66% of those in the lower class, and

TABLE 6. Father's Social Class (Warner Index of Status Characteristics), By Use, Self-Designation and Sex, in Per Cent

	Nonusers		Users			
			Nondrinkers		Drinkers	
	Boys	Girls	Boys	Girls	Boys	Girls
Upper class	2	0	0	0	5	6
Middle class	50	52	46	34	38	28
Lower class	42	41	42	60	44	57
Unclassified	6	7	12	6	13	8
Totals	100	100	100	100	100	100
N	104	161	172	107	129	48

49% of those whose class position could not be classified because one or another crucial piece of information was not reported. Correspondingly, 91% of the middle-class girls, 80% of the lower-class, and no upper-class ones were nonusers.

Status Aspirations and Expectations

While an adolescent receives his socioeconomic position in the community from the status of the father, a young person may also aspire to and identify himself with a socioeconomic position he prefers as well as the one he himself expects to achieve as an adult. For example, the son of a factory operative may aspire to a professional occupation or to be in a social class higher than the one his family currently occupies. He may have as the preferred model of his behavior in such a case not his father but the image of an adult or adults occupying the status positions to which he aspires. A similar observation might be made of the girl whose status aspirations, which are expected to be realized in a career or in marriage, do not coincide with her present social status. The following paragraphs will explore the relevance of status aspirations vis-à-vis status expectations for understanding the drinking behavior of high-school teen-agers.

When the father's occupation is projected as a possible occupation for self or for husband, users were more likely than nonusers to evaluate this possibility as "poor" or "very poor" (Table 7). This is consistent with the observation that users are more likely than others to come from families in which the occupational status of the father is predominantly low. Among boys, 46% of the nonusers considered the

TABLE 7. Student Estimates of Acceptability of Father's Occupation for Self or Spouse, By Use, Self-Designation and Sex, in Per Cent

	Nonusers		Users			
			Nondrinkers		Drinkers	
Estimates	Boys	Girls	Boys	Girls	Boys	Girls
Good–very good	46	58	43	49	36	35
Fair	27	22	27	25	27	29
Poor–very poor	23	18	22	22	34	30
No answer	4	2	8	4	3	6
Totals	100	100	100	100	100	100
N	104	161	172	107	129	48

father's occupation as "good" or "very good" as a possibility for themselves in contrast to 36% of the drinkers and 43% of the nondrinkers. More than half of the girl nonusers considered the father's occupation as "good" or "very good" for themselves or their spouses in contrast to one in three of the drinkers and slightly less than half of the nondrinkers.

Users and nonusers had different occupational expectations. For example, among boys, 40% of the nonusers in contrast to 30% of the nondrinkers and 33% of the drinkers expected professional–managerial occupations for themselves (Table 8). When this expectation is compared with the reported occupational status of the father (Table 5), the number of nonusers expecting this classification is about equal to those whose fathers actually have this classification. The number of users expecting these occupational classifications, however, reflects upward occupational aspirations for many. Among nondrinkers, the number of students who expect top level occupations was greater (30%) than

TABLE 8. Students' Occupational Expectations for Self or Spouse, By Use, Self-Designation and Sex, in Per Cent

	Nonusers		Users			
			Nondrinkers		Drinkers	
Expectations	Boys	Girls	Boys	Girls	Boys	Girls
Professional–managerial	40	30	30	16	33	29
Clerical–sales	3	33	4	37	2	23
Craftsman–operative	17	4	35	4	22	6
Other	5	6	6	19	4	8
No answer	35	27	25	24	39	34
Totals	100	100	100	100	100	100
N	104	161	172	107	129	48

the number reporting such occupations for the father (21%). Among drinkers the discrepancy is even greater (33% compared to 15%).

The differences between the expected (for self or spouse) and the reported occupational classification of the father among the boys are also found among the girls. Thirty per cent of the nonusers expected a professional or managerial occupation for self or spouse, while 16% of the nondrinkers and 29% of the drinkers had this expectation. Again the expectation of upward mobility is more apparent among the users (compare Table 5). On the assumption that the father's occupation is a fair indicator of a son's probable occupation or the probable occupation of a daughter's spouse, these students seem realistic in stating their occupational expectations.

As might be expected in a society in which white-collar jobs are available to women in increasing numbers and in which there is the general expectation that a woman should marry up the status ladder, all the girls expected upward social mobility. Sixty-three per cent of the nonusers, 53% of the nondrinkers and 52% of the drinkers expected a white-collar occupation for self or spouse. Of the girl nonusers, 21% more expected a white-collar occupation for self or spouse than had fathers in such occupations. Similar discrepancies of 16% and 19% were found among nondrinkers and drinkers, respectively.

Evidence of the relationship between class and use or nonuse of alcohol among these teen-agers in high school may be summed up as follows. When the occupation of the father alone serves as an indicator of status, users are more likely than others to come from a family in which the father has a blue-collar occupation. However, when additional criteria are used to place students in a hierarchy of social classes, users are more likely to be found in upper and lower classes, the nonusers in the middle class. Among boys, use of alcohol appears to be related to the preference and expectation of upward social mobility. Among girls, the relationship between potential upward social mobility and use of alcohol is less clear. Girl nonusers, however, are more likely than others to expect such mobility.

Among users, the nondrinkers and drinkers were not sharply differentiated from each other in terms of the various indicators of status used. Characteristically, however, in any comparison of status characteristics between nonusers and users the greatest differences were found between nonusers and the self-designated drinkers.

SUMMARY

This chapter has concentrated on the patterns of teen-age drinking and abstinence. The focus of attention has been on the two acts: (1) the use or avoidance of alcohol; and (2) the self-designation of the *user* as *drinker* or *nondrinker*. A second focus has been on the location of the teen-agers in the community in terms of sex, age and socioeconomic status.

Most teen-agers in the study were found not to use alcohol either frequently or in quantity. Drinking for them was not experimental or occasional, as appears to be the case for most drinking nondrinkers. For the self-designated *drinker* the use of alcohol appeared to be a normal part of his behavior. He was most likely to drink with his peers in situations in which adults were absent, particularly at a party. The surreptitious aspects of his drinking behavior are in large part explained by the recognized disapproval of adolescent drinking by adults and his assumption that such behavior is generally disapproved in the community.

The North American adolescent occupies a somewhat anomalous position in our society. He is no longer a child but not quite an adult. Appropriate behavior for men and women is defined differently. Both these facts have significance for understanding his use or avoidance of alcohol. Regardless of use or nonuse of alcohol and of his self-designation as a *drinker* or a *nondrinker*, the teen-agers studied perceived the adult as a person who drinks at least sometimes. But only the *users* who designated themselves as *drinkers* perceived most other adolescents as persons who drink sometimes. This means that the teen-ager's conception of himself primarily as an adolescent or an adult should be closely related to his use or nonuse of alcohol and his self-designation as a *drinker* or *nondrinker*. The data tend to support this conclusion.

Those teen-agers who are older; who, for whatever reason, are playing or expect soon to play adult roles; who prefer adult models of behavior; and who are least active in organized teen-age activities—these are the teen-agers who are most likely to be *users* and, if *users*, to designate themselves as *drinkers*. While some teen-age peer groups in some cases support the *drinker's* conception of himself, this is clearly not the case for most teen-age peer groups. A distinctive widely shared "youth culture" supporting drinking among these adolescents is not apparent.

The *drinker* seems best described as a person whose preferred groups are primarily adult oriented. But the groups within which he interacts most frequently are necessarily largely composed of adolescents. His claims to adult status, or at least to the adult's right to discretion about his drinking or abstinence, are acknowledged by neither adults nor most other adolescents.

From the little evidence which is available on the drinking mores of the different classes in American society, it appears that drinking is most common among the "upper class" and the "lower class." The results of this study give tentative support to this observation. In addition, use of alcohol and the designation of self as a drinker is related to expectations of social mobility among boys. Whether or not this relationship can be explained in terms of the presumed ability of drinking to facilitate this mobility requires further investigation.

Juvenile Delinquency Among Middle-Class Girls

NANCY BARTON WISE

Female delinquency is a virtually neglected aspect of the study of criminology. The reiteration of official statistics has led some criminologists to accept the contention that female delinquency is both negligible in volume and different in quality from male delinquency. It is commonly asserted that girls commit predominantly sex delinquencies while boys engage in especially "masculine" offenses such as theft, assault, and vandalism.[1] Some writers have even concluded that the difference in quality is so great between male and female delinquency that different research methods are required for studying the delinquency of each sex. In addition, since official sources indicate that girls constitute a small proportion of the total number of delinquents, female delinquency is often considered a fruitless area for research. Consequently, there is little information on female delinquency, and data are virtually nonexistent on delinquency among middle-class girls.

Official statistics regarding female delinquency in general are both inaccurate and unreliable. Newly emerging evidence about the character of middle-class delinquency, and the modification of sex roles among middle-class adolescents, challenge popular notions about the quantity and quality of middle-class female delinquency in particular. If middle-class girls engage in nonviolent forms of delinquency, they participate also in a wide variety of essentially masculine delin-

Written especially for this volume.

quent acts including certain kinds of theft. Consequently, departing from popular criminological views, this paper suggests that *in the middle class* female delinquency closely resembles male delinquency in form and quantity.

THEORY

Contrary to official records and popular beliefs, there is some evidence suggesting that teen-age boys are as sexually delinquent as girls, and that many girls engage in typically male kinds of delinquency.[2] It is also true that much of the female delinquency that is considered typically male in quality is deliberately overlooked by officials and escapes official recording. Were identical criteria employed by law enforcement agents in making arrests of boys and girls, there would undoubtedly be less variation in delinquency rates between sexes. On the basis of these observations, a greater similarity can be expected in the form and the amount of male and female delinquency than is reflected in official statistics.

There is even greater reason to believe that delinquency among middle-class girls resembles that of middle-class boys. Descriptive accounts of American society frequently emphasize two major points about American culture: (1) that there exist marked differences between the working-class and middle-class cultures, and (2) that middle-class norms, having become widely institutionalized, are routinely enforced by the police. Law in America is very likely to be middle-class law, and is apt to treat middle-class deviance with greater leniency than deviance within the working class. Whereas working-class culture tends to emphasize verbal and behavioral spontaneity, and place nominal restraint in daily social interaction, middle-class culture stresses the importance of rationality, subtlety, and control in social behavior.[3] Therefore, middle-class behavior is apt to be less violent or aggressive, and unlikely to attract the attention of law enforcement officers. By contrast, working-class behavior is more likely to be noticed, disapproved, and officially recorded.

The delinquent behavior of youths tends to reflect their social class backgrounds. Delinquency among middle-class youths is typically daring, perhaps ingenious, often feigning sophistication, and usually avoids the violence, coercion, and impulsiveness allegedly characteristic of working-class youths.[4] Because ours is largely a "middle-class society" delinquent behavior which conforms to typically middle-class patterns will seldom be labeled "delinquent" by law enforcement agents. On the other hand, the police are prone to arrest and record working-class youths whose behavior is both typically working class in quality *and* delinquent. Middle-class girls, with both sex and social class biases in their favor, will constitute the smallest category of delinquents among official statistics.

If the delinquencies of middle-class boys reflect dominant middle-class values of nonviolence and social control, and rely upon ingenuity rather than physical force, middle-class girls ought to be equally capable of performing the same delinquent acts. Moreover, their motivation for delinquency and the kinds of delinquency they adopt ought to mirror their social class background. Despite the limited research data, there is some indication that the behavior of middle-class boys and girls is growing increasingly similar in form.[5] Recent studies have shown that teen-age and college girls harbor some resentment toward traditional female role obligations. Such girls might easily take on masculine aspects to their own routine behavior. Furthermore, studies of the contemporary middle-class family document a gradual convergence in parental sex roles whereby parents provide similar models of behavior for their offspring. There is evidence that parents hold approximately similar expectations of the behavior of adolescent boys and girls, and that these adolescents demonstrate a pronounced similarity in their attitudes, tastes, and practices. Despite sex differences one might reasonably expect middle-class youths to adopt generally similar patterns of conduct. Such a similarity can be anticipated also in the delinquency of middle-class boys and girls.

In summary, four observations have been made: (1) official delinquency statistics are inaccurate and generally favor middle-class youths, particularly females, (2) middle-class youths will commit delinquencies consistent with their class cultural values, (3) middle-class girls are physically capable of committing delinquencies considered typical of the middle-class boy, and (4) middle-class girls and boys, exposed to changing male and female role definitions, are adopting similar patterns of nondelinquent and delinquent behavior. Given these observations the null hypothesis was formulated that among middle-class adolescents, girls will not differ significantly from boys in either the volume or the type of their reported delinquent behavior.

RESEARCH

In order to overcome the limitations of police and court statistics regarding middle-class female delinquency, a check list was constructed of 37 delinquency items. Since school authorities objected to items inquiring directly about sex, two items were used which inferred sex delinquency. All but these two items were considered delinquent acts under Connecticut law. The check list was designed to reveal the nature, scope, and frequency of the delinquency of each respondent and contained an equal number of typically working-class and middle-class delinquent acts. Response categories included never, once or twice, several times, and quite often. Precautions were taken to maximize the reliability of data, and to identify dishonesty and inaccuracy in the responses. These included assurances of anonymity as well as checks for consistency, overconformity, and exaggeration.

The questionnaires were administered simultaneously to 1,079 sophomores and juniors attending the single public high school in a Connecticut suburban community. Although the community was predominantly middle class, it contained a large number of upper middle-class and upper-class families. A modified Hollingshead Index of Social Position, employing occupational, educational and ecological indices, was used to select a sample of 589 middle-class boys and girls ranging in age between 15 and 18. A comparative study of male and female delinquency was undertaken.

RESULTS

Contrary to the hypothesis, the data indicate significant differences between male and female delinquency. With few exceptions significantly more boys than girls reported committing each offense. The exceptions included sex and alcohol delinquencies and those offenses seldom reported by middle-class boys and girls. Table 1 lists the general offense categories and indicates that boys outnumber girls in all but two offenses. Boys and girls participated about equally in sex and alcohol offenses.

TABLE 1. Proportion of General Offenses Committed by Middle-Class Boys and Girls

Offense Category	Number of Acts Committed by			Percentage of Acts Committed by	
	Boys	Girls	Total	Boys	Girls
Sex	196	195	391	50.1	49.9
Alcohol	334	323	657	50.8	49.2
Driving	491	318	809	60.7	39.3
Ungovernability	356	202	558	63.8	36.2
Theft	568	304	872	65.1	34.9
Vandalism	540	219	759	71.1	28.9
Assault	356	97	453	78.6	21.4
		$N = 589$			

Although more boys than girls committed delinquent acts, the difference in ratio between the volume of male and female delinquency was not as great as official statistics suggest. Official estimates range from 1:3 to as low as 1:10. Table 2 presents the ratios when delinquency items are combined for general offense categories, and reveals that in all but two offenses female delinquency is comparatively higher than the 1:3 official estimate. Although vandalism and assault account for the greater difference in male and female offenses, these offenses were committed by the fewest number of middle-class youths. Therefore, the difference in

TABLE 2. Ratios of Male and Female Offenders According to Offense Derived from Self-Reported Data

Offense Category	Percentage Committing Offense			Ratios–Girl: Boy	
	Girls	Boys	Total	Actual	Approximate
Sex Offenses	33.2	36.6	34.7	99:100	1:1
Alcohol Offenses	54.7	63.7	58.8	96:100	9:10
Driving Offenses	27.1	46.9	36.0	65:100	3:5
Ungovernability	13.7	26.6	19.8	56:100	3:5
Theft	14.7	30.5	22.1	54:100	1:2
Vandalism	9.3	25.2	16.8	41:100	2:5
Assault	6.6	26.6	16.1	27:100	1:4
		$N = 589$			

TABLE 3. Comparative Rank Order of Offenses Committed by Boys and Girls

Rank Order of Delinquent Acts Committed by Boys	Percent of Total Boys Admitting	Rank Order of Delinquent Acts Committed by Girls	Percent of Total Girls Admitting
1. Fist fighting	84.0	1. Given or attended parties where liquor was served	58.5
2. Skipped school without excuse	66.0	2. Bought or drunk beer, wine, or liquor	51.4
3. Taken something from a store	64.6	3. Skipped school without excuse	41.3
4. Bought or drunk beer, wine, or liquor	64.3	4. Taken things of little value	34.9
5. Given or attended parties where liquor was served	61.0	5. Stayed through the last movie at a drive-in	34.5
6. Taken things of little value	60.9	6. Entered a private home or building when it was supposedly locked	34.2
7. Entered a private home or building when it was supposedly locked	57.1	7. Taken something from a store without paying for it	33.6
8. Sat on fenders or bumpers of moving vehicles	49.3	8. Driven or been in a car participating in a "drag race"	32.1
9. Purposely damaged or destroyed public or private property	47.4	9. Had mixed groups in home without parents' permission	31.9
10. Driven or been a passenger in a car participating in a "drag race"	47.0	10. Driven a car without a driver's license	31.0
11. Driven too fast or recklessly in an automobile	44.0	11. Painted and chalked trimmings on buildings or statues	28.5
12. Driven a car without having a driver's license	43.3	12. Driven too fast or recklessly in an automobile	23.4
13. Stayed through the last movie in a drive-in with a mixed crowd	40.7	13. Sat on fenders or bumpers of moving vehicles	21.8
14. Painted and chalked trimming on statues or buildings	39.2	14. Taken things of medium value	21.7
15. Removed traffic signs or placed them in positions not intended	38.4	15. Fist fighting	21.3
16. Broken street lights or windows in		16. Removed traffic signs or placed	

17.	[illegible] want that did not belong to you	35.0	17.	[illegible] public or private property	15.3
18.	Had mixed groups in your home without your parents' permission	32.5	18.	Taken things you really didn't want that did not belong to you	15.0
19.	Concealed a weapon on your person	29.4	19.	Run away from home	13.9
20.	Stayed out all night without your parents' permission	24.6	20.	Stayed out all night without your parents' permission	9.8
21.	Purposely damaged lawns, trees, gardens, or shrubbery	22.0	21.	Sneaked into a drive-in movie without paying	8.8
22.	Taken things of medium value	21.7	22.	Taken part in gang fights	4.4
23.	Sneaked into a drive-in movie without paying	21.3	23.	Purposely damaged lawns, trees, gardens, or shrubbery	4.4
24.	"Beat up" on kids who hadn't done anything to you	17.9	24.	Taken a car for a ride without the owner's knowledge	4.1
25.	Physically hurt someone just to see them squirm	13.1	25.	Physically hurt someone just to see them squirm	4.1
26.	Run away from home	12.7	26.	Broken street light or windows in a public building	3.7
27.	Taken part in "gang fights"	12.7	27.	Set fires in buildings or on grounds where they were not intended	3.7
28.	Been placed on school probation or expelled from school	11.2	28.	"Beat up" on kids who hadn't done anything to you	2.7
29.	Set fires in buildings or on grounds where they were not intended	11.2	29.	Been placed on school probation or expelled from school	2.7
30.	Taken a car for a ride without the owner's knowledge	7.0	30.	Concealed a weapon on your person	1.7
31.	Entered a commercial or public building and wrecked-up things	6.0	31.	Used force to get money from another person	1.4
32.	Used force to get money from another person	5.2	32.	Entered a commercial or public building and wrecked-up things	1.0
33.	Taken things of large value	3.0	33.	Sent in false fire alarms	0.7
34.	Sent in false fire alarms	1.5	34.	Taken things of large value	0.0
35.	Used or sold narcotics	0.0	35.	Used or sold narcotics	0.0

Rho = .871 $N = 589$

boy–girl ratio between official statistics and these self-reported data cannot be explained by the volume of delinquencies in these two categories. The self-reported data suggest that the overall ratio of girl to boy offenders is 3:5 or 1 girl delinquent to every 1.7 boy delinquents. At least in the middle class, a much higher proportion of girls committed delinquencies than official statistics usually acknowledge. Far from being negligible in volume, middle-class female delinquency closely resembles male delinquency in the number of youths taking part.

A partial explanation for the discrepancy between the self-reported data and official statistics may be the difference in frequency with which boys and girls committed offenses. This evidence suggests that girls seldom repeated their offenses more than once or twice, whereas a fairly high percentage of boys frequently repeated the same delinquent act. This suggests that girls tend to experiment with delinquency, but are less likely to persist in their offenses. Official statistics usually refer to apprehended delinquents, and since boys repeat their delinquencies more often than do girls, they are more likely to be caught committing a delinquent act. Perhaps official records are a more accurate representation of the overall number of male and female delinquencies committed than of the number of boy and girl offenders.

The evidence provides greater support for the second part of the hypothesis than the first. It indicates that middle-class boys and girls engaged in similar kinds of delinquency. In contrast to official statistics which indicate that sex offenses and ungovernability are typically female delinquencies, the self-reported data show that sex offenses were committed equally by girls and boys, and that proportionately two of every three delinquencies of ungovernability were male offenses. Nor was theft the most typical male offense. Few acts of assault and vandalism were reported, but there was a proportionately greater difference between male and female participation in these offenses than in theft. Alcohol offenses, petty theft, and sex offenses were the most common delinquencies among girls.

Inspection of Table 3 reveals a similarity in the rank order of "popularity" of reported delinquencies between boys and girls (Rho = .871). Moreover, high-ranking delinquencies for both boys and girls were characteristically nonviolent and noncoercive in quality. Delinquency such as assault, serious theft, narcotic use, and gang fighting, perhaps more common among working-class youths, was comparatively rare among these teen-agers.

Two conclusions can be drawn from the data: (1) in the middle class boys commit more delinquencies, more frequently, than girls, yet more middle-class girls commit delinquencies than official statistics would suggest, and (2) middle-class boys and girls engage in essentially noncoercive, nonviolent forms of delinquent behavior and participate about equally in sex and alcohol delinquencies.

SUMMARY AND DISCUSSION

Additional information obtained from the questionnaire suggests several explanations for the findings of this study. Of major interest is the fact that a relatively small segment of the sample committed any single delinquent act. Drinking, truancy, minor forms of vandalism, and fist fighting comprised the most frequent offenses. Although theft figured prominently among the offenses of these youngsters, serious theft was seldom reported. Narcotic use was emphatically disapproved. While a large majority of the sample reported some delinquency, few reported committing a serious offense, experimenting widely with delinquency, or frequently repeating their offenses. These data suggest that middle-class children are not especially delinquent. Both the unserious nature and infrequency of their offenses may account for their failure to appear in greater numbers in official statistics.

The fact that middle-class boys and girls engage in similar kinds of delinquency indicates, perhaps, that they are not strongly influenced by traditional sex roles. Traditional role expectations have always permitted boys greater laxity of behavior. Fist fighting, acts of daring, and "sowing one's wild oats" have often been permitted, if not prescribed, among middle-class boys. Stricter obligations have governed the customary roles of girls in the middle class. Even minor forms of deviance are considered more serious for girls than for boys. The considerable amount of female delinquency reported in this study suggests strongly that a change is occurring in expectations associated with the social roles of middle-class girls.

In contrast to the past, contemporary boys and girls in the

middle class are expected to engage on an equal basis in a wider variety of activities. They are encouraged to compete directly in the world of work and scholarship, and in leadership and social activities such as dating, parties, and other uniquely social events. With these changes taking place in role expectations, a role convergence may be occurring among these youngsters which includes both nondelinquent and delinquent kinds of activity.

This study provides evidence that female delinquency can no longer be overlooked as a matter of investigation. Although these data reveal a similarity in the delinquency most often practiced by boys and girls, more research is required to confirm these results. Especially needed are data on the conditions under which delinquency occurs among middle-class youths, the sex composition, and comparative sex roles of youths engaged in delinquent activities. Furthermore, future studies of middle-class delinquency would do well to include comparative analyses of the behavior of adolescent boys and girls in their daily legitimate and illegitimate activities.

The Suburbs

HARRISON E. SALISBURY

The two boys were a little tight when they came out of Freddy's Bar & Grill and got into the new cream-and-green Buick sedan. It was spring vacation and both were home in South Neck from college. Roy was a junior at Union College and Ralph was a sophomore at Cornell. Roy was twenty; Ralph, nineteen.

"You're sure she'll have a friend," Ralph asked nervously as Roy started the car.

"She better, the black bitch," the older boy said. "If she doesn't you can have her when I'm through."

The boys drove in silence through the spring evening. South Neck is a rather large suburb of New York, about forty-five minutes' ride from Grand Central. Twenty years ago it was quite exclusive. Today it is predominantly middle-class and upper middle-class. Most housewives in South Neck do their own work with the aid of a girl once or twice a week. These domestic workers are Negroes for the most part. Lately, more and more have been young girls, some still in their teens, newly arrived from Florida and Georgia. These girls, new to the North, work for slightly lower wages until they learn the ropes.

Among some of the middle-class boys of the late teens and early twenties a fad has sprung up of "dating" these Negro girls. The boys pick them up, usually by prearrangement, buy them a few drinks in a highway tavern, take them to the drive-in movies or park with them in lovers' lanes. They deposit the girls at the station in time for a late train back to New York.

"It's a big thrill for the girls," one of the boys explained. "Most of them are from the South. They've never been out with a white man before. It's a kick."

The kick, it is apparent, works both ways.

When Roy and Ralph got to the meeting place only one girl, a thin, rather good-looking light tan girl of eighteen or nineteen was standing there. Her girl friend, she explained, couldn't come.

Roy turned the wheel over to Ralph and got into the back seat with the girl.

"Just drive around," he ordered. "I got business to attend to."

The girl giggled nervously. "Where's this place you said we would go to?" she asked.

"You'd be surprised," Roy said, pulling her over to him.

Later, Ralph told the boys at Freddy's what had happened.

"Geez," he said, "don't tell Roy but I was kinda scared. I didn't know what to do. They were all quiet in the back seat. Then, I heard a noise like the girl was being sick or something. Kind of a choking noise. There was a slap and I looked back and Roy was belting the hell out of her."

Ralph said he had slowed the car for a turn when he heard the door slam and the girl scream at almost the same time. He turned his head and saw that the girl was gone.

"I said, 'What happened, Roy,' and he said, 'I kicked her the hell out of the car.' I said why and he said, 'I didn't like the way she was doing it, that's all.' I asked him about the funny noise and he laughed. 'Oh, I just choked her a little to see if she'd get any better. She didn't so I threw her the hell out.' "

The South Neck police say that there have been several complaints in the last six months by Negro girls who reported that they had been assaulted by white teen-agers. One girl said she was standing on a corner waiting for a bus. A car with six white boys in it, all under twenty, pulled up beside her. A boy said: "Come on with us." The girl refused. Three boys jumped out of the car, pulled her into the rear seat and held her down. They drove to a deserted lane outside town, ripped off her clothes and raped her while one boy held a knife against her throat.

"We don't want no trouble around here," a police sergeant said. "We try to discourage them from filing complaints. This is a quiet community and we aim to keep it that way. We have some fine people here. Of course, sometimes, the kids get a little wild. But we try to keep things in the family you might say."

There have been no arrests in the assault complaints.

I asked the officers whether there were any gangs in South Neck.

"No, sir," he said. "There's none of that cowboy stuff like they have in New York. We wouldn't allow that. Not for a minute."

What, I said, about a report I had heard that a gang of Negro boys had driven down one of the main streets of town on a recent evening, firing shots in the air, and stopping to beat up two boys who were walking home from the railroad station.

That had happened, he conceded. But those "hoods" better not try it again. They'd get what they had coming. He didn't think the Negroes were from New York. Probably from Newport, a nearby suburban town with several factories and a small Negro population.

Perhaps there is no connection between the assaults on

Negro girls by the white boys of "good" family and the incursion of the Negro gang. The police think not. But there is no doubt that in a deeper sense the two phenomena are intimately linked. Both are part of the pattern of delinquency in a middle-class setting, the manifestation of the shook-up generation in the American suburb.

No subject is more difficult to analyze or even to get information on than the extent and nature of antisocial activity by the children of white-collar families, the "better class" people in medium-sized communities, the families which make up 90 per cent of the population of so many suburbs and residential developments.

It is the thesis of Dr. Walter B. Miller, director of a special research project on youth in middle-class Roxbury, Massachusetts, a suburb of Boston, that much public concern over delinquency stems not from an increase in antisocial conduct but from the fact that patterns of conduct formerly exclusive to poor, working-class or lower-middle-class youngsters, have spread to the middle-class as a whole and to upper-class youth, as well.

This, he believes, has aroused middle-class anxiety. He cites the rock 'n' roll fad as an example of how lower-class culture and speech patterns have engulfed all American youth regardless of social status.

There may be some truth in Dr. Miller's idea. But there is reason to believe that there has always been much more antisocial conduct among children of better families than is generally known, largely because these families possess the ability to conceal or wipe out the evidence of what their children do.

When twelve-year-old Peter and his friend, thirteen-year-old John, walk into Kresge's on the main street of South Neck and swipe some candy bars off the counter and are caught as they try to sneak out the manager doesn't call the police. He knows the boys. He has seen them often with their mothers who are good customers. He bawls the kids out and sends them home. If he is thoroughly annoyed (because children's shoplifting goes on every day of the week) he may call up the mothers. But he does not think of arresting the youngsters. But if the same thing happens in Bedford-Stuyvesant and the kids are caught the policeman is called in, the kids are dragged off to the station house, they are sent up to

Children's Court, put on probation and classified as juvenile delinquents.

If sixteen-year-old George and three of his friends "borrow" a nice-looking Pontiac convertible from the country club parking lot and set off on a joy ride and are caught speeding by the county police they are taken to the station house, all right, but nothing goes on the blotter. The parents come down, there is much talk, the fathers bawl the daylights out of the boys, the kids promise to be good, any damage to the car is paid for by the parents, the owner wouldn't think of making any charge and by two o'clock in the morning everyone is back home, peacefully sleeping. At Christmas time the police captain gets several very nice presents. There's no case, no record, no statistics, "no delinquency."

When seventeen-year-old Joan gets pregnant after letting eighteen-year-old Denis "fool around" at a beach party one summer night she isn't sent to Youth House. Nor is Denis confronted with the dilemma of marrying the girl or facing a charge of statutory rape. There is an angry dispute between the two families. Joan's family blames Denis. Denis's family blames Joan. In the end Joan's father finds a doctor who takes care of Joan for $750. Joan is a month late starting school in the fall because, as her mother explains to the principal, she had such a bad reaction from the antibiotics they gave her at the camp up in New Hampshire where she went in August.

This is the classic middle-class way of dealing with the problems of antisocial conduct which when they arise in the slum become the bread-and-butter business of the police, the courts and the social agency.

As Professor MacIver of the New York Delinquency Evaluation Survey puts it:

"There is much more upper-class gang activity than is realized. There is more delinquency. But it is covered up. It is almost impossible to get statistics on it. We know that it exists. We know that there is much theft by middle-class children. We know there is much sex deviation. But it is all nicely covered up. A middle-class child has to act much worse than a poor boy before his conduct becomes the subject of a notation on the police blotter."

The chief of detectives of a large Middle Western city with a commendably low juvenile delinquency record says privately that he has more cases and more trouble in the district of the town's most fashionable high school than in any other section.

"It's so," he said. "But for heaven's sake don't quote me. I have enough trouble from the mothers and fathers already."

Does this mean that there is today more delinquency than before among children from so-called better homes? Is the middle-class component of the shook-up generation growing? I think the answer is yes to both of those questions.

The first scientific, sociological studies of this problem are just beginning to be reported. They show that the supposed immunity of "better" families to delinquency is an illusion. Albert K. Cohen, the author of classic studies on delinquency and teen-age gangs, selected a group of 337 college students, representing a cross-section of better economic and social strata. None of these youngsters had a criminal record. They were given a list of fifty-five offenses—the fifty-five for which slum children are most often arrested—and asked to check any which they had ever committed. Every boy checked at least one offense. James F. Short of the Washington State College sociology department has just completed a comprehensive study of the relationship, if any, between income, social status and delinquency.

"The traditional assumption of a higher incidence of delinquent behavior among members of the lower socioeconomic group; based on official statistics, is not substantiated," he reported.

Mr. Short compared youngsters from three Western cities of ten to twenty-five thousand population with a control group in the Washington State training schools. He found virtually no difference in the incidence of delinquency. Kenneth Polk of the University of California at Los Angeles sampled San Diego youngsters and came to the same conclusion—no correlation between economic status and delinquency. This does not mean that there is not more delinquency in a slum than in a first-class residential area; that children fortunate enough to have good, warm, interested families are as subject to delinquency as those who come from broken homes; that children who play freely in open spaces are as subject to trouble as those who live on streets ruled by gangs. What it means is that neither money nor social status, per se, affords a clue to delinquency liability.

Take, for instance, what happened in Massapequa, Long Island. Massapequa is a good middle-class suburb of New

York. Families move there from Manhattan to get their children away from the "bad" conditions in the New York City schools.

A few months ago two fifteen-year-old boys were living in Massapequa with their families. One boy lived with his father, manager of a New York trucking company, his mother and his twelve-year-old sister in a pleasant white Cape Cod house. The other lived in a new ranch-type house on a quiet tree-lined street with his father, a photoengraver in New York, his mother, an older brother and three younger sisters. The two houses were about three miles apart. Both boys went to Massapequa High School. Both were in ninth grade.

One day in the washroom of the school Bruce Zator, who was the boy who lived in the ranch-type house, had a fight with a boy named Butch O'Malley. The boy from the Cape Cod cottage, Timothy Wall, intervened. According to Butch, Timothy knocked a knife out of Bruce's hand. Bruce, he said, warned them: "I'll get you two."

Bruce, a curly-haired, rather quiet boy, had not been doing well in his studies. He had been getting poor grades and lately had failed in two subjects. Because of this he was referred to the school psychologist. But he had never had any kind of disciplinary trouble.

About the time that Bruce and Butch had their fight in the washroom Bruce's father brought him a present from New York—a new shotgun. Bruce and his father planned to go hunting for rabbits.

For some reason, possibly because he was afraid of repercussions from his fight with Butch, Bruce stayed away from school for about five days. Finally, on a Tuesday he returned to school with his parents. On Wednesday morning Bruce got to school bright and early. By a little after eight in the morning he was in the lavatory where he had had the fight two weeks before.

According to the police Bruce went into one of the lavatory stalls. Presently Tim came into the room, went to the washbasin and started to comb his hair. A moment later, according to the story a third boy told the police, a voice rang out: "This is for you, Timmy, you creep."

Tim turned from the mirror at the sound of the voice, a gun roared, and he fell to the lavatory floor. He died a few minutes later in the school infirmary. Half an hour later police captured Bruce. He was wearing a raincoat under which, they said, he had concealed a single-barrel 12-gauge shotgun with a 12-inch stock. The barrel had been filed down to two inches.

Police charged that on the day before Bruce returned to school he filed down the gun and provided himself with some Double-O shells. They arrested Bruce and held him on first-degree murder charges.

Both school and police officials went to some pains to emphasize that this was not a "gang" killing, that it resulted from personal differences. While it was acknowledged that there was a "club" called the Clovers at the school the authorities said this had nothing to do with the case.

This insistence on the part of the authorities seems rather facile since regardless of whether there was an organized teen-age gang in the school the whole affair was permeated with gang morals, gang tactics and gang technique. The sawed-off shotgun from the time of Al Capone and George (Bugs) Moran has been the favored weapon of gangland. And only by the intrusion of the mores of the street could a schoolboys' lavatory quarrel turn into a fatal affair. The best that could be said is that the killing of one schoolboy did not lead to a whole series of attacks as might have been the case in a street fighting area of Brooklyn.

Massapequa, unfortunately, is not the only quiet, middle-class suburb which has been shocked into awareness of the violence of which the shook-up generation is capable. Suburban communities all over the country have been building new schools at an unprecedented rate to cope with rising school populations. Repeatedly, communities which have invested hundreds of thousands or millions of dollars in new school structures have seen these fine new buildings assaulted by youthful vandals. Damage has run to tens and even hundreds of thousands of dollars. These are not schoolboy pranks. They are vicious gang assaults. Whether the youngsters call themselves Bishops or Rovers makes no difference. Their tactics would be the envy of their slum comrades. The school vandalism fever seems to have started on the Pacific Coast and spread east. It has virtually died out in the West. But it is in full flower in the East, particularly around New York.

A typical outbreak occurred at Maplewood, New Jersey, a fine community of middle-class families, proud of a low juvenile delinquency rate. A gang of boys broke into the Maplewood Junior High School and sacked it. They destroyed the principal's office, wrecked classrooms, carried kerosene and alcohol from the art department into the library, toppled books from the shelves, poured inflammables over them and set fire to the place. School authorities estimated the damage at $300,000. The school had to be closed for a week to make repairs.

Only after this outrageous attack did the community discover that there had been some signs that gang behavior was infecting the younger generation. There had been an increase, police said, in thefts of auto accessories and cars. Not long before the attack on the school a highway ice-cream parlor was wrecked one night after closing.

The Maplewood attack is outstanding only because of the extent of the damage. During a three-months period in the New York suburbs there were at least six similar outbreaks. Youngsters attacked a new $3,900,000 high school at West Islip, Long Island, smashing furniture, windows, throwing typewriters and tape recorders into the swimming pool, breaking up the principal's office and stealing the school station wagon. Another gang set four fires in the Uniondale, Long Island, High School, apparently in an effort to destroy truancy and grade records. A gang of seventeen youngsters attacked cars parked in the Valley Stream, Long Island, High School lot. They smashed windshields, slashed tires and tops. Two police cars parked on the lot were vandalized among the rest. A gang broke into the Memorial Library at Bellmore, Long Island, and set it afire, causing $65,000 damage. A gang broke into the new $3,500,000 high school in Passaic, New Jersey, spilling acid over the science laboratories, smashing bird specimens, breaking fish tanks, ripping down shelves and hurling India ink over walls and books.

Schools were not the only target of adolescent gang attacks. Teen-agers hurled smoke grenades into the swank Parkway Casino on the Bronx River Parkway while a high school dance was in progress. Fortunately, no one was injured. Another gang near Merrick, Long Island, killed a group of swans in a reservoir by hurling lighted sticks at them. Several youngsters from good families at Greenpoint, Long Island, took a car and spent a whole evening shooting out street lights and smashing school windows with air guns. A gang of ten youngsters broke into a beer warehouse at Sayville, Long

Island, and set fire to it "to conceal their fingerprints" after making off with several cases of beer.

Youngsters of middle-class families have greater material resources than their young comrades in the street gangs. They usually employ a car in their escapades and manage to rove about the countryside to a startling degree. A group of three boys, fifteen, sixteen, seventeen, from good families in a nice suburb of San Antonio, Texas, ran away from their homes in mid-winter. They had a car and carted along with them more than three hundred pounds of canned goods and other supplies, apparently intending an extended stay in the wilderness. They drove to Florida, where one night they forced their way aboard a forty-foot yacht, terrorized a family of six to whom it belonged, and set sail for Cuba or Mexico—they weren't exactly sure which. In another day these boys might have wound up in the California gold rush or rounding the Horn in the forecastle of a four-masted sailing ship. But in this era they stole a cabin cruiser at gunpoint. The families said all of the boys were good youngsters. However, as is so often the case with the middle-class delinquent, there had been a trouble signal which was ignored. One of the boys had been arrested in a stolen car case, months before, it was revealed, but the case was not pressed.

There seems to be no limit to the sadistic ingenuity of teen-age delinquents. Possibly inspired by some comic strip adventure or the belated influence of a Pearl White serial, a bunch of boys in Norwalk, a suburb of Los Angeles, bound seven-year-old Michael Evans to the Santa Fe Railroad tracks. He was rescued by his father a minute or two before the express was due to whiz past.

It was in suburban Yonkers that some young gang boys got into an argument with four national guardsmen while their cars were waiting at a stoplight. When the light changed they swerved their car, forced the guards to the curb, leaped out and beat the militiamen badly with tire irons and jack handles. It was in suburban Belleville, New Jersey, that eighteen-year-old Nicholas Ucci lost an eye when he was dragged from the car in which he was riding and beaten by a rival gang in another car. And it was in West Hempstead, Long Island, that two cars laden with teen-agers were returning from a dance after midnight. The drivers began the dangerous game of veering at each other, turning at the last moment to avoid a collision. Finally the cars halted, nine youngsters, including two girls, piled out and a general melee ensued. Police halted the brawl after one boy was badly knifed.

These are just run-of-the-mill incidents in the better suburbs, for the most part, of the New York metropolitan area—the incidents which got on the record, which were not hushed up.

It is not only what is happening today which worries many social workers acquainted with suburban conditions. What alarms them most is what lies just ahead. In the years immediately after the war enormous numbers of jerry-built mass suburban developments sprang up on the flat sands of Long Island, the Jersey countryside, the vacant lands between Washington and Baltimore, the areas around Chicago and the endless vistas that surround Los Angeles. These cheaply built homes are largely populated by young working-class and lower-middle-class couples who started their families at about the same time, just after World War II. The birth rate in these communities is far higher than the national or the urban rates. The children of these families are just beginning to reach the age at which delinquency begins to manifest itself in more violent and destructive form. Thousands of these youngsters are moving into adolescence week-by-week and step-by-step together. Many of these communities are deficient in facilities for recreation for older children. Many of the families are not as strong or capable as they might be. Trouble, social workers fear, lies ahead in serious form.

This problem of the future is going to be much more like the delinquency problems of California than those of the teen-age gangs of Brooklyn. This new crop of mass-delinquents-to-be are going, for the most part, to be equipped with cars. They will be highway delinquents. Not street gangs. But the problem will be just as serious. Possibly more so.

PART IV

Theories of Middle-Class Juvenile Delinquency

INTRODUCTION

Theory of middle-class juvenile delinquency has been delayed long by the absence of empirical research. Recent interest in the youth culture, and sudden concern over delinquency among middle-class boys have produced a number of separate theories of the phenomena. This augurs well for the future and should stimulate research. But how different are the explanations of middle-class delinquency from the theories of delinquency in the lower class! Here there is no malice or rebelliousness, no status deprivation, or emotionally starved children; poverty, broken homes, and "bad" companions do not account for middle-class delinquency. In contrast, delinquency is pleasure-seeking, and becomes almost a side issue. The youth culture is characteristically wholesome, fun-loving, respectable, and often receives the approval of parents. According to the theories, middle-class boys become delinquent by enjoying the best of both worlds, the high school and the drive-in; by coming from upwardly mobile working-class families, and thereby being unfit to adjust to new middle-class surroundings; by conformity to legitimate teen-age activities; by imitating the current fads and practices of the lower class. Indeed, one looks hard for "bad" boys doing wrong. Perhaps this is a function of the scarcity of data on these youths. Perhaps the acts of middle-class youths are *less aggressive and damaging and, therefore, more difficult to visualize as "delinquent." Or, do we tend unconsciously to blunt the wrongdoing of children who resemble our own?*

Nevertheless, the following theories reveal an overlap in conceptual interest. There is a pronounced concern in the youth culture and in recent changes occurring in the social structure and in middle-class values. Also emphasized are the importance of status, the quest for masculinity, and the problems of adjustment among these youths. This theoretical focus hints that already an integrated framework is in the making. If future research tends to support these ideas, we are on the right track.

In the first article Albert K. Cohen accounts for delin-

quency in the middle class in terms of structural change in society. This has resulted in a multiplicity of youth cultures, and a shift from a pattern of deferred gratification to one of immediate, hedonistic gratification among middle-class youths. Scott and Vaz contend that delinquency among middle-class youths is understood best through examination of the everyday legitimate youth culture, and that to explain what is "bad" in the culture first we ought to look at what is "good."

Status inconsistency is at the core of Robert Bohlke's theory. Bohlke sees delinquency as a function of the social marginality of the nouvelle bourgeoisie*—newly arrived families in the middle class who possess the financial resources, but lack the social graces for adequate social adjustment. Children from these families may be rejected by "old middle-class" cliques which could generate rebellious behavior among aspiring youths.*

Other theorists, such as William Kvaraceus and Walter B. Miller, posit the upward diffusion of working-class values and behavior patterns into the middle class as a major source of middle-class delinquency. When middle-class boys imitate the delinquency of lower-class youths, the characteristic qualities of bravado and violence of lower-class boys become subdued.

The importance of the youth culture is evident in the formulation by Ralph England. This theory states that the teen-age culture is populated by immature, inexperienced youths, whose motivation for delinquency arises in the adaptive process of selecting adult values which have a strong hedonistic potential for exploitation. Conduct in terms of these values leads often to delinquency.

pleasure seeking

Middle-Class Delinquency and the Social Structure

ALBERT K. COHEN

This paper is an attempt to explain a fact whose existence has not yet been established, namely, the increase in middle-class delinquency rates. My evidence that middle-class delinquency rates have increased, and possibly contributed disproportionately to the overall increase in delinquency as measured by official delinquency statistics, is not the sort that will hold up in court. It consists entirely of the impressions of police, court workers, social workers and school authorities, but there is enough consensus among these people to create a strong presumption that such an increase has actually occurred. Pending research of a more conclusive nature, we shall assume that this is so and attempt to explain it. Parenthetically, it is noteworthy that, despite all that has been written on the causes of juvenile delinquency, there has been hardly any serious thought given, in recent years, to explaining changes in delinquency rates over time.

In the writer's book, *Delinquent Boys*, and elsewhere in the literature, it is suggested that the middle-class boy—and also the upwardly mobile working-class boy who has elected what William Foote Whyte has called the "college-boy" way of life—has traditionally been insulated from delinquency by what has been referred to as the deferred gratification pattern: the subordination of present hedonic satisfactions and immediate impulse to the rational pursuit of long-run goals. A boy committed to such a deferred gratification pattern cannot afford to be a member of a delinquent group,

Printed by permission of the author. Paper read at the annual meeting of The American Sociological Association, August, 1957.

because such groups make demands upon their members which are incompatible with middle-class goals and middle-class ways of striving for them. The delinquent gang demands loyalty, reciprocity, sharing and mutual aid, that is to say, the subordination of one's own long-run aspirations to the claims and the welfare of the group. Needless to say, it makes enormous demands upon the boy's time. The delinquent gang is notoriously street-centered: it "hangs around the corner"; it "fools around"; it "kills" and "wastes" time in the streets, in the alleys, in the candy store. Delinquent subcultures do more than provide a social support for delinquency; they provide a design for living, a way of life. And to the degree that one is committed to either way of life—the delinquent or the middle-class way—he is restrained from participating in the other.

Now this deferred gratification pattern used to be more than just a middle-class tradition. It was supported by a social structure in which achievement of middle-class goals was actually heavily dependent upon conformity to such a pattern. In a society of relative scarcity and one not so technologically advanced as present-day American society, there was a huge demand for relatively unskilled labor and great pressure to turn young people into the labor market at an early age. The schools were under no great pressure to cater to the unambitious and the dullards, and neither parents nor the state were willing or able to assume the continued tutelage and support of young people unless they showed special ambition, seriousness and promise. Adults could dictate the terms on which young people could remain in school and the "undeserving" were unsentimentally dumped on the labor market. Ambitious young people danced to the tune the adults played. Good grades and graduation went to those who were talented or hard working or both.

Recent social changes, however, have weakened the nexus between the deferred gratification pattern and the goals to which it was formerly instrumental. These changes have included: phenomenal increases in productivity of labor, an increased demand for labor in the higher status occupations, an increased ability of the government, through increased revenues, to assume new responsibilities, increased pressure to keep young people out of the labor market and a general improvement in family resources. In consequence, the functions of the schools have undergone change. They are now charged with the responsibility of keeping the children off the streets and out of the labor market—and "children" are increasingly defined as anybody up to the age of eighteen or nineteen. "Dropouts" from school under the age sixteen, regardless of their origins, ability or aspirations, are increasingly thought of as "failures" on the part of the school.

This means that the schools are no longer in a strong position to impose high standards of performance and achievement. Children can no longer be readily sloughed off if they fail to meet such standards. In fact, in order to avoid an intolerable accumulation of pupils in the lower grades, they must be promoted regularly regardless of performance. The schools are required to process vastly increased numbers of students, and these include large numbers of children who formerly have left school or been expelled because of lack of interest, incompetence, or behavior problems. The schools are faced with an unprecedented problem of maintaining order. Deprived of their principal sanctions—expulsion and refusal to promote to a higher grade—they must seek to make school a *pleasurable* experience rather than a *discipline*. Increasingly the adults in authority are forced—often with great reluctance—to take their cues from their charges, to find out what the children want to do and help them to do it. Status in the school is increasingly defined in terms of the standards and values of the adolescent peer groups, and the role of the adult becomes to create a benign atmosphere in which every child can integrate happily with some group. Modern philosophy and psychology of education have commended themselves and caught on, we suggest, because they rationalize and legitimize this situation, this *fait accompli*.

It is difficult for a school system like ours to maintain a double standard for children of lofty aspirations and high ability and children who are just marking time. Standards of academic performance tend to drop for all categories of children, and the child of just modest talents and middle-class aspirations can achieve at least his proximate goals of good grades, promotion and graduation with just a moderate investment of time and effort. Getting into college—the great gateway to middle-class occupations—also becomes easier, since many colleges require little more than graduation from high school for entrance; and, in these times of full employment, and high prosperity, financial barriers to higher education are greatly reduced.

The general effect of all this is to produce, in the eyes of middle-class children with middle-class aspiration, a picture of the world in which the attainment of their future goals does not appear so contingent upon what they do *now* as it did to their predecessors of a generation or two ago. The structural props of the deferred gratification pattern have been greatly weakened. (It is too early to assess the effect of the impending crisis in the ability of the colleges to accommodate greatly increased numbers of students. Apparently colleges are beginning to become more selective, to tighten up their standards, and young people or at least their parents are becoming anxious about admission to college. This could result in an attitude of heightened seriousness in the high schools.)

To the extent to which these changes have occurred, there has resulted a weakening of one of the principal insulators against juvenile delinquency. It becomes possible to be middle-class in terms of aspirations and at the same time to "hang around the corner." Middle-class youth turn increasingly to hedonically oriented "youth cultures." These youth cultures are not necessarily delinquent but they are generally characterized by pleasure seeking and emancipation from adult controls. We have middle-class "corner-boys."

With respect to delinquency, however, the new situation is more than merely permissive. It also contains certain positive motivations to delinquent behavior. In the "old-fashioned" system, the subordination of consumption activities and temptations to sober, productive, "constructive" activities was a legitimate and recognized way of establishing and vindicating one's masculinity and maturity. It becomes a task of the youth cultures to provide a means for doing this same thing within their own hedonically oriented framework. The youth cultures tend to place a high value, therefore, on those traits and activities which, in our culture, are symbolic of masculinity or adulthood or both, but which do not require self-discipline, deferred gratification, sobriety and diligence. Recklessness, prowess and the courting of danger ("Chicken!") are safely masculine and may take the specific form of predatory and destructive behavior. The simulation and compulsive exaggeration of certain patterns which are symbolically adult, especially those connected with liquor, sex and automobiles, also lend themselves to the requirements of the youth cultures and easily take a specifically delinquent form.

In conclusion, we want to emphasize that we have treated but one mechanism through which social changes have contributed to middle-class delinquency. Some of the same structural changes in American society, through their impact on family life, have contributed in other ways as well, but these matters fall outside the scope of this paper.

A Perspective on Middle-Class Delinquency

JOSEPH W. SCOTT AND EDMUND W. VAZ

Most literature on juvenile delinquency describes it as essentially a product of the lower socioeconomic classes. While there has been some speculation over the incidence and quality of middle-class delinquency, what evidence exists is largely impressionistic. Nevertheless, the prevailing view is that delinquency among middle-class youth has increased in recent years. The present paper seeks a sociological and theoretical perspective to help account for the dominant forms of juvenile delinquency among middle-class youth. It attempts also to explain the emergence and the particular qualities of middle-class delinquency as a consequence of structural changes taking place in the larger society.

Accounting for middle-class delinquency in North America

Reprinted by permission of the authors and of the editor from *The Canadian Journal of Economics and Political Science*, Vol. 29, No. 3 (August, 1963), 324–335.

requires an understanding of the dominant culture of middle-class youth. Structural changes in society over the last half-century have produced opportunities for extensive adolescent peer-group participation and the emergence of a mass youth culture. During the growth of this youth culture, in which the majority of middle-class teenagers participate, there have emerged, jointly, both delinquent and non-delinquent patterns of behavior. It is the thesis of this paper that the bulk of middle-class delinquency occurs in the course of *customary, non-delinquent* activities and falls within the limits of adolescent group norms. Moreover the knowledge of both delinquent and non-delinquent patterns in the youth culture is widely shared among middle-class teenagers. Thus, in order to account for middle-class delinquency one need not look for a separate "delinquent subculture."

Any explanation of the emergence and growth of the contemporary middle-class youth culture must first consider the changes which have occurred in society over the past seventy-five years. The social and economic structure has undergone vast transformation. The first half of the period was an era of rapid expansion, of untempered competition, with increasing opportunities for the accumulation of wealth, vertical mobility, and employment based on technical skills. The economy had an almost limitless capacity for absorbing unskilled and semi-skilled labour, and it was viewed as a mine of opportunities and rewards for men of "good character." David Riesman has suggested that the old middle class was ideologically equipped to exploit such opportunities.[1] Imbued with the importance of integrity, self-discipline, and hard work, and the conviction that what it was doing was morally right, it possessed the resiliency and enterprise necessary for confronting and overcoming the challenges of the economy. It can truthfully be said to have striven with self-reliant and dedicated individualism.

To inculcate the energy, determination, and moral fortitude to meet the widening frontier of economic and occupational opportunity, considerable attention was given in the home to the formal character training of children. It soon became an integral part of the education of the child, and parental demands for conformity at this time were for "characterological fitness and self-discipline." At the same time, because of their diligence and effort at work, fathers often cut themselves off from friends and family. Indeed the middle-class father, instilled with industry and frugality, was preoccupied with production, self-help, and the "character-conditioned need to test and discipline himself." For these reasons he was largely incapable of casual relationships even with his own children. However, with the expansion of the occupational structure, the father's absorption in his work pointed up clear-cut goals for his children; thus they were not only motivated, but also shown the way to get ahead.

While parents emphasized the "building" of character and moral principles in the upbringing of their children, the formal educational system concentrated upon the teaching of ideas and the disciplined pursuit of learning. As Riesman writes, this procedure "affirms to the child that what matters is what he can *accomplish* and not how nice is his smile or how cooperative his attitude."[2] Formal education was prized and the significance of university training was reflected in hours of rigorous self-application. In school the teacher held undisputed authority, discipline was harsh, and scholarship was encouraged. The whole system neatly fitted the child for the emerging needs of a growing economy.

Home life precluded the development of extensive peer-group relationships. Parental emphasis upon ambition and achievement, and character-forming behaviour patterns such as "saving for college" and "working after school," modelled after parental patterns of "hard work and hard saving," served to keep middle-class youth occupied, indoors, and off the streets. Playmates were usually brothers and sisters. Peer-group associations were time-consuming and often costly, and middle-class youth were disinclined to waste either time or money.

It seems clear that on all fronts the middle-class boy was prevented from forming a "street-corner society." His diurnal round of activities, his duties in the home, his role as student and the expectations associated with it, besides the consumption of his time, all tended to divert him from peer-group affiliations. Such activities as "vandalism," gambling, widespread drinking, "partying," and sex activities on a large scale would have conflicted with his daily routine.

After the First World War the American economy underwent significant change. Of great importance was the growth of technology and technological efficiency. Coupled with a declining demand for unskilled and semi-skilled labour was a decline in the number of proprietors, and the massive centralization of industry. More and more people were corralled into large-scale organizations. C. Wright Mills writes: "In 1939, 1 per cent of all firms in the country—27,000 giants—engaged over half of all the people working in business."[3] This structural upheaval severely restricted upward mobility for the lower-placed worker. With an increase in life expectancy and a decrease in the birth rate, the population pyramid soon showed an increase of persons in the productive years of life. Furthermore, the levelling of income and social resources favoured the mass production of educated and specialized personnel for the labour market. Concomitantly industry could afford to become highly selective in its choice of personnel[4] which meant that the criteria for recruitment and promotion underwent change, and factors other than technical expertise became crucial. William H. Whyte quotes excerpts from his research: "We used to look primarily for brilliance," said one president. "Now . . . we don't care if you're a Phi Beta Kappa or a Tau Beta Phi. We want a well-rounded person who can handle well-rounded people."[5] Thus conformity to the norms of the Protestant ethic became impracticable and gave way to the structurally generated social skills and social values of a new morality—the social ethic.

Under changing social and economic conditions there occurred, also, a gradual transformation in the make-up of the nuclear family, family patterns, and child-rearing practices. The traditional, patriarchically-controlled family soon gave way to the more "democratic" unit in which parents and children shared in the decision-making process. Standards guiding parent-child relationships became blurred, and the family atmosphere became increasingly "permissive." In contrast to the acquisition of technical skills and ethical values for the achievement of goals, the institutionalized means for "getting ahead" and for gaining prestige are, under such circumstances, elusive, subtle, and difficult to teach. "The loss of old certainties in the spheres of work and social relations is accompanied by doubt as to how to bring up children."[6] Under such circumstances parents can hardly be expected to instruct their offspring in the adolescent role. Thus, the definition of the adolescent role is vague, and standards of behaviour, moral prescriptions, and the traditional distinctions between right and wrong are necessarily soft-pedalled.[7]

The school, meanwhile, has not remained unchanged. The

new requirements of corporate business and industry have made themselves felt. The hallmarks of the modern educational process are "group adjustment," success, and controlled individuality. Moreover, there has been a shift in power from teachers to pupils, a move in the direction of adult deference to the inclinations and interests of the pupils.[8] Gradually, "the school . . . begins to parallel the career pattern of the adult, particularly that of the male, in that it now absorbs more and more of the personality of the child."[9] This change in focus of the school has been noted by Seeley in the study of Crestwood Heights: "The educational system of Crestwood Heights is becoming, to a greater and greater degree, responsible for the successful 'adjustment' of the child, as a person, to the culture in which he lives."[10] The school, in socializing the "whole" child, neatly prepares him to meet the newly developing requirements of large-scale business and industry. In emphasizing the "socially adjusted," effective personality, the contemporary school system satisfies the "Organization's" needs for a "well-rounded person who can handle well-rounded people."

Under such circumstances the school becomes noticeably more "permissive," fixed standards of performance are abandoned on the grounds that they "straitjacket the child," and the whole learning experience, slowly but ineluctably, becomes a "painless process."[11] With drastically relaxed academic expectations, schoolwork for the teenager becomes routine, and, since household chores have become minimal, the middle-class adolescent has little work to absorb his time throughout the day or evening. With leisure time, peers become available and the emergence of peer-groups possible. In fact, there gradually emerges a middle-class street-corner society. The teenager, reared witness to the daily significance of social standing and the peer-group mentality of the parents, is also peer-group oriented. Furthermore, parental emphasis on group-belonging soon becomes a moral imperative, and prevailing teaching encourages dependence on adolescent peer-group affiliation for social prestige and recognition.[12]

The adolescent conspicuously lacks an exact definition of the expectations and obligations attached to his role in society and he is left to define for himself what is "right" conduct. However, the peer-group begins to exercise an inexorable influence upon the teenager and to substitute for the ambiguity in family relationships. But the peer-group cannot state explicitly what "ought to be," that is, what the content of the general normative system is, and each individual must learn to conform to whatever behaviour patterns happen to prevail. In contrast to an earlier era of individual initiative, there is now little justification for non-conformity, and the violation of group norms becomes a serious offence.

To understand the development and maintenance of the middle-class youth culture it is necessary to examine the functions of the contemporary high school. In a rapidly changing, highly industrialized society like ours, the high school has become the principal social setting for a system of informal relationships and a fabric of social norms which help knit teenagers together. Besides providing the opportunity for formal learning, the modern high school acts as a central agency in the socialization process, and in the informal distribution of satisfactions for the teenager. The setting apart of adolescents in schools (which constantly take on more functions, more extracurricular activities) for an ever-increasing period of training has a singular impact on a youth.[13] He is divorced from the remainder of society, and more or less compelled to carry out his whole social life with others of his own age, that is, within his peer-group.

It is within the peer-group that the teenager first feels his independence, tries out new ideas, and shares secret emotions. Here, for example, he can pry and probe with impunity into the much tabooed secrets of sex while the nagging, if uncertain, intervention of adults is absent. So important is the peer-group for the middle-class teenager that his success and failure in the classroom cannot be explained irrespective of his peer-group affiliations.[14] Conformity to peer-group norms is rigidly required, and the norms decry scholastic effort. Thus, nowadays, it is almost a commonplace that there is in the schoolroom restriction of scholastic output.[15] The old refrain, "I never crack a book," and the opprobrium attached to the "damned average raiser" are classic testimony to the informal system in operation.

It is abundantly clear that peer-group attachment confers social approbation on the teenager and gives notice (to peers and parents alike) that the teenager is socially adjusted. Thus Coleman writes, "even the rewards a child gains from his parents may help reinforce the values of the adolescent culture . . . because parents want their children to be successful and esteemed by their peers."[16] More significant, however, is the increase in social status derived from conformity to peer-group expectations. Peer-group membership offers the adolescent access to teenage parties, "high-ranking" girls, "big dates," the latest style, esteemed events, and other "social objects." Conversely the student who persists in conforming to other standards, through concern for studies and good grades, is seldom sought after by the opposite sex. In the contemporary high school it is the "active" student, the boy or girl who engages in social affairs, extracurricular activities, and athletics, who ranks highest within the adolescent culture and, often, among the teachers as well.

It is precisely because they symbolize membership and prestige in the peer groups that such events and activities as parties, dances, dates, and "socials" become especially instrumental for the middle-class teenager. In familiar fashion, an increase in prestige elicits greater social approval from the group which, in turn, evokes further status-rewarding opportunities, activities, and relationships within the youth culture. Moreover, because teenage participation in social activities is rewarded, conformity to peer-group expectations assures a stable group status. Under these conditions deviance becomes costly and cannot be tolerated since it might result in the loss of social honour and the downfall of the group. The maintenance of social status depends, therefore, upon the continuation of conformity to group norms and expectations.

MIDDLE-CLASS DELINQUENCY[17]

While adolescent conduct within the middle-class youth culture seems to be infinite in variety, dominant themes include "joy-riding," "drag-racing," "partying" (which means late hours), drinking, gambling, and variations of sex behaviour. Such activities usually involve both sexes and present adolescents with the opportunity for status gain and social success among their peers. If such behaviour were altogether unacceptable to the group, adolescents would be unlikely to participate for fear of lowering the group's status. In fact, however, teenagers who engage in these activities are neither rebuked for their acts nor especially condemned by the group.

Since conformity is the keynote within the youth culture,

the question of change and cultural variation arises. From our perspective delinquent behaviour evolves from such non-delinquent, legitimate activities as dating, parties, dances, and possession of an automobile, within the adolescent youth culture. We have already noted the gradual transformation—the democratization of family relations, the ambiguity in traditional distinctions between right and wrong, and the concomitant undermining of parental authority and teaching—in the make-up of the nuclear family. We have also suggested that parental behaviour indicates the need to acquire social skills and competence and the importance of the responses of others in determining one's behaviour. Under these circumstances "operating inventions"[18] (behavioural innovation) among adolescents become probable. Indeed the pursuit of scarce desired goals among adolescents makes innovation likely, since it is socially rewarded so long as it meets the expectations and demands of peer-group members. And it is precisely because peer-group expectations *are* middle-class that innovating behaviour must not transgress the adolescent, middle-class value system. Thus, whatever deviation emerges must not jeopardize group status, and is tolerated by group members only within the limits of socially acceptable youth culture activities. So we find that violence, armed robbery, and the carrying of lethal weapons fall outside the prescribed boundaries, but "joy-riding," drunkenness, and sexual intercourse are variations on conduct patterns which fall within the limits.

In the course of legitimate, everyday activities and relationships within the middle-class youth culture, "veiled competition" for status leads to varying efforts at innovation. Such innovation covers a wide range of exploratory acts and is likely to be tentative, uncertain, and ambiguous. Yet because there is "mutual exploration and joint elaboration" of behaviour among adolescents, such small, almost unobtrusive, acts gradually lead to unanticipated elaboration beyond the limits of legitimacy—into the realm of delinquency and the illegitimate. But since each succeeding exploratory act is so small an increment to the previously acceptable pattern, at no stage in the process need the behaviour be perceived as "delinquent."[19] Once these patterns develop and are socially rewarded they generate their own morality, norms, standards, and rewards. It is in this manner that delinquent behaviour gradually emerges from socially acceptable, non-delinquent, activities among adolescents within the middle-class youth culture.

At this point we address ourselves to some of the socially acceptable activities among middle-class adolescents and attempt to show how delinquent behaviour arises from respectable behaviour.

In the larger middle-class society the party is a prominent, socially structured situation for learning particular attitudes and forms of behaviour. Similarly, within the youth culture the party is a group event where the learning and transmission of conduct patterns occur. Such behaviour habitually is first taught in the home where, at an early age, the child is introduced to the vignettes of culturally approved conduct. By acting as "junior host" and "helping out" at adult gatherings the youngster soon learns the appropriate behaviour, skills, and demeanour for such occasions. At the same time he also learns the "party games," and the "party drinks" which are served at such times. With the added significance given adolescent participation in social activities, the increase in adolescent prerogative, and the tacit approval given to "having a taste" or "spiking" the party punch, drinking becomes acceptable. The phrase, "a glass of beer won't hurt him," reflects the approval given by parents to teenage drinking in the home on special occasions. As the drinking pattern develops among adolescents it generates its own morality, its special game rules, standards, and its particular rewards. Among older adolescents, informal drinking bouts to test one's capacity for alcoholic beverages are certainly not alien to the youth culture. Indeed the approval given to the adolescent who can "hold his liquor" follows adult lines, and reflects such practices and games among middle-class teenagers. And adolescent intoxication is not altogether disapproved since it simply represents an unsuccessful attempt to conform to the rules of the game.

The possession of an automobile is one of the crowning symbols of distinction among teenagers. It is a core cultural element and gives meaning to social events and practices integral to the youth culture. "Without a car a boy must be chauffeured to movies, sports events, and—most embarrassing of all—to dates."[20] Highly visible, easily presented, the automobile is a unique means of self-distinction and an extension of one's self-image. Indeed the possession of a car is often the accolade of social status among both male and female teenagers. While changes in clothing styles among adolescents often mirror changes in self-conception and the silent struggle for status,[21] so too, the presentation of car and its manipulation along the highway undergo change. Here behavioural innovation varies from the initial efforts at "dressing" the automobile to sporting "duals or Hollywood mufflers," "joy-riding,"[22] "drag-racing," and ultimately, to "playing chicken" at a hundred miles an hour. This form of marginal differentiation reflects the effort for prestige among such adolescents. While some of the practices are functionally related to the masculine, middle-class value of courage and "daring," others are linked to the equally important value of possessing a "social personality." Such conspicuous, yet limited, innovation is significant evidence of the "antagonistic co-operation" for social recognition among middle-class adolescents.

That dating is a socially rewarding activity in the middle-class youth culture cannot be gainsaid. Moreover, dating and varying degrees of "friendship" between sexes are encouraged by parents and teachers alike as respectable, "healthy," "normal" activities for adolescents. Furthermore, restricted forms of physical contact between sexes are approved. Thus, holding hands, dancing, good-night kisses and, under certain conditions such as "going steady," initial stages of "necking" are condoned as indications of "social maturity," and part of "growing up."

Delinquent sex behaviour among middle-class adolescents emerges from culturally approved activity, and can be explained as a variation on the encouraged patterns of dating. In this regard girls face a dilemma in having to use sex appeal and glamour as the chief way of attracting and holding the opposite sex, yet simultaneously endeavouring to maintain their reputation. In the absence of firmly established moral rules and clearly defined role patterns, rules and norms develop in the course of resolving the dilemma which help govern the sex game among adolescents. The value of these game rules is illuminated by Coleman's remarks: "In very early adolescence, before courtship has begun in earnest, kisses flow freely at party games. They have not yet become currency in the competition for status and control. Later, the girls who once played post office with abandon now dispense their kisses much more strategically."[23] No less than in other areas, innovating and exploratory behaviour emerges from the dating relationship. Under these conditions it is likely that succeeding degrees of physical intimacy can be correlated with succeeding stages in the "romantic" attachment. For each stage there may come to exist a corresponding normative expectation of physical intimacy. If the good-night kiss is correlated with the "first date," "going steady" may be expected to result in efforts at sexual intercourse. Moreover, whatever factors tip the scales in favour or rejection of sexual intercourse among adolescents must also be normatively influenced. The give-and-take between sexes, the degree of intimacy, types of kissing, the extent of physical contact and, eventually, the sex act gradually become circumscribed by game rules.

While both boys and girls engage in the dominant behaviour patterns and activities in the youth culture, in the daily course of events there are recurrent situations in which only boys participate. Here rules and forms of social control applicable only to boys are likely to develop and different role-expectations and behavioural configurations emerge. Yet the veiled quest for social recognition is no less important. Here we should expect behavioural innovation to take another form, conceivably of less "sophisticated," more "masculine" quality. Thus, groups of boys "hanging about" at night, returning from a football match, or simply wasting time "rough-housing," often engage in acts of destruction such as "stomping" on the hoods and roofs of automobiles, letting air from tires, ripping antennae from automobiles, and breaking street-lights. However, "muggings," "rolling drunks," and "breaking and entering" rarely occur among middle-class boys. Such behaviour of a violent nature usually undertaken to steal money reflects values foreign to the middle-class culture. This type of activity is noticeably absent from the daily routine of middle-class teenagers, and roundly condemned within the middle-class youth culture.

The learning of delinquent behaviour is an insufficient condition to insure its performance. There must be an opportunity to carry out the learned activity. That is, the structure of opportunity—the particular form of social organization—must support the actual role performance.[24] In this case it is the opportunity structure for *legitimate* behaviour which is necessary for the performance of illegitimate, disapproved conduct.

If the daily round of activities of middle-class adolescents includes delinquent patterns of behaviour, the more a middle-class adolescent is immersed in the youth culture the more likely he is to become involved in juvenile delinquency. Some adolescents will have greater opportunities for delinquency than others. The question now is: under what circumstances is the middle-class teenager most likely to become involved in delinquent behaviour?

One condition for delinquent conduct among middle-class adolescents is access to the requisite physical objects for participating in the teenage youth culture. We have suggested that prominent behaviour patterns among middle-class teenagers spotlight such "things" as the possession of a car, accessibility to teenage girls, alcoholic beverages, pocket money, the latest style, and so forth. Therefore, access to one or all of these "social objects" is extremely important for participation in the middle-class adolescent culture. Indeed it is difficult to conceive of an adolescent's becoming part of the middle-class teenage crowd if he has neither control over nor access to some of these "objects." For example, dating is a highly valued experience within the youth culture, and the possession of an automobile is a symbol of social rank; thus the youth who owns or has access to a car has an obvious advantage in dating. To the extent that the means of participation in teenage activities are not equally available to all, participation in the youth culture and involvement in juvenile delinquency will likely be unevenly distributed.

A second contingency is a receptive attitude towards youth cultural activities on the part of the individual adolescent. Since participation in the prevailing network of legitimate activities within the youth culture results in favourable responses from his peers, the adolescent will likely derive social and emotional satisfaction from it, and define it as "normal" or as "having fun." But what aspect of participation he stresses is important. Thus we find that some teenagers believe that "stirring up a little excitement"[25] is crucial for participation in the teenage crowd. Others accept the car as the only "right" way to be "in with the crowd." Physical attractiveness, "personality" characteristics, and athletics are also significant for success in the middle-class youth culture. So also, for others, are "sociability," or sex activity with girls, or money, or clothes, or a "flashy appeal." In brief, to the degree that an adolescent favours all or various combinations of such characteristics and activities as means of participating in the youth culture he is likely to become involved in delinquent behaviour.

The social organization and "cultural flavour" of the "big city" differ greatly from the semi-rural and "main street" atmosphere of the small town. The presence of night-clubs, jazz-dens, "bohemian" coffee-houses, bars, "artistic" restaurants, theatres and the like in a metropolis serve as organized opportunities for middle-class adolescents to engage in a wide variety of "sophisticated" and novel behaviour with members of the opposite sex. If a teenager resides in a rural area, his choice of activities will be restricted.

Finally, the price for non-participation in the contemporary youth culture is likely to be inordinately high for the average middle-class adolescent. Today it is not easy, if it is possible at all, to shrug off the responses of others and the judgements and respect of our peers and schoolmates. Hence Gordon tells us that "an 'isolate' views her lack of clique membership as the major failure of her high school career."[26] Is it any wonder, then, that the teenager who is in a social setting where he must engage in youth culture events or else lose access to desirable, satisfying experiences, will have little choice but to act in a delinquent manner if such opportunities arise in the *routine* course of events?

If we are correct, the opportunities which exist for the middle-class adolescent to engage in legitimate, approved activities will greatly influence the probability of his becoming involved in illegitimate, disapproved behaviour. Easy access to the means for participation in the youth culture, highly desirable physical and "personality" qualities, the appropriate psychological definition of youth culture activities, residence in or near a metropolitan area, and active participation in the middle-class youth culture—all are important conditions determining the opportunities for the individual adolescent to engage in middle-class delinquency.

INTEGRATION AND STABILITY OF THE YOUTH CULTURE

As the emerging network of contacts and relationships becomes established over time, culturally approved patterns of behaviour and norms arise, the youth culture takes shape, and tends to persist irrespective of the initial forces giving rise to it. Although the variables "causing" its appearance remain and help maintain the cultural system in operation, other variables are recognizable which contribute to its stability.

By continuously pointing up the importance of internal group relations and morale, the adult community alerts the adolescent to the significance of peer-group membership and conformity to youth culture activities. The schools have been quick to underline conformity and adjustment to the peer-group as characteristics of adolescent growth. With heavy emphasis on the pragmatic and the social, the concept of "adjustment" soon becomes the over-arching criterion in evaluating the student's maturity. More specifically, profound parent-teacher concern over teenagers who do not "mix with the others" imposes on adolescents the moral obligation to engage in youth culture events. Under such circumstances, "the child who tends to be withdrawn is given special attention."[27] Furthermore, the deeply felt importance of sustaining "high morale" among "our children" underscores the necessity of peer-group association.

In a limited, yet significant, way the adult community creates structured opportunities for adolescents to engage in youth culture activities, that is, in "wholesome" recreation. Organized dances, high school "formals" and informal "hops," church "socials," and athletic events reflect this structural link between the youth culture and the adult community, and reveal especially cherished values and expectations sustained by adults.

The age-sex roles of adolescents are equally important for understanding the increasing stability and permanence of the middle-class youth culture. Adult expectations of middle-class teenage behaviour involve a growing concern for contact and interaction with members of the opposite sex. At a very early age a network of organized events begins to surround the child, activities *formerly* associated with an older age group. Dating, parties, dances, "socials," and kissing games begin at eleven or twelve years of age, and sometimes earlier. While parents might not always approve of all such activities, they are nevertheless "committed to the notion that both sexes should learn to adjust to each other by boy-girl participation" in social activities.[28] Indeed, in pre-teen years, steps are taken to develop in the child qualities which are considered prerequisite for social success later on. Once adolescence has been reached, increased participation in dating and other social events involving both sexes and the use of "dad's car" are culturally recommended. With the increase in leisure time and the greater possibility of spending this time together, stable conduct patterns among adolescents become entrenched. In this way adolescent adaptation to structured, age-graded expectations is a major contributory link towards increased stability of the middle-class youth culture.

The conditions which give rise to the adolescent youth culture are typically urban and most teenagers in metropolitan areas are exposed to the youth culture. Merely by association with the multiplicity of cultural sources and social groups, middle-class youngsters, at an early age, become influenced by, sensitive to, and later recruited into the adolescent youth culture. For example, teenagers have become increasingly active consumers. The increased spending power of the teenager over the past fifty years or so is likely to govern the nature, organization and prosperity of certain types of small and large businesses. Furthermore, the teenage youth culture has contributed to the birth and popularity of a variety of new occupations and associations in society, such as counseling and guidance officers, recreation "leaders," "disc jockeys," and "Little League" sports. This widespread transformation has made the youth culture conspicuously important and a full-fledged institution of the society. It has become an approved and encouraged segment of the community and cannot escape the recognition of the mass media of communication. The popularity of the adolescent market, and the dissemination of information about the teenage youth culture, publicize its existence and call the attention of the adolescent community to the prominence and rewards of membership therein.

A major implication of this paper is that a special set of motives need not be recruited to explain delinquent behaviour within the middle-class youth culture. At no time does the middle-class teenager turn from legitimate to illegitimate means in order to attain his ends. In terms of a means-end schema, this can only make sense if there has been neither a rejection of cultural goals nor frustration in the employment of legitimate means. The seeds of middle-class delinquency reside in the prominent, culturally esteemed patterns themselves. Therefore, delinquent behaviour can best be

understood through knowledge of the structure and content of the *legitimate* youth culture and its structural connections to the community within the larger historical transformation taking place.

Social Mobility, Stratification Inconsistency and Middle Class Delinquency

ROBERT H. BOHLKE

Within the past few years a number of observers have taken the position that juvenile delinquency may be increasing among middle class youth.[1] Although the evidence is highly impressionistic[2] five explanations have been offered to account for this phenomenon. First, it is seen as the result of the diffusing of working class values and behavior patterns to middle class youth, a process greatly aided by the mass media.[3] Second, it is considered to be a product of a weakening of the deferred gratification pattern in middle class families,[4] which, in turn, stems from a complex of changes in the educational system,[5] in the economy, and in child rearing patterns.[6] Third, it is viewed as reflecting the increasing difficulty that sons have in trying to match the mobility of their fathers who had been able to do much better than their rural- or foreign-born parents.[7] Fourth, it is seen as stemming from the fact that new suburban communities lacking "community services or tradition may be limited in their capacity to promote acceptable social behavior."[8] Fifth, it is perceived

Reprinted by permission of the author and of the editor from *Social Problems*, Vol. 8, No. 4 (Spring, 1961), 351–363.

as originating in part from the development in communications since World War II—advertising directed toward teenagers, disc jockey programs, and teenage TV shows and magazines. These innovations function to heighten in-group feelings among teenagers which together with those American cultural values reflecting hedonistic qualities serves to motivate delinquent behavior among middle class youth who are more closely tied to the communications network and more subject to the status ambiguity of youth than their counterparts in the working class.[9] For the most part this paper will not concern itself with the foregoing,[10] but, instead, will seek to delineate an hypothesis that has generally been overlooked in the recent speculation about an increase in middle class delinquency.

All of the accounts thus far written on middle class delinquency, with one exception,[11] have neglected one of the most significant, and fundamental, changes that has taken place in America in the past 20 to 25 years. Millions of Americans are now in the middle income group whereas in 1935 or 1940 they were in the low income brackets.[12] It would seem rather probable that many of these families while middle class in income are not so in terms of values, beliefs, attitudes and behavior patterns. In essence, such families would represent a group whom we can call the *nouvelle bourgeoisie*.[13]

To be sure, the socially mobile person or family has always faced problems of adjustment and the task of learning a new culture, but I would say that the process of income mobility in recent years is considerably different from that of 50 years ago when in an economy of scarcity, vertical mobility—income-wise—was likely to be predicated upon the adoption of middle class values. In other words, the person went up the occupational and income ladder by demonstrating the virtues of thrift, individual responsibility, hard work, etc. This is not to say that if he demonstrated these virtues he automatically "moved." But if he did "move" the chances were high that he had given evidence of middle class values.

On the other hand, since the late 1930's we have under the impetus of war and defense spending become an economy of abundance. Now the process of mobility *vis-à-vis* the Protestant Ethic has been changed. Today a person can move income-wise without necessarily demonstrating middle class virtues, and he may or may not adopt the full complement of middle class values subsequent to his rise in income. Income mobility for the groups with which I am concerned appears to have become increasingly dependent upon the strength of the union of which a person is a member and upon the degree to which the corporation where he is employed is "tied to" armament production. This means that income mobility is less dependent upon individual traits than formerly; it is a less selective process. Thus people who rise in income today are less likely to differ in personality from those who do not than was the case a generation or two in the past. A person "succeeds" today not because of the kind of personality he is but to a greater extent because of impersonal societal forces.

When Miller's analysis of middle class delinquency as a phenomenon resulting from the diffusion of behavior patterns from the working class to the middle class and a weakening of the middle class deferred gratification pattern[14] is viewed from the above perspective his hypothesis would seem to be an illustration of the error of treating two dimensions of social stratification—the economic and the social—as one.[15] The phenomenon that we choose to call stratification inconsistency[16]—a condition resulting from people being mobile, either upward or downward, in one stratification dimension without a concomitant change in another stratification dimension[17]—would appear to provide insight into middle class delinquency.[18]

Hence, instead of speaking of middle class delinquency as being the result of cultural diffusion from the working class I would hazard the guess that the middle class youth who appear to have taken on working class values and behavior patterns are in reality boys from families who were in the lower income group until fifteen to twenty years ago. Rather than saying that the boys have taken on working class culture, I believe it would be more accurate to hypothesize that they *have not yet* taken on middle class values and behavior patterns because their families, despite a dramatic rise in income, have not had to renounce working class values in the cultural context of economic abundance.

In his penetrating work on delinquency Cohen notes that ". . . many families which are middle class in economic terms and live in what are known as middle class neighborhoods may be decidedly working class in terms of the experiences they provide their children."[19] It is interesting that Cohen, after noting the phenomenon of stratification inconsistency, fails to exploit this idea in either *Delinquent Boys* or in a later paper wherein he seeks to explain the rise in middle class delinquency.[20]

The foregoing discussion serves to point up the rather surprising fact that specialists in the analysis of juvenile delinquency, with one exception, have given no attention to the possible relationship between it and social mobility.[21] This is all the more puzzling because within recent years social mobility has been emphasized as an important variable in connection with such phenomena as prejudice,[22] mental illness,[23] marital instability,[24] family limitation,[25] family disunity,[26] and the new conservatism in politics.[27] This omission becomes even more critical inasmuch as Peter Blau has hypothesized and found some evidence to support the principle ". . . that many beliefs and practices of the upwardly and downwardly mobile are intermediate between those of the stationary highs [high socio-economic status] and those of the stationary lows [low socio-economic status]."[28]

Blau's synthesis of considerable research on social mobility thus lends support to the generally accepted idea that delinquency has a higher incidence among working class boys and yet, at the same time, it is compatible with the recent speculation that delinquency is increasing among middle class youth. Also it is consistent with my thesis that the rise in middle class delinquency is in part related to the income revolution characterizing World War II and the post-war period in America. Assuming that the highest incidence of delinquency is found among working class youth, Blau's formulation would lead us to expect the incidence of delinquency among youth of mobile working class families to be less than that characterizing the youth of stationary working class families but more than that which is true of the youth of stationary middle class families.[29]

To the degree that income mobility is followed by residential mobility—that is, movement of the family from a working class neighborhood to a middle class neighborhood, or movement from the city to the suburb—there then arises the possibility that delinquency among "middle class" youth is a function of marginality.[30] In the first place, their parents may not be accepted by the middle class people into whose neighborhood or suburb they move. This failure to be given prestige correlative with income could foster tension within the family[31] with subsequent repercussions for the behavior of the adolescent. In the second place, the adolescent may find himself excluded from "old middle class" peer cliques. Given a number of adolescents, subjected to similar experiences in a given neighborhood or community, their response may be to join together and display the hedonistic culture that Cohen analyzes in *Delinquent Boys*. This culture could be said to be a product of two forces—a symbolic "thumbing of the nose" at the middle class culture of those adolescents who won't accept the youth of the *nouvelle bourgeoisie* as well as a reflection of working class culture not yet discarded. In essence, there develops a "self-fulfilling prophecy." The boy of working class background who has moved to the middle class neighborhood or suburb behaves in a way that affronts those youth who are middle class in attitudes and values, and the social rejection employed by the latter simply serves as a stimulus to evoke further working class behavior.

To be sure, there are diverse reactions to marginality. The writer would not maintain that all marginal youth become delinquent, but he would hypothesize that in a given number of middle income youth the probability of delinquent behavior would be greater among marginal adolescents than among non-marginal adolescents.

It is of interest to relate the foregoing analysis to Merton's model of deviant behavior.[32] At first glance it might appear that my thesis is at odds with Merton's, for he views obstacles to mobility as primary factors generating deviance. However, in the sense that mobility may be "partial"—that is, a change of occupation, or a rise in income, and a correlative shift in residence without a concomitant shift in prestige or social acceptance—this analysis would seem to be consistent with Merton's model.[33] It might be said that in a society where everybody is expected to be a "king" many people in the past 15 to 20 years have acquired the material symbols of "kingship," but they are nevertheless not treated as "kings" by those "born to the purple" or those whose middle class status goes back several generations.

What of Cloward and Ohlin's[34] further elaboration of Merton's thesis? Their analysis of delinquent behavior focuses on lower class youth and their main concern is with that category of lower class youth who desire a change in economic position, who are *not* interested in membership in the middle class, but who fail to succeed economically.[35] This group is obviously excluded from this writer's analysis. In fact, Cloward and Ohlin's discussion seems to assume that all lower class families are at the lower level of both the economic and status hierarchies whereas I have sought to underline the thesis that there are many families who have risen to a middle position in the former hierarchy but not in the latter. Thus, the need for a new term: the *nouvelle bourgeoisie*. To oversimplify the two arguments somewhat, it might be said that Cloward and Ohlin emphasize the consequences of the failure to be mobile whereas I am emphasizing the consequences of being mobile. To summarize my thesis to this point: delinquent behavior among *nouvelle bourgeoisie* youth is seen as arising from any one or a combination of the following—failure to adopt middle class values, attitudes and behavior patterns, rejection by the youth of the "old middle class," and reaction to intra-familial stress resulting from the fact that while their parents have "succeeded" (economically) they are not accepted.

On the other hand, what of the white collar workers whose position in the income hierarchy has not remained consistent with their place in the prestige hierarchy?[36] Such people may be said to be accepted but they have not "succeeded." This, of course, is the counterpart of the income revolution which has lifted the income of many people. In fact, it represents partial downward mobility. In an economy of abundance to "stand still" in terms of income is in reality to "fall." It would seem that this could be as pregnant with stress as partial upward mobility. Could this lack of stratification consistency among the "old middle class" make their youth more delinquent prone than previously? The common sense view sees delinquency as emanating from the failure of the parents to set a good example, to fail to "practice what they preach." I would be inclined to say that the white collar parents often do "practice what they preach," but their adolescent sons become aware of the fact that their parents' "practices" have not "paid off." What I am suggesting here is that "old middle class" adolescents may be revolting against the traditional middle class values which, in terms of the typical American measuring rod—money—have failed to bring "just rewards" to their parents.[37]

The foregoing analysis suggests at least five types of research in the area of middle class delinquency. First, there should be studies aimed at determining the amount and nature of middle class delinquency over the past ten to twenty years. In an effort to determine whether middle class delinquency has been increasing three approaches might be employed: (1) a repetition of several studies that were made one or two decades in the past and which, with one exception, represented attempts to measure more than court delinquency;[38] (2) studies of the delinquency rates in 1960 in middle income[39] census tracts in such cities as Baltimore, Boston, Chicago and Cincinnati, compared with the delinquency rates in 1950, or 1940, in middle income census tracts, and the relationship of change, or the absence of change, in these rates to the occupational and/or educational background of the families residing in such tracts at the two points in time; and (3) studies of self-admitted delinquencies by middle class high school students in given communities today compared with retrospective studies of self-admitted delinquencies during high school days by a group of adult males today who, when in high school in 1940 or 1950, belonged to middle class families. The delinquency scale developed by Nye and Short,[40] or a revision of it, would serve as the basic instrument for such studies.

The second type of research needed are studies through time in various types of communities using a sample of middle income families who, at the time of the initiation of the research, have boys in the age range 15–18. The following data should be collected on each family: (1) its income history for the period between the middle 1940's and the year of the study; (2) the occupational history of both parents during the period; (3) the values, beliefs, attitudes and behavior of the parents in such areas as education, consumption and saving, use of leisure time, participation in civic affairs, etc.;[41] (4) the pattern of informal and formal associations participated in by the parents at the time of the study; (5) the "social acceptance" or "social rejection" of the parents, to be determined by a comparison of their associational reference groups (informal groups and formal associations with whom they would like to interact) and their membership groups; and (6) a history of the juvenile court appearances and social agency referrals involving the sons, as well as self-testimony of delinquent acts by the sons by means of the Nye-Short Scale.

A number of hypotheses are suggested by the above but to save space only two will be presented.

1. Boys from blue collar families who have moved into the middle income bracket without a change in occupation and whose values, beliefs, attitudes and behavior reflect a minimum of traditional middle class culture, and who either do not seek social acceptance from white collar groups or are rejected if they do, will be more likely to have engaged in delinquent behavior than boys from former blue collar families who have moved into the middle income bracket, who have been occupationally mobile into the white collar group, whose culture reflects a middle class orientation, and who both desire and receive social acceptance from other white collar families.

2. Boys from white collar families whose incomes have remained relatively stable, or have declined, whose culture reflects a middle class orientation, who desire but are denied "social acceptance" from white collar groups, will be more likely to have engaged in delinquent behavior than boys from white collar families who have had a moderate rise in income, whose culture reflects a middle class orientation and who desire and receive "social acceptance."

Of course, longitudinal studies similar to the above but beginning in 1961 or 1962 and running for a period of ten or fifteen years would be possible, and, in some respects, preferable because those designing the studies could very likely then insure more accurate data collection. Furthermore, a longitudinal study of middle income blue collar and white collar families which "picked up" a sample of boys as they began school would enable the researcher to get some insight into the problem of "relating social system variables to psychological system variables" which Moles, Lippitt and Withey[42] see as crucial in causal process analyses in delinquency studies and the lack of which Blumer saw as a deficiency in many sociological studies.[43]

A third type of research could be focused on the school experiences of the sons of blue collar and white collar parents. Such studies could serve to bring about a convergence of two approaches that are highly relevant to the problem of delinquency, but which have neglected it: (1) studies of the achievement motivation and/or aspirations of high school students,[44] and (2) studies of middle class bias in the public schools.[45]

The following model illustrates the nature of the data that would have to be collected and the hypotheses to be tested:

Father's Occupation	Aspirations of Son	Rewards[a] Received By Son	Probability of Delinquent Behavior By Son[b]
Blue collar	Working class	Few	Medium to high
Blue collar	Middle class	Many	Low
Blue collar	Middle class	Few	High
White collar	Working class	Few	Medium to high
White collar	Middle class	Many	Low
White collar	Middle class	Few	High

[a] High academic grades, academic awards, athletic letters and awards, offices held in student organizations, and social acceptance by peers and by school personnel.

[b] Juvenile court appearances, social agency referrals, deviant behavior in school, and self-testimony of deviant behavior outside of school.

Other variables that should be incorporated in the study design are test intelligence, the student's perceptions regarding the question of "bias" by the faculty and administrative personnel,[46] the nature of the adolescent subculture(s) prevailing in the school, and the degree of socio-economic heterogeneity characterizing the school.[47]

Such studies of the educational opportunity system could either be cross-sectional—that is, a sample of the entire student body of a junior or senior high school—or a longitudinal study which would "pick up" a group of boys as they entered seventh grade and "follow them" until the age of eighteen. Once again it should be noted that the latter approach would enable the researcher to deal with the problem of intervening variables, previously referred to,[48] by analyzing the existing adolescent subculture(s) in a given school, the boy's aspirations, his self-image, and his perceptions of the subculture(s) as he enters the social system, and by studying the developing interrelationships between the subculture(s), the boy's aspirations, his self-image, his reference groups, his relative success, or failure, in achieving his goals, and his behavior—conforming or deviant—within the school and in the community.

The fourth type of research studies should be directed at comparing the amount and types of delinquency in diverse kinds of suburban and satellite communities such as those made up largely of middle income blue collar families, those primarily white collar in composition, and others that are a mixture of the two occupational groups. In the latter case it would be particularly important to compare the delinquency in a community like Ventura, California, where Sargent[49] found little evidence of class consciousness and in another city of similar size where class divisions were considerably more apparent.

The fifth type of research that should be initiated is suggested by the previously mentioned study of status disequilibria in Chicago by the Duncans.[50] A cursory examination of occupational distribution by census tracts in the city of Baltimore[51] in 1950 indicates that the following types of "occupational mixes" are likely to be found in any large city:

Occupational Group	Types of Occupational Mixes					
	A	B	C	D	E	F
Professional & technical workers	–	+	0	+	+	–
Clerical & kindred workers	–	–	0	–	+	+
Operatives & kindred workers	+	+	0	–	–	+

– Proportionately few members of a given occupational group.
\+ Proportionately many members of a given occupational group.
0 Approximately equal proportions of the three occupational groups.

What do these various types of "occupational mixes" mean to the family life of clerical workers—that is, parent-child relationships and husband-wife relationships—and to the behavior of their adolescents? More specifically, are cross-pressures[52] on the parents more operative in one type of "mix" than in another? Do different mixes generate different kinds of cross-pressures? What types of intra-familial stresses are generated by what kinds of cross-pressures, and how do these stresses affect the behavior of the teen-ager? Is one type of "mix" more related than others to delinquent behavior among the youth of clerical workers?[53]

Studies of the nature of those outlined above are needed in

part because we cannot assume that explanations of working class delinquency will also apply to middle class delinquency.[54] Furthermore, to the degree that we come to grips with the latter we will likely shed light on sociological theory concerning such phenomena as social mobility in its various dimensions, stratification inconsistency, and its relationship to inter-personal stress and deviant behavior.

The practical need for such research is also pressing.[55] Accelerating technological change as represented by automation is likely to increase social mobility and stratification inconsistency, at least as far as the number of people affected is concerned. Some analyses of automation see it as tending to upgrade jobs,[56] but one study raises serious questions on this score.[57] There is also some evidence that the impact of automation on clerical and office workers may serve to increase the stress which is already part of their world.[58] Whatever view turns out to be correct it appears fairly safe to conclude that the further development and spread of automation will have major consequences for the stratification dimensions of both factory workers and white collar workers.[59]

And it seems a reasonable guess to assume that the income revolution will continue.[60] This factor together with a rapidly growing population and the increasing disorganization of our large central cities will likely spawn increasing numbers of new communities composed of people, who, although having similar incomes, are likely to reflect important subcultural differences in social class backgrounds. If middle class delinquency[61] is not increasing at the present time it may well do so in the future unless we begin to study it. It would seem to be a fairly safe assumption to hold that middle class delinquency, like working class delinquency, will not be reduced or held in check by conventional and commonsense social nostrums.

Norm-Violating Behavior in Middle-Class Culture

WILLIAM KVARACEUS AND
WALTER B. MILLER

Norm-violating behavior occurs in all segments of American society. However, the largest volume of crime and delinquency which comes to the attention of official agencies involves residents of lower-class communities. As pointed out in the previous section, lower-class cultural concerns serve as a generating force for a range of law-violating acts. Nevertheless, it must be emphasized that the choice between law-abiding behavior and law-violating behavior is primarily a choice *within* lower-class culture rather than a choice between lower- and middle-class concerns.

LOWER INCIDENCE OF MIDDLE-CLASS DELINQUENCY

There is a prevalent impression that middle-class delinquency has increased substantially. It is difficult to appraise the strength of this trend, if indeed it exists, for it involves the problem of actual and apparent delinquency, which will be discussed further in Chapter 12. The middle and upper classes control various means of preventing detection, influencing official authority, and generally "taking care of their own" through psychiatrists, clinics, and private institutions,

Reprinted by permission of the authors and of the publisher from *Delinquent Behavior: Culture and the Individual*, Washington, D.C.: National Education Association of the United States, 1959.

thus avoiding the police and courts—the official recording agencies. In this situation, delinquency appears less as a "social problem" and more as a "home problem," which is handled by the family and its circle of influential friends. The middle-class family tries to resolve the situation with a minimum of official help or intrusion of social and legal agencies. In contrast, the lower-class youngster, once he is apprehended, is more likely to become the concern of an official agency, and hence a recorded statistic.

Much norm-violating behavior in the middle class is more easily handled and concealed than in the lower class, since it tends to be more sporadic and less patterned. Only when the middle-class crime is of the more serious type (stabbing, rape, homicide, grand larceny) does it move into a visible orbit. When this happens, the resulting upsurge of publicity and concern creates the impression of serious delinquency permeating the adolescent middle class.

To some extent the lower frequency of actual as well as apparent delinquency among middle-class youth can be explained both in terms of who writes the laws and where officials look to find delinquency. These two factors are closely related, for laws are written by legislators who reflect and support middle-class norms.

MIDDLE-CLASS CONCERNS

What are the special concerns of the middle-class individual as compared with lower-class concerns such as trouble, toughness, smartness, fate, and autonomy? Middle-class concerns appear to be centered around the following: achievement through directed work effort, deferment of immediate pleasures and gains for future goals, responsibility, maintenance of the solidarity of the nuclear family, child rearing, accumulation of material goods and conscientious maintenance of property, education and the improving of the mind, formal organizations, cleanliness, and ambition to get ahead. The orientation of middle-class parents toward these concerns tends to deter their youngsters from norm-violating behavior, particularly where the middle-class norm is clearly buttressed by the legal code.

Differences in focal concerns influence differential allocation of income by lower and middle classes. In lower-class culture most individuals orient more to immediate gratification from immediately available objects and experiences. This group is more vulnerable to direct salesmanship—"We'll bring in this big, shiny TV set, and you can turn it on and have a swell time." In contrast, the middle class is more inclined to defer gratification and to ask, "How is this going to fit into paying for our insurance premiums?" or "How is this going to go when the dentist's bills come in?" or "What will happen to Billy's college fund?" The bank book comes to symbolize impulse control and a long look at future family goals.

Money, in lower-class culture, is spent almost as soon as it comes in on goods and experiences that bring immediate emotional returns—betting on the horses, going out and drinking, taking in a carnival or penny arcade, or visiting a honky-tonk. Lower-class adults are generally able to tolerate long periods of essentially repetitive and routine work which demands considerable impulse control, but such "control" is not ordinarily exerted to defer present pleasure for anticipated future gain.

In contrast, the customary middle-class pattern is to subordinate present gratification to future goals. It is this group that purchases life insurance policies, establishes savings accounts for its children, and invests in education. This tradition has proved highly valuable for society in general and accounts for much of the "American success story." The strong middle-class cultural system has instilled a capacity for impulse control and self-denial in a large number of youngsters, and this has not been an easy job. If there is an increase in middle-class delinquency, it may be accounted for, in part, by a weakening of this tradition.

Achievement in school, on the job, and in the home is heavily dependent on maintenance of the difficult pattern of directed work effort, focus on future goals, high aspiration, and deferment of immediate pleasure. But there is evidence today that the strength of this pattern is lessening in some sectors of middle-class society. The steady increase in installment-plan financing as well as "impulse" buying can be viewed as a phenomenon approaching the "have-it-now" pattern of lower-class culture. At the same time, compulsory education and a continuous promotion policy tend to keep all youngsters in school regardless of effort, achievement, or future goal. These forces have tended to diminish the perception of middle-class youngsters that success is achieved through deferred gratification, frustration-tolerance, hard and sustained work, and self-discipline.

Other trends which go counter to traditional middle-class ideals can be observed in emphases on war (hot or cold), on armament, on defense, on military might—which place heavy stress on force rather than rational mediation. This stress on "might makes right" on the international scene is, to some degree, similar to the focus on "toughness" so prevalent in street-corner society. Several authors have pointed to an increase in "white-collar" crime, as evidenced by publicized cases of defrauding the government through income-tax evasion, embezzling of private and public funds, and gift-giving by businessmen in return for governmental "favors."

INFLUENCE OF LOWER-CLASS CONCERNS ON MIDDLE-CLASS BEHAVIOR

Much has been written and implied concerning the influence of middle-class standards on lower-class youth. However, relatively little attention has been paid to the influence of lower-class behavior on patterns of middle-class youth and adults through a process of "upward diffusion." At least a part of the current apprehension expressed over the "increase in middle-class delinquency" represents a fright-reaction of many parents and youth workers who perceive that lower-class conduct is being manifested by large numbers of middle-class youth. Seeing and fearing this, many middle-class adults have been cracking down on the manner of dress, coiffure, language, and entertainment of their adolescents. How much of this irritating and borrowed behavior represents merely a passing fad and how much portends a real shift in the direction of lower-class tradition?

Dr. Miller has traced the impact of lower-class culture on middle-class youth through an analysis of trends in jazz music over the past 50 years. Jazz in its original form is a product of the lower-class Southern Negro community. Its form and lyrics reflect classic concerns of lower-class Negro culture in such Southern cities as New Orleans and Memphis. These deal with the female-based household, serial mating, masculinity and toughness, cheating, rent parties, and "easy riders" (unmarried lovers). As this form has developed over the years, it has been progressively adopted by middle-class society. Each time it has been taken over—in a succession of fads—it has undergone some modification to make it palatable to middle-class Whites, but, at each successive repetition of this cycle, the form has been less modified.

When New Orleans jazz first came to Chicago in 1917–18, it took on certain typical "White" characteristics, and the result was ragtime. The second round came in the swing era of the 1930's. Here again there was considerable attenuation and adulteration of the Negro forms to make the music more acceptable in White middle-class terms. But common to both cycles were loud laments of middle-class adults over "flaming youth," "youth gone wild," "loss of all restraint," "disappearance of respect for good taste and morality," "corruption of our youth," and "flagrantly immoral songs and dances." However, jitterbugging, the type of Negro dancing which accompanied swing and which was regarded as a form of "youth madness," is now acceptable even at a church club dance.

Finally, as Dr. Miller's analysis shows, the third and current resurgence of this type of music, rock and roll—with its two basic components of classic Negro blues and White "hillbilly" or "barn-dance" music—has been taken over by middle-class youth as much more of an unadulterated lower-class tradition than was either ragtime or swing. Now specifically lower-class concerns and an associated cluster of cultural accretions involving language, dress, and speech forms are much more in evidence than before. Rock and roll represents lower-class Southern culture, both Negro and White. It is taken up as a fad by middle-class White youngsters who become, in turn, influenced by lower-class language, dress, and song; and it is transmitted from the lower-class Negro musician to the lower-class White musician, and through the disc jockey to the adolescent. The power and the prestige of the disc jockey as an agent of cultural transmission, although much in evidence in all parts of the country, is generally underestimated and unappreciated by parents and school personnel.

As this upward-diffusion trend occurs, one can hear adult demands and pleas that the line be held on hair styles, dungarees, tight-fitting sweaters and skirts, and language. Many middle-class adolescents appear to have oriented to values centering around toughness, hardness, excitement, present pleasure—all reflecting the focal concerns of lower-class culture. Many of these values are also strongly reinforced by the steady fare offered on the wide movie screen, on TV, and in contemporary literature. Parents and teachers, seeing these patterns among middle-class youth, naturally react with concern, apprehension, and even horror. They often conclude that delinquency has increased by leaps and bounds. How serious or dangerous is this strange and difficult-to-accept behavior now prevalent among the middle-class teen-agers?

Lower-class behavior patterns, which are characterized by toughness, excitement, chance-taking, indulgence, "conning," autonomy and hardness, represent the real thing and are played for keeps. This behavioral patterning is rooted in the subculture and is meaningful and significant for the lower-class youngster. In the middle-class community, however, the appearance of such behavior generally assumes the quality of an adolescent fad.

In the United States every generation of youngsters espouses a current fad which will distinguish it from the adult population. One function of such fads is to provide a vehicle of rebellion against parents; the fad is effective to the degree that it succeeds in shocking and dismaying the older generation. Today's middle-class youngster finds that he cannot get much of a rise out of his parents by "free" sexual references; Freud is too well known and accepted. Nor can he shock them by political radicalism; this is currently too dangerous. But he has discovered that one *really* effective way to appall his parents is to assume behavior patterns characteristic of lower-class culture. The black leather jacket, tight dungarees, a D.A. haircut, a Marlon Brando intonation pattern, or James Dean stance—as concrete symbols of lower-class culture—or truanting, failing grades, threatening to quit school, or belittling the worth of college—as indications of a general lower-class set—are sure-fire methods for producing maximum parental agitation.

Another function of the adolescent fad relates to its "exclusiveness" value. Adolescents frequently adopt a secret language or special means of communication that can be understood only with great difficulty by many adults. Thus, what appears to be a "bizarre" espousal of rock and roll music, together with a strong emphasis on certain patterns of dress, dance, and "jive talk" ("Crazy, man. I dig it the most," "Like, wow, man, I'm hip!") actually fulfills two important functions. It provides, first, the exclusivity that adolescents want and need, and second, it serves as a means of customary rebellion against adults. One way to indicate emancipation from the paternal yoke is to adopt a parentally disapproved style of living.

Before teachers and parents despair altogether of the future of these youngsters, they should remember that the "flaming youth" and "lost" generation of the 1920's turned out to be good, substantial citizens who, in turn, became incensed at their own youngsters as they danced to the "wild Benny Goodman swing music" of the thirties. Just so will the many middle-class youngsters now addicted to rock and roll become substantial, albeit complaining, parents of the next generation.

There is much selling and buying of lower-class concerns and values to middle-class consumers. All mass media today dig deeply into lower-class culture, wrapping their plots and characters around force, trouble, excitement, chance or fate, autonomy, and present pleasure. A few examples will indicate how the media have exploited lower-class characteristics and how these have permeated the screen, the air waves, and the printed page.

Mickey Spillane's Mike Hammer personifies the masculine qualities of the "tough man" school. Mike operates on force and duplicity. He must outsmart the crooks and murderers, but he also has a lot of excitement, which usually includes a drink and a willing dame. Some middle-class book-club members may not relish the literary style of Spillane, but the tough-man theme has also been exploited by such representatives of the "better" literary school as Ernest Hemingway and Tennessee Williams. The movie version of Williams' *A Streetcar Named Desire* brings out vividly many of the features (gambling, toughness, excitement) which have been identified with the lower-class pattern. On the other hand, the film *High School Confidential* tells the story of marijuana and heroin addiction among middle- and upper-class adolescents, a rarity in real life. Yet such patterns, adult-created images of lower- and higher-class contemporary youth, are held up for all youth to see and for some to follow. The deluge of horror films of the "monster" variety, including *Teen-Age Monster* and *Teen-Age Werewolf*, lean heavily on force, masculinity, smartness, and fate, in the form of magic and the supernatural. The many detective stories and westerns making up an evening's TV diet also play with the same themes. These concerns, found in their "purest" form in lower-class society, provide identification patterns for some segments of the middle class and are the basis of some of the customs of the "beatniks" (the middle-class intellectual equivalent of lower-class, gang-type culture).

Much that is written about characters in lower-class society carries a strong element of truth. Mass media bring this very much into the open. Some of the message is also "created" by the mass media. Youth always manifests a "normal" flexibility, unpredictability, and rebellion. Adolescents are often ready to "buy" what is so vividly and clearly portrayed and to assume the visualized role, even when it includes violence and wildness. With such images before them as models, youngsters can give violent substance to their ordinary tendencies.

YOUTH WORKERS AND THE DELINQUENT

Many middle-class adults work with delinquent youth, either professionally or on a lay-volunteer basis. The motivations of youth workers who are trying to help the underprivileged, particularly the delinquent, are a subject of concern. There are many valid, explicitly stated motivations—"to help the unfortunate," "to do unto others," "to share what I have with those who have not"—that stir the middle-class youth worker to great sacrifice. However, in addition to such expressly stated motives for working with the delinquent, there is another set of motivations for this type of work. It provides, for some, a means of dealing with unconscious emotional conflicts relating to sex roles or repressed aggressive impulses.

It is important to be concerned not only with the expressed motives of those planning to work with delinquents of either sex, but also their inner motivations. More attention should be given to the problem of selection and screening of those who work closely with delinquent youngsters. Disturbed delinquents can attract disturbed workers. Those for whom youth work reflects significant elements of inner disturbance may do much harm.

RECAPITULATION

Norm-violating behavior, usually fairly well concealed in middle-class culture, quite possibly will become more prevalent in the future. If this happens, more attention will be given to the delinquency problem. One incident involving sex, stabbing, or stealing in a middle-class community arouses more fear and concern than do many similar episodes in a lower-class area. At present it is difficult to ascertain whether actual delinquency among middle-class youth is really increasing or whether middle-class concern with the problem makes it appear to increase. Most official juvenile delinquency occurs within lower-class communities. However, there is some borrowing of lower-class concerns by middle-class youth related to an "upward diffusion" of lower-class cultural concerns into the middle-class community and, in addition, there appears to be a general societal trend for upward diffusions into the middle-class community of many of the concerns of lower-class culture. Some of this represents a fad, but other aspects of the adoption of lower-class patterns of behavior may have more serious consequences for some segments of the middle class. When serious delinquency occurs in middle-class groups, it may be a portent of pathological behavior, since this type of conduct runs counter to the definitions of many of the youngster's most significant reference groups. The middle-class youngster who engages in norm-violating behavior may often be viewed more usefully as a "behavior problem" than as a "delinquent." This is not to deny, however, that some norm-violating behavior in lower-class society also reflects pathology. To what degree and in what ways does emotional disturbance or behavioral pathology enter into delinquency for both middle- and lower-class youngsters?

A Theory of Middle Class Juvenile Delinquency

RALPH W. ENGLAND, JR.

Since 1948 the number of children aged ten to seventeen coming before juvenile court authorities has more than doubled, while the number of children within these ages in the total population has increased by only 19 percent.[1] Despite the caution with which one must regard juvenile court data, police arrest statistics and the testimony of numerous persons working with youth support the Children's Bureau figures.[2] There exists non-statistical evidence that an unprecedented share of the apparent increase in delinquency is being contributed by "normal" youngsters from middle class families in communities and neighborhoods lacking previous experience with serious misbehavior among their children. Rowdiness in and out of school, abuse of driving privileges, joy-riding thefts, excessive drinking, vandalism and sexual misconduct are among the principal forms of disapproved acts seemingly becoming more frequent among teenagers from "better" backgrounds. And the problem is not merely a phenomenon of metropolitan areas: towns and smaller cities in which delinquency of any kind was nearly non-existent before the war are reporting similar difficulties.

A number of researches have shown the existence of considerable unrecorded delinquency among socially advantaged youths,[3] but few theoretical attempts have been made to explain such behavior. In an article published in 1942

Reprinted by permission of the author and of the editor from *The Journal of Criminal Law, Criminology and Police Science*, 50 (March–April, 1960), 535–540.

Talcott Parsons touched briefly upon the existence and nature of a "youth culture."[4]

"Perhaps the best single point of reference for characterizing the youth culture lies in its contrast with the dominant pattern of the adult male role. By contrast with the emphasis on responsibility in this role, the orientation of the youth culture is more or less specifically irresponsible. One of its dominant notes is "having a good time" in relation to which there is a particularly strong emphasis on social activities with the opposite sex.

". . . it is notable that the youth culture has a strong tendency to develop in directions which are either on the borderline of parental approval or beyond the pale, in such matters as sex behavior, drinking and various forms of frivolous and irresponsible behavior.

"[The youth culture] shows strong signs of being a product of tensions in the relationships of younger people and adults."

The last sentence foreshadows his later theory that in the process of acquiring a masculine role-identity middle class boys react against the feminine identification of their childhoods by engaging in "masculine protest" behavior of a rough, destructive kind. The relative inability of youths today to observe directly their fathers' occupational roles, coupled with the ubiquity of feminine roles in the home, forces an eventual rebellion not only against "feminineness" but against the "goodness" which seems to the child an integral part of femininity.[5]

A number of objections to this theory can be raised. (a) In the process of "protesting masculinity" why is the trait of adult male responsibility shunned while other presumed traits of the male (loud, aggressive, rambunctious behavior) are adopted? (b) One can imagine middle class boys who live in dormitory suburbs and large cities having some difficulty picturing their fathers' occupational roles, but this may not be true in smaller cities and in towns where the fathers' places of work are more readily accessible for visits, and where their roles are less likely to be obscured by employment in bureaucratic organizations. (c) How can the participation of girls in the youth culture be explained by Parsons' theory? (d) Are mothers' roles especially ubiquitous in communities where commuting time for the father is not so great that he cannot be with his family meaningfully except on weekends? "Catching the 7:05" each morning before the children are up and returning in the evening shortly before their bedtime is a pattern found only in our largest cities. (e) Is it to be assumed that the seeming increase in middle class delinquency since the Second World War is the result of a post-war increase in sons' difficulties in identifying with their fathers' roles, in the absence of basic post-war changes in our society's occupation structure?

The present paper begins with a backtrack on Parsons' thinking to his idea that hedonistic irresponsibility characterizes the youth culture of the United States, and a departure from this in another direction from that taken by him. The theory to be presented here is that some middle class delinquency is the result of an interaction between certain aspects of our general cultural system and an emerging teenage system, producing norms entirely functional to the latter but not to the former.

THE TEENAGE SYSTEM

The groundwork for the emergence of a teenage culture in our society was laid a century and more ago when youngsters were gradually removed from functional roles in the economy through restrictive apprenticeship codes, protective labor legislation, the compulsory education movement, and the withdrawal of children from agricultural activities attendant upon urbanization. However diverse the forces were which led to this removal from productive roles, the result was that for probably the first time a major society deactivated a large and energetic segment of its population without clearly redefining the status and function of that segment. The resulting ambiguity of status, the blurring of the lines separating childhood from youth and youth from adulthood, has been commented upon by many observers; the middle class teenager, with his typically lengthened period of ambiguous status compared with working class youngsters, is faced with contradictory expectations. He is not expected to engage in productive labor, but neither is he encouraged to loaf; he is discouraged from early marriage, but is allowed to engage in proto-courtship; he cannot vote, hold public office, or serve on a jury, but is expected to be civic-minded; he is given many privileges and a large measure of individual freedom, but without the obligatory ties to significant others which, for the adult, help keep privilege and freedom from deteriorating into license.

Bloch and Neiderhoffer[6] have recently suggested that certain attributes of adolescent life (tattooing, hazing, the adoption of nicknames, etc.) serve as latter-day rites of passage into adolescence to lessen the anxiety-producing absence of adult-sponsored rites. For several generations the teen years have been a singularly faddist time of life, and peculiarities of dress, speech, values and interests are increasingly conspicuous among this population group. It seems reasonable to presume, as have Bloch and others, that these widely-shared peculiarities are highly functional to teenagers, and are not simply youthful fancies. Some might, indeed, be the equivalent of primitive rites of passage; others might serve to maintain the new status; still others might be the ordinary *impedimenta* of a burgeoning youth cultural system.

It is the writer's contention that certain post-World War II changes—mainly in communications—have speeded the development of long-nascent tendencies arising from the ambiguous status of our teenage population. These changes have had the general, if inadvertent, effect of making teenagers newly aware of themselves as a nation-wide segment of our society by fostering communication within this population group. Probably none of these changes singly could have produced this effect, but their conjuncture following the war provided means for teenagers to enter into at least secondary contact far beyond the pre-war confines of their respective communities.

1. Perhaps basic is the exploitation of an enlarged market for teenage goods and services following our post-war rise in living standards and the consequent possession of large amounts of spending money by youngsters. An estimated nine billion dollars are spent annually by teenagers.[7] National advertising campaigns, many found only in the new teen magazines, publicize products tailored to the interests and needs of this age group: motor scooters, acne creams, portable phonographs and radios, western and rock-and-roll movies, auto accessories, hot-rod conversion kits, unusual clothing, mail-order dance lessons, etc. The wide distribution of these items is contributing to the growth of a nationally shared but age-restricted material culture.

2. Post-war changes in local radio broadcasting with in-

creased reliance on canned material, particularly popular music, has brought into prominence the disc jockey, whose seeming chumminess with entertainers gives him some of the glamour of show business. Despite competition from television the number of operating commercial broadcasting stations increased from 890 to 3,680 between 1945 and 1958,[8] many of them being located in smaller communities throughout the country. The number of disc jockeys has been estimated at 2,500,[9] compared to a handful before the war, and their audiences apparently are drawn mainly from among persons in their teens and early twenties. The recent disturbance in Boston where a disc jockey was accused of inciting his young followers to riot, and the power of these men to stimulate teenage interest in charity drives, contests and the like, are suggestive of their role in teenage communications.

3. Similar to the above, but with the added element of visual impact, is TV programming of teen dance shows, from Dick Clark's nationally broadcast American Bandstand to the one-channel town's airing of the local equivalent with a lone disc jockey providing the recorded music. The particular image of teenage life thus promulgated by many of the country's 544 operating commercial television stations (contrasted with six in 1945[10]) probably reaches a large audience.

4. Young people's magazines have been published for many decades in the United States. With few exceptions, their common stamp was one of staid, moralistic conservatism which viewed adolescence as a period of preparation for an adulthood of similar qualities. Since 1944, however, when *Seventeen* began publication, a number of magazines have appeared whose kinship to the older *Youth's Companion* and *American Boy* is only faintly discernible. At least eleven of these are currently in the market, led by *Seventeen*, whose monthly circulation is slightly over one million copies. *Co-Ed*, *'Teen*, *Cool*, *Hep Cats*, *Modern Teen*, *Ingenue* and *Dig* have combined circulations of about 1,500,000.[11] These publications are similar in format to movie and TV magazines read by many adults, but their picture stories emphasize younger personnel from the entertainment industry, and they contain a thin scattering of teenage love stories, youth "forums," puzzles and articles on automobiles and high school sports. In sharp contrast with the moralistic flavor of earlier youth magazines, the post-war group is distinguished by its por-

trayal of hedonistic values within an essentially amoral setting: the teen years are not ones of preparation for responsible adulthood, but of play and diversion.

5. A final influence contributing to the teenagers' awareness of themselves as a distinct population group may be the very fact that the post-war years have seen public attention directed increasingly toward our youth because of the apparent increase in juvenile problems. Teenagers seem very much aware that such problems exist, even if their outlines are not clear to the youngsters.[12]

Given the existence of a large population segment permeated with anxiety arising from its ill-defined status, and communicating, however imperfectly, on a national scale, one observes elements necessary for the development of something akin to a minority group psychology: a shared sense of grievance and alienation among substantial numbers of persons readily identifiable by some conspicuous trait—in this case, being in the teen years. Listing further points of similarity between minority groups and today's teenagers, one could mention *leaders and spokesmen* in the persons of disc jockeys, young entertainers and some educationists; a distinctive set of material and non-material *culture traits; sentiments of exclusiveness* toward most adults and toward "square" (*i.e.*, adult-oriented) youngsters; and *culture heroes*, selected mainly from among entertainers and athletes.

While the theory being presented here does not hinge on teenagers constituting a true minority group, it does assume that on a national scale there is evolving a complex of attitudes and values tending to control and motivate teenagers in ways consonant with the role implied by their position as a youthful group having leisure, relatively ample spending money and few responsibilities. The theme of this emerging culture seems to be one of an increasingly institutionalized but immature and irresponsible hedonism, as Parsons suggested.

It is evident that not all teenagers behave as if they were participants in such a culture. The degree to which any particular youth is controlled and motivated by the norms of the teenage system may be a function of the extent and intensity of his affiliation with youthful autonomous cliques, for these, rather than individuals, appear to be the social units of the teenage world. The relative importance of clique-membership may in turn be inversely related to a teenager's commitment to groups—usually adult-dominated—which purvey conventional normative systems, and which have the inherent disadvantage, in competing for teenagers' loyalties, of requiring accommodation to adult demands.

While strong peer-group appeal is exhibited among both working class and middle class youngsters, there may exist class differences both in the content of the youth culture shared by teenagers from the two strata, and in the duration of the culture's importance in the lives of its followers. Those teenagers currently labeled "hoods" by other youngsters are marked by levis and leather jackets, motorcycles and jalopies, frankly promiscuous girl friends, truculent, aggressive behavior in school, and a sneering avoidance of extracurricular school social activities. For these youngsters delinquent motivations may indeed stem from their experiences with snobbish discrimination within the high school social structure, as Cohen maintains.[13] But their earlier entrance into the labor market and their lower age at marriage enable them to acquire adult roles—and to become saddled with adult responsibilities—sooner than middle class teenagers. By contrast, the middle class "social crowd"—more seemly and fashionably dressed, smoother mannered, driving late-model cars, peopling the parties and proms in their communities, and indulged by their prosperous and permissive parents—constitute the spending market alluded to earlier, and may be proportionately greater participants in the teenage communications network and in that part of the teenage culture depicted in it.

DELINQUENCY AND THE TEENAGE CULTURE

An ethos of irresponsible hedonism is not in itself productive of delinquent motivations, and I am not suggesting that middle class delinquency is simply a manifestation of unchecked impulses, as the term "irresponsible hedonism" connotes. The relationship between this ethos and delinquency is more complex. If the teenager's urgent need for status affirmation is met by the teenage culture, then it becomes necessary for him to reject influences from the adult world which threaten it, and to accept only those giving it support. The threatening influences are attitudes and values running counter to short-run, irresponsible hedonism, such as hard work, thrift, study, self-denial, etc., while those supportive of it are cultural elements adaptable to it. It is the writer's contention that delinquent motivations among middle class teenagers arise from this adaptive process, in which the teenage world, peopled by immature and inexperienced persons, extracts from the adult world those values having strong hedonistic possibilities, with the result that the values of the teenage culture consist mainly of distorted and caricatured fragments from the adult culture. These highly selected and altered values then serve to motivate and give direction to members of the youth world, sometimes in ways adults define as delinquent. Some examples of such value transformation will make my meaning clear.

1. Abuse of driving privileges by some teenagers is a persisting problem in most communities. Open mufflers, drag-racing, speeding, playing "chicken," or just aimlessly driving about constitute nuisances and sometimes dangers on public streets and highways. To emotionally mature adults automobiles primarily represent—and are operated as—means of transportation, but in the process of adaptation to the adolescent ethos they are redefined as playthings whose important qualities are less those pertaining to getting from place to place than to glitter, power and speed, and teenagers tend to operate them in ways appropriate to these qualities. Youth's intense interest in cars is reflected in the current number of magazines (twenty-one) devoted to the automobile. Eighteen of these were founded since 1945, and fourteen since 1950. Their reported combined monthly circulation is about 2,300,000. *Hot Rod Magazine* leads this group, with about 490,000 paid monthly circulation.[14] Some 2,000 so-called "speed shops" supplied by 100 manufacturers distribute parts and accessories for youth car enthusiasts.[15]

A more serious problem with respect to automobiles is the increasing number of cars "borrowed" for joy rides by middle class (or at least "favored group") teenagers.[16] Larceny is customarily defined as taking another's property with intent to deprive the owner permanently of its use; joyride thievery seldom involves this criminal intention, and apprehended youngsters are quick to point out—quite accurately—that they were "merely having a little fun." (It is worth noting that cars borrowed for joy rides almost invariably embody qualities extraneous to mere transportation. Flashy convertibles are especially vulnerable.)

2. The competitive spirit, valued in our larger society as a spur to achievement, but hedged about with customary and legal restrictions, becomes productive of bitter and childish rivalries when it is applied to high school intermural contests. The youngsters, aroused by pep committees, coaches and alumni, transform competition into a hedonistic travesty: witness the growing problem of fights, car chases and vandalism attendant on important games.

3. Whether or not we are a sex-obsessed society, as European observers sometimes contend, the meaning of sex to our teenagers is confused and contradictory. On the one hand, pre-marital chastity and forbearance are upheld as prime moral values. On the other, sex is heavily exploited in most of the popular media of entertainment. The image of sex, love and romance presented by these media is one rejected by most adults whose views have been tempered by the realities of life, but the middle class youngsters of the teenage world, bemused by their burgeoning sex drives in the prolonged and presumably chaste interval between puberty and marriage, and betrayed by their inexperience, are inclined to accept this image as valid. More importantly, this image is considerably more congenial to their ethos than one conveying restraint and self-control; sex and love are redefined as ends in themselves, and have acquired sufficient preeminence in the teenage system since 1945 to motivate youngsters of twelve to begin "going steady," and of sixteen to contemplate marriage seriously.

4. Among the adult values attractive to the teenage ethos, the use of alcoholic beverages is perhaps the one most readily lending itself to distortion, for the temperate use of alcohol by adults themselves requires a degree of restraint seldom found in youngsters. Normatively, alcohol is utilized by the middle class as a social lubricant and as an adjunct to food, and strong social pressures help limit its use to those functions. By custom (as well as by law) teenagers are forbidden generally to use alcoholic beverages on their own for any purpose. But its fundamental hedonistic quality—its capacity to intoxicate—makes it so highly adaptable to the teenage ethos that when alcohol is used, this quality is emphasized, and drinking to excess becomes the norm. A further

difficulty arises from the obligatory secretiveness of teenage middle class drinking: it must be done quite apart from adult eyes in automobiles, public parks, rented cottages and motels where drinking parties can easily get out of hand.

SUMMARY

Post-war changes in communications processes are heightening in-group feelings within a large population segment which, during the last one hundred years, has experienced increased status ambiguity as the productive roles of this group have diminished. The intensive preoccupation with play among today's teenagers results from the circumstance that hedonistic pursuits, evoked by the youngsters' present position in the social structure, are becoming the status-defining "function" of this emerging national interest group. In order to retain the need-satisfactions produced by this new status clarification, the group's values and norms must support its play function by constituting a hedonistic ethos, and must neutralize non-hedonistic pressures from the adult world either by denigrating them entirely or by altering them to conform with the teenage culture. Once incorporated into that culture, they become controlling and motivating forces for those teenagers sharing the system, but in directions sometimes inconsistent with adult norms.

Selected Readings

Cavan, Ruth, *Juvenile Delinquency*, Philadelphia: J. B. Lippincott Co., 1962. This general textbook in juvenile delinquency contains a chapter on middle-class delinquency.

Cohen, Albert K., *Delinquent Boys: The Culture of the Gang*, Illinois: The Free Press of Glencoe, 1955. A sociologically sophisticated account of the delinquent subculture according to the status deprivation of lower-class boys. Contains a description of the "middle-class ethic." Especially well written.

Cohen, Albert K. and James Short, Jr., "Juvenile Delinquency" in *Contemporary Social Problems*, ed. by Robert K. Merton and Robert A. Nisbet, New York: Harcourt, Brace and World, Inc., 1961. An excellent brief review of the field of juvenile delinquency.

Coleman, James, *The Adolescent Society*, Illinois: The Free Press of Glencoe, 1961. This is the best study of the content and structure of the cultures of adolescents.

Greeley, Andrew and James Casey, "An Upper Middle-Class Deviant Gang," *American Catholic Sociological Review*, Vol. 24, No. 1 (Spring, 1963). A group of disturbed boys who have difficulty maintaining their social position turn to delinquency in a new upper middle-class community.

Matza, David and Gresham M. Sykes, "Juvenile Delinquency and Subterranean Values," *American Sociological Review*, Vol. 26, No. 5 (October, 1961). The values characteristic of juvenile delinquency resemble closely those of the larger leisure-oriented society. This provides a basis for examining the similarity of all adolescents—delinquents and nondelinquents—as members of a "leisure class."

Musgrove, F., *Youth and the Social Order*, Bloomington: Indiana University Press, 1965. The changes in status of young people in Western society are traced over the past 200 years. The scene is England.

Parsons, Talcott, "Certain Primary Sources and Patterns of Aggression in the Social Structure of the Western World," *Psychiatry*, Vol. 10, No. 2 (May, 1947). The author links successfully the "masculine protest" motif to the family and occupational structures of modern society.

Porterfield, Austin, *Youth in Trouble*, Fort Worth: Leo Potishman Foundation, 1946. An early study of the self-reported offenses of college students the majority of whom were likely middle class.

Reiss, Albert J. and Albert Lewis Rhodes, "The Distribution of Juvenile Delinquency in the Social Class Structure," *American Sociological*

Review, Vol. 26, No. 5 (October, 1961). A well-executed technical study of the relationships between delinquency rates and occupational status groups, and the ascribed status of schools. The status of the school a boy attends exercises considerable effect on the likelihood of his becoming delinquent.

Seeley, John R., R. Alexander Sim and Elizabeth W. Loosley, *Crestwood Heights*, New York: Basic Books, Inc., 1956. Little is left to chance in the socialization of children in an upper middle-class Canadian community. An insightful study.

Shoham, Shlomo and Meir Hovav, "'B'Nei-Tovim'—Middle and Upper-Class Delinquency in Israel," *Sociology and Social Research*, Vol. 48, No. 4 (July, 1964). A survey of middle- and upper-class juvenile delinquency in Israel.

Ten articles on "Youth: Change and Challenge" are found in *Daedalus: the Journal of the American Academy of Arts and Sciences*, Vol. 91, No. 1 (Winter, 1962).

Notes

The Protective Environment and Adolescent Socialization

WILLIAM A. WESTLEY AND FREDERICK ELKIN

1 F. Kluckhohn and J. P. Spiegel, "Integration and Conflict in Family Behavior," *Group for the Advancement of Psychiatry* (August 1954), p. 16. See also M. Mead, *Coming of Age in Samoa* (New York: W. W. Morrow Co., 1938); K. Davis, "Adolescence and the Social Structure," *Annals of the American Academy of Political and Social Science* (November 1944); T. Parsons, "Psychoanalysis and the Social Structure," *Psychoanalytic Quarterly* (1950), pp. 371–384; M. A. Elliott and F. E. Merrill, *Social Disorganization* (New York: Harper & Row, 1941), pp. 83–101; E. W. Mowrer, *Disorganization: Personal and Social* (New York: J. B. Lippincott and Co., 1942), pp. 54–59.

2 See F. Elkin and W. A. Westley, "The Myth of Adolescent Culture," *American Sociological Review*, 20 (December 1955), pp. 680–684.

3 We cannot be certain that the sample is representative of adolescents in the community. However, the relative size of the sample, the consistency of the findings, the support of case-history material of college students reared in Suburban Town, and the agreement with the description of adolescents in Elmtown (Hollingshead, *Elmtown's Youth* and Warner, *Democracy in Jonesville*), temper the significance of this methodological deficiency.

4 Preliminary results of a comparative study in a working-class section of Montreal suggest sharp class difference in this regard. In the working-class section children report few details of their behaviour to their parents and are not expected to do so.

5 The average allowance among a comparable age group in a working-class section of Montreal is $2.00 per week.

6 For a broader discussion of the significance of sacrificing for future gains, see A. Davis and J. Dollard, *Children of Bondage* (Washington, D.C.: American Council of Education, 1940).

7 There are a few "wild" individuals; however they represent a very limited proportion of the adolescents in the community. It is possible that, in many communities, a few "wild" individuals receive so much attention that others mistake them for typical residents.

Teen-Age Culture: An Overview

JESSIE BERNARD

1 This figure includes Alaska but not Hawaii. It was arrived at by assuming that the proportion of 13- and 14-year-old youngsters in the

10–14 age bracket was the same in 1959 as in 1950 and applying it to 1959 estimates.

[2] The proportion of teen-age males in school rose between 1930 and 1958 from 93 to 99 per cent for 14-year-olds, from 85 to 96 per cent for 15-year-olds, from 66 to 88 per cent for 16-year-olds, from 47 to 74 per cent for 17-year-olds, and from 31 to 43 per cent for 18-year-olds.

[3] Young women under 20 spend 4½ billion dollars, and, as one of the editors of *Seventeen* points out, they have no income taxes, no rent, no insurance premiums to take out of this sum; they have it all for themselves. Sigana Earle, in a talk at the Michigan Home Economics Association convention, April 30, 1960, at Michigan State University.

[4] Allegedly $20,000,000 is spent annually on lipstick, $25,000,000 on deodorants, and $9,000,000 on home permanents.

[5] They spent 38 per cent of their money on such items as transportation, grooming, books, newspapers, magazines, school supplies; 25 per cent on food; 16 per cent on entertainment; 15 per cent on clothes; and 9 per cent on sports. *Life Magazine*, August 29, 1959, pp. 78–85.

[6] Ross A. McFarland and Roland C. Moore, "Youth and the Automobile," in *Values and Ideals of American Youth*, Eli Ginzberg, ed. (Columbia University Press, 1961), pp. 171, 172.

[7] *Ibid.*, pp. 173, 176.

[8] *Life Magazine*, August 29, 1959, pp. 78–85.

[9] Sigana Earle, of *Seventeen, loc. cit.*

[10] *Chicago Tribune*, reporting on Park Forest, cited in *Population Bulletin*, October 1960, p. 140.

[11] Joseph Welch once pointed out that, in the tobacco advertisements beamed at teen-agers, the choice seems to them to be between brands rather than between smoking and not smoking. *New York Times*, February 26, 1961.

[12] *Life Magazine*, August 29, 1959, p. 78.

[13] Teen-agers share with adults moving pictures and television programs. These media must reach as wide a public as possible, adult as well as adolescent; no American studio specializes in pictures for young people only. Although teen-agers go to movies about twice as often as the 20–29 age group and three times as often as the 40–49 age group, their taste is not markedly different from that of adults of the same class. Television viewing declines between childhood and adolescence; preferences for blood-and-thunder, mysteries, cowboy stories, comedy, family programs remain but make way in part for sports and adult drama. See George Gerbner, "Mass Communications and the Citizenship of Secondary School Youth," mimeographed report for the Interdisciplinary Study Group, Tufts Civic Education Center.

[14] Donald Horton, "The Dialogue of Courtship in Popular Songs," *American Journal of Sociology*, Vol. 62 (May 1957), p. 575.

[15] These studies are summarized in *Recognition of Excellence* (Glencoe: Free Press, 1960), pp. 57–63.

[16] James S. Coleman, "The Adolescent Subculture and Academic Achievement," *American Journal of Sociology*, Vol. 65 (January 1960), pp. 346–347.

17 Erving Goffman, *The Presentation of Self in Everyday Life* (Garden City, N.Y.: Doubleday Anchorage, 1959), p. 238.

18 George Gerbner, *op. cit.*, p. 10.

19 In 1937–1938, the most frequent part-time jobs of boys were paper boys, sales clerks, filling-station attendants, theater ushers and assistants, and delivery jobs. For girls, the commonest part-time jobs were sales clerks, housework, nursemaids, waitresses, musicians, and music teachers. In 1942, 28.7 per cent of a sample of boys and 9.0 per cent of a sample of girls had after-school jobs; 41.6 per cent and 12.5 per cent respectively had Saturday jobs; and 57.6 per cent and 14.4 per cent had summer jobs. Miller and Form, *Industrial Sociology* (New York: Harper & Row, 1951), Chap. 16. For an excellent analysis of "culture shock" as the teen-ager moved from his school culture to the work culture, see pp. 610–632.

20 But note current trends in teen-type magazines described below.

21 Seymour Martin Lipset, *Political Man* (Garden City, N.Y.: Doubleday, 1960), Chap. 4.

22 A. B. Hollingshead, *Elmtown's Youth* (New York: Wiley, 1949).

23 H. H. Remmers and D. H. Radler, *The American Teenager* (Indianapolis: Bobbs-Merrill, 1957), pp. 80–85.

24 Burton R. Clark and Martin Trow, "Determinants of College Student Subculture," in *The Study of College Peer Groups: Problems and Prospects for Research*, a volume based on the work of the seminar sponsored by the Social Science Research Council, Ann Arbor and Berkeley, 1959–1960 (mimeographed), p. 2. See Davie and Hare, "Button-down Collar Culture: A Study of Undergraduate Life," *Human Organization*, Vol. 14 (Winter 1956), pp. 13–20, for a picture of collegiate culture.

25 Clark and Trow, *op. cit.*, p. 6.

26 *Ibid.*, p. 7.

27 *Ibid.*, p. 8.

28 *Ibid.*, p. 16.

Athletics in High School

JAMES S. COLEMAN

1 See James S. Coleman, *The Adolescent Society* (Glencoe: The Free Press, 1961), pp. 70–71, 88–90.

2 In certain cases, random variation due to the small number of students in the smallest school prevents separate conclusions about it.

3 Other areas of achievement were included in the questionnaire, for example, knowing about cars and being most attractive to the girls. The visibility for both of these was far below that for athletes or scholars.

4 The number of cases was over 800 in each grade, so the difference reported is significant beyond the .001 level.

5 This question was studied only in four of the five smallest

schools; technical problems prevented it in the large schools, and the smallest school had no distinct crowds.

[6] The ranks average to 3.3 rather than 3.5 as they should, because not every boy assigned all ranks.

[7] Abraham J. Tannenbaum, "Adolescents' Attitudes Toward Academic Brilliance" (unpublished Ph.D. dissertation, New York University, 1960).

[8] For further discussion of this point, see Coleman, *op. cit.*, p. 303.

[9] When a union becomes merely a business union, no longer actively fighting for collective worker benefits, it survives in name, but it can no longer depend upon its members for active support. This, in fact, is the fundamental problem of many unions at the present time.

[10] This can be illustrated by the story, perhaps apocryphal, of the employer who paid every second worker on an assembly line a higher rate, so that every worker's neighbors received rates different from his own. A similar mechanism has been documented in department stores, where clerks are given marginal differentiations in title and pay to keep them divided. See Carl Dreyfuss, "Prestige Grading: A Mechanism of Control," in R. K. Merton and Others, *Reader in Bureaucracy* (Glencoe: The Free Press, 1952), pp. 258–264.

[11] One of the important reasons that incentive pay, in the form of commissions, has always worked well for salesmen is that their active work in selling the company products to doubtful customers generates in them a positive identification with the company. Another reason, of course, is that they are usually dispersed, not in contact with one another.

[12] This is not to say that the absence of athletic emphasis in these institutions has principally bad consequences. Many colleges have, rather, compromised their original goals through the power and interest of their athletically involved alumni. But the withdrawal from interscholastic athletics without the substitution of other bases for institution-inspired pride and identification leaves the institution weaker and less likely to survive.

[13] This suggests that high schools in Europe, which are coming to enroll larger and larger proportions of adolescents, will increase the emphasis upon athletic contests, unless they find another mechanism to accomplish the same end.

[14] The sense of shock and disbelief in Brooklyn when the Dodgers moved to Los Angeles is a measure of Brooklynites' identification of the team with their community. On the other side, it has been said that Los Angeles ceased to be a collection of suburbs and became a city for the first time when "their" Dodgers won a pennant.

[15] This pattern is being replaced by a pattern of promoting assistant principals or guidance counselors, who have administrative training in schools of education. There is no evidence that they make better principals than coaches do.

The Rating and Dating Complex

WILLARD WALLER

1 James G. Leyburn quotes an old-fashioned Boer mother who said, "I am sick of all this talk of choosing and choosing . . . If a man is healthy and does not drink, and has a good little handful of stock, and a good temper, and is a good Christian, what great difference can it make to a woman which man she takes? There is not so much difference between one man and another." (*Frontier Folkways*, p. 129.) Such an attitude was possible in Boer society as it is not in ours.

2 Folsom, who has studied this same process, has come to essentially similar conclusions concerning the exclusion of certain persons from the dating process: "This factor is especially prominent in state universities with a vigorous fraternity culture and social stratification. Such institutions are attended by students from an unusually wide range on the social scale; there is a tendency to protect one's social ranking in college through a certain snobbishness, and there is also a great drive toward social climbing. Fraternities are important agencies in this struggle for prestige. The fraternities and sororities apply considerable pressure to the 'dating' of their members. One gets merits, whether formally recorded or not, for dating with a coed of a high-ranking fraternity, demerits for association with a non-fraternity person. The net result of this competition might seem to be to match each person with one of fairly equal rank, as happens in society in general. But there is another result. It is to discourage matching altogether among the lower ranks. The fire of competitive dating burns hot at the top, smoulders at the bottom. The low-ranking student often has more to gain by abstaining from dating than from dating with a person of his own rank." (J. K. Folsom, *The Family*, p. 341.)

Sexual Codes in Teen-Age Culture

IRA L. REISS

1 Albert J. Reiss, "Sex Offenses: The Marginal Status of the Adolescent," *Law and Contemporary Problems*, Vol. 25 (Spring 1960), pp. 309–334.

2 Of course, there is a biological basis for sexual behavior, but social scientists seem generally agreed that the specific way the sexual drive expresses itself is learned. The wide variety of sexual codes throughout the world testifies to the fact that whatever differences exist biologically between men and women can be compensated for by cultural training. The best brief source for cross-cultural information is Clellan S. Ford and Frank A. Beach, *Patterns of Sexual Behavior* (New York, 1954). For a discussion of this entire issue, see Ira L.

Reiss, *Premarital Sexual Standards in America* (Glencoe, Ill., 1960), Chap. 1.

[3] For evidence, see Maureen Daly, *Profile of Youth* (Philadelphia, 1951), p. 30. It may be well to note here that the author has conducted a pilot study to test the hypothesis that the advent of the junior high school has spread heterosexual knowledge and behavior to younger age groups and thus encouraged earlier dating. In support of this, one may cite Dr. J. B. Connat's belief that the junior high imitates the high school in its social characteristics. In addition, the anticipatory socialization of sex games like "spin the bottle," "post office," and "flashlight" begin today prior to junior high levels and thus prepare students for dating in junior high. The author's evidence indicates a connection between junior high school and early dating patterns.

[4] Robert D. Herman, "The Going Steady Complex: A Re-Examination," *Marriage and Family Living*, Vol. 17 (February 1955), pp. 36–40.

[5] For evidence on this point, see Winston W. Ehrmann, *Premarital Dating Behavior* (New York, 1959), p. 141.

[6] Alfred C. Kinsey and Others, *Sexual Behavior in the Human Female* (Philadelphia, 1953), Chap. 7.

[7] *Ibid.*, p. 244.

[8] This investigation is supported by a Public Health Service research grant (M-4045) from the National Institute of Mental Health, Public Health Service.

[9] Alfred C. Kinsey, *Sexual Behavior in the Human Male* (Philadelphia, 1948), p. 550.

[10] For a full discussion of this standard, its historical sources and reasons for being, see Ira L. Reiss, *Premarital Sexual Standards in America* (Glencoe, Ill., 1960), Chap. 4.

[11] Lester Kirkendall has conducted extensive research on the nature of the interaction process in sexual relations, and his evidence to date seems to support my position here. He will soon publish a book on this topic.

[12] Ira L. Reiss, *op. cit.*, Chap. 6, for a full discussion of this standard.

[13] For a book containing many of these "stories," see Shailer U. Lawton, M.D., and Jules Archer, *Sexual Conduct of the Teen-Ager* (New York, 1951).

[14] Ehrmann, *op. cit.*, pp. 263–266.

[15] Lester A. Kirkendall and A. E. Gravatt, "Teen-Agers' Sex Attitudes and Behavior," in Evelyn M. and Sylvanus M. Duvall (eds.), *Sexways in Fact and Faith* (New York, 1961), pp. 115–129.

[16] Kinsey, *Sexual Behavior . . . Female*, *op. cit.*, p. 173. See also William R. Reevy, "Adolescent Sexuality," in A. Ellis and A. Abarbanel, *The Encyclopedia of Sexual Behavior* (New York, 1961), pp. 52–67.

[17] For an interesting article discussing shifts in male and female attitudes, see J. P. McKee and A. C. Sherriffs, "Men's and Women's Beliefs, Ideals and Self Concepts," in Jerome M. Seidman (ed.), *The Adolescent* (New York, 1960), pp. 282–294.

[18] One of the major efforts of my book is to demonstrate the evidence for this trend. See Ira L. Reiss, *op. cit.*, Chap. 10.

[19] Kinsey, *Sexual Behavior . . . Female*, *op. cit.*, pp. 275, 339 *passim*.

[20] Kingsley Davis, "The Sociology of Parent-Youth Conflict," *Ameri-*

can Sociological Review, Vol. 5 (October 1940), pp. 523–535; Talcott Parsons, "Age and Sex in the Social Structure of the United States," *American Sociological Review*, Vol. 7 (December 1942), pp. 604–616.

21 H. H. Remmers and D. H. Radley, *The American Teen-Ager* (Indianapolis, 1957), pp. 83, 225–236.

22 R. D. Hess and I. Goldblatt, "The Status of Adolescents in American Society," in Seidman, *op. cit.*, pp. 321–333.

23 Kinsey, *Sexual Behavior . . . Female*, *op. cit.*, Chaps. 5, 7, 8.

24 August B. Hollingshead, *Elmtown's Youth* (New York, 1949), p. 227. See also Maxine Davis, *Sex and the Adolescent* (New York, 1960), p. 136.

25 T. Lefoy Richman, *Venereal Disease: Old Plague—New Challenge* (Public Affairs Pamphlet No. 292; New York, 1960), p. 7. For more technical data, see T. Lefoy Richman (ed.), *Today's Venereal Disease Control Problem* (New York: American Social Health Association, 1961), especially pp. 36–43.

26 Richman, *Venereal Disease . . .*, *op. cit.*, pp. 6, 20.

27 Paul H. Gebhard and Others, *Pregnancy, Birth, and Abortion* (New York, 1958), pp. 45, 160.

28 Clark E. Vincent, "Illegitimacy in the United States," in Duvall (eds.), *op. cit.*, p. 143.

Socioeconomic Status and Delinquency Behavior

F. IVAN NYE, JAMES F. SHORT, JR., AND VIRGIL J. OLSON

1 Ernest W. Burgess, "The Economic Factor in Juvenile Delinquency," *Journal of Criminal Law and Criminology and Police Science*, XLIII (May–June, 1952), 29–42; Cletus Dirksen, *Economic Factors in Delinquency* (Milwaukee: Bruce Publishing Co., 1948); Bernard Lander, *Juvenile Delinquency* (New York: Columbia University Press, 1954); J. B. Maller, "Juvenile Delinquency in New York City," *Journal of Psychology*, III (January, 1937), 1–25; Earl R. Moses, "Differentials in Crime Rates between Negroes and Whites in Comparisons of Four Socioeconomically Equated Areas," *American Sociological Review*, XII (August, 1947), 411–420; W. C. Reckless, *Vice in Chicago* (Chicago: University of Chicago Press, 1933); Clifford R. Shaw and H. D. McKay, *Juvenile Delinquency and Urban Areas* (Chicago: University of Chicago Press, 1942); T. Earl Sullenger, *Social Determinants in Juvenile Delinquency* (New York: John Wiley & Sons, 1936), 170–180; William W. Wattenberg and J. J. Balistrieri, "Gang Membership and Juvenile Delinquency," *American Sociological Review*, XV (December, 1950), 744–752; Paul Wiers, *Economic Factors in Michigan Delinquency* (New York: Columbia University Press, 1944).

2 Clement S. Mihanovitch, "Who Is the Juvenile Delinquent?" *Social Science*, XXII (1947), 45–50; Sophia M. Robison, *Can Delinquency Be Measured?* (New York: Columbia University Press, 1936); Edward Schwartz, "A Community Experiment in the Measurement of Juvenile Delinquency," *National Probation Association Yearbook*, 1945,

pp. 157–182; Thorsten Sellin, "The Basis of a Crime Index," *Journal of Criminal Law and Criminology and Police Science*, XXII (September, 1931), 335–356; Jeremiah Shalloo, "Youth and Crime," *Annals of the American Academy of Political and Social Science*, CXCIV (November, 1937), 79–86; Henry D. Sheldon, "Problems in Statistical Study of Juvenile Delinquency," quoted in Edwin H. Sutherland and Donald R. Cressey, *Principles of Criminology* (Chicago: J. B. Lippincott Co., 1955).

[3] Austin L. Porterfield, *Youth in Trouble* (Fort Worth: Leo Potishman Foundation, 1946).

[4] Fred J. Murphy, M. Shirley, and H. L. Witmer, "The Incidence of Hidden Delinquency," *American Journal of Orthopsychiatry*, XVI (October, 1946), 686–696.

[5] James S. Wallerstein and C. J. Wyle, "Our Law-abiding Lawbreakers," *Probation*, XXV (April, 1947), 107–12.

[6] James F. Short, Jr., "A Report on the Incidence of Criminal Behavior, Arrests, and Convictions in Selected Groups," *Proceedings of the Pacific Sociological Society*, 1954, pp. 110–18 (published as Vol. XXII, No. 2, of "Research Studies of the State College of Washington" [Pullman, Wash., 1954]).

[7] Cletus Dirksen, *Economic Factors in Delinquency* (Milwaukee: Bruce Publishing Co., 1948).

[8] E.g., Bernard Lander, *Juvenile Delinquency* (New York: Columbia University Press, 1954).

[9] Albert K. Cohen, *Delinquent Boys: The Culture of the Gang* (Glencoe, Ill.: Free Press, 1955), pp. 37–41.

[10] *Ibid.*, pp. 170–171.

[11] LaMar T. Empey, "Relationship of Social Class and Family Authority Patterns to Occupational Choice of Washington High School Students" (unpublished Doctoral dissertation, State College of Washington, 1955).

[12] The actual items in the delinquency check list are as follows: defied parents' authority; taken things you didn't want or need; "beat up" on kids that hadn't done anything to you; hurt or inflicted pain on someone just to see them squirm; purposely damaged property; taken things under $2.00 in value; taken things between $2.00 and $50.00; taken things $50.00 and over; driven recklessly in a car; bought or drank intoxicants; used or sold narcotics; homosexual relations; heterosexual relations; taken someone's car without asking; taken part in gang fights; run away from home; had a fist fight; and probation or expulsion from school.

[13] Empey, *op. cit.*; see also LaMar T. Empey, "Social Class and Occupational Aspiration: A Comparison of Absolute and Relative Measurement," *American Sociological Review*, XXI (December, 1956), 703–709.

[14] Raymond B. Cattell, "The Concept of Social Status," *Journal of Social Psychology*, XV (May, 1942), 293–308; Joseph A. Kahl and J. A. Davis, "A Comparison of Indexes of Socio-economic Status," *American Sociological Review*, XV (December, 1955), 317–325; National Opinion Research Center, "The Quarter's Polls—Occupations," *Public Opinion Quarterly*, XI (1947–48), 138–171.

[15] This assumes independence of variables and of each of the tests.

The assumption in this case is valid except where boys and girls are combined following tests performed on data for boys and girls separately. For a summary of significant differences see Table 3 and comment below.

16 The combination of table cells serves to increase the *n* within each cell. *If* the distribution of responses of the two samples is similar in adjacent cells, the combination of such cells increases the *n* per cell without diminishing percentage differences between samples. As a result, differences previously not significant become significant. Total sample *n* is not increased, but, by decreasing the degrees of freedom, the end result is somewhat similar.

17 Hovland and Linquest have cautioned against detailed tests following a general test which proved not significant. In each case, however, the caution appears to be directed against using such double tests in a search for support of a positive hypothesis. Hovland is particularly concerned about possible "false validities." We have guarded against false validities by discounting significant differences to the number of 5 per cent of the total tests made. As the tests are employed here, the analysis goes considerably beyond usual practice in exhausting every possibility for disproving our null hypothesis and providing support for the opposed traditional theory. For Hovland's and Linquest's discussions see Carl Hovland, A. A. Lumsdaine, and F. D. Sheffield, *Studies in Social Psychology in World War II*, Vol. III: *Experiments on Mass Communication* (Princeton, N.J.: Princeton University Press, 1949), p. 297, and E. F. Linquest, *Statistical Analysis in Education Research* (Boston: Houghton Mifflin Co., 1940), pp. 296–297.

18 For a description of the construction of the delinquency scale see F. Ivan Nye and James F. Short, Jr., "Scaling Delinquent Behavior," *American Sociological Review*, XXII (June, 1957), 326–331.

Middle-Class Delinquency and Specific Offense Analysis

ROLAND J. CHILTON

1 William W. Wattenberg and James Balistrieri, "Automobile Theft: A 'Favored-Group' Delinquency," *The American Journal of Sociology*, 57 (May, 1952), pp. 575–579.

2 See William S. Robinson, "Ecological Correlations and the Behavior of Individuals," *American Sociological Review*, 26 (June, 1950), pp. 551–557.

3 See Sophia Robison, *Can Delinquency Be Measured?*, New York: Columbia University, 1936, pp. 124–125.

Differences in the Conception of Self as a Male Among Lower and Middle Class Delinquents

LEON F. FANNIN AND MARSHALL B. CLINARD

1 Some of the studies that have focused upon the self include Marsh Ray, "The Cycle of Abstinence and Relapse Among Heroin Addicts," *Social Problems*, 9 (1961), pp. 132–140; Frank R. Scarpitti, Ellen Murray, Simon Dinitz, and Walter C. Reckless, "The 'Good' Boy in a High Delinquency Area: Four Years Later," *American Sociological Review*, 25 (1960), pp. 555–558; John W. Kinch, "Self-Conceptions of Types of Delinquents," *Sociological Inquiry*, 32 (Spring, 1962), pp. 228–234. Much of the theoretical and empirical work dealing with self-conception during the last 15 years has been in the area of clinical psychology, with a strong emphasis usually upon the discrepancy between self and ideal self as an index of adjustment. See, for example, Victor C. Raimy, "Self Reference in Counseling Interviews," *Journal of Consulting Psychology*, 12 (1948), pp. 153–163; Rosalind F. Dymond, "Adjustment Changes over Therapy from Self-Sorts," in Carl R. Rogers and Rosalind F. Dymond (eds.), *Psychotherapy and Personality Change*, Chicago: University of Chicago Press, 1954, pp. 76–84; Renate G. Armstrong, William O. Hambacher, and James F. Overley, "Self Concepts of Psychiatric and Normal Subjects as Revealed by the Way Test," *Journal of Clinical Psychology*, 18 (1962), pp. 271–276.

2 Thus, the "social self" is considered by various writers to include not only self-conceptions, but a number of "elementary selves," conscious and unconscious evaluation of behavior through role taking, consequent feelings of gratification or mortification, stabilized and unstabilized internalized "others" as standards, and a built-in component of indeterminacy, the "I." In addition, all these are in a state of flux, as the self is a process, not a static entity. See George H. Mead in C. W. Morris (ed.), *Mind, Self, and Society*, Chicago: University of Chicago Press, 1934, pp. 47, 68–69, 136–138, 142–144, 154, 178; Anselm L. Strauss, *Mirrors and Masks*, Glencoe, Ill.: The Free Press, 1959, pp. 49ff.; Tamotsu Shibutani, *Society and Personality*, Englewood Cliffs, N.J.: Prentice-Hall, 1961, pp. 214–236; and S. Frank Miyamota and Sanford M. Dornbusch, "A Test of Interactionist Hypotheses of Self-Conception," *American Journal of Sociology*, 61 (1956), pp. 399–403.

3 See Morris Janowitz, *The Professional Soldier*, Glencoe, Ill.: The Free Press, 1960, pp. 228–229; Charles H. Coates and Roland J. Pellegrin, "Executives and Supervisors: Contrasting Self-Conceptions and Conceptions of Each Other," *American Sociological Review*, 22 (1957), pp. 217–220; Peter F. Merenda and Walter V. Clarke, "Influence of College Experience on the Self-Concepts of Young Male Job Applicants," *Journal of Psychological Studies*, 12 (1961), pp. 49–60.

4 See Walter B. Miller, "Lower Class Culture as a Generating Milieu of Gang Delinquency," *Journal of Social Issues*, 14 (1958), pp. 5–19; Albert K. Cohen, *Delinquent Boys*, Glencoe, Ill.: The Free

Press, 1955, pp. 24–32; Albert K. Cohen and James F. Short, Jr., "Juvenile Delinquency," in Robert K. Merton and Robert A. Nisbet (eds.), *Contemporary Social Problems*, New York: Harcourt, Brace, 1961, pp. 77–126; Marvin E. Wolfgang, *Patterns in Criminal Homicide*, Philadelphia: University of Pennsylvania Press, 1958, pp. 188–189; also see Leon F. Fannin, "A Study of the Social Class Affiliation and Societal Reaction to Convicted Sex and Non-Sex Offenders," unpublished Ph.D. dissertation, University of Wisconsin, 1962, pp. 169–171, 178–179. For a broader perspective concerning the possible relationship between self-conception and stratification, see G. Morris Carstairs, *The Twice-Born: A Study of a Community of High-Caste Hindus*, London: The Hogarth Press, 1961; Hugh H. Smythe, "The Eta: A Marginal Japanese Caste," *American Journal of Sociology*, 58 (1952), pp. 194–196. On the basis of such data, it might be hypothesized that the more discontinuous a stratification system, the more each stratum will generate disparate self-conceptions over a wide range of traits.

5 To avoid repetition, lower-middle class will be referred to hereafter as middle class.

6 Edward Bennett, *Personality Assessment and Diagnosis*, New York: The Ronald Press, 1961, pp. v, 69–80, 173–187, 253–270.

7 Miller, *op. cit.*

8 Gresham M. Sykes, *The Society of Captives*, Princeton: Princeton University Press, 1958.

9 The functions of the "tough guy" self-conception need thorough study if only because there are probably others in addition to status acquisition-retention and defense.

10 See Clark E. Vincent, "Ego Involvement in Sexual Relations: Implications for Research on Illegitimacy," *American Journal of Sociology*, 65 (November, 1959), pp. 287–295. It has also been suggested that attitudes of females toward premarital sex relations are related to class: see Eugene J. Kamin and David H. Howard, "Postmarital Consequences of Premarital Sex Adjustment," *American Sociological Review*, 23 (October, 1958), pp. 556–562, and J. C. Ball and N. Logan, "Early Sexual Behavior of Lower-Class Delinquent Girls," *Journal of Criminal Law, Criminology and Police Science*, 51 (1960), pp. 209–215.

11 Other types of female roles which these delinquents recognized, however, were much the same across class lines, and similar to those described by: William Foote Whyte, "A Slum Sex Code," *American Journal of Sociology*, 49 (July, 1943), pp. 24–31.

12 Edwin M. Lemert, "An Isolation and Closure Theory of Naive Check Forgery," *Journal of Criminal Law, Criminology and Police Science*, 44 (1953), pp. 296–307.

13 Richard R. Korn and Lloyd W. McCorkle, *Criminology and Penology*, New York: Henry Holt, 1959, pp. 336–339; John Paul Scott, *Aggression*, Chicago: University of Chicago Press, 1958, pp. viii, 5–6; Arnold H. Buss, *The Psychology of Aggression*, New York: John Wiley and Sons, 1961, p. 28.

Field Observations of Middle Class "Gangs"

HOWARD L. MYERHOFF AND BARBARA G. MYERHOFF

1 Albert K. Cohen, *Delinquent Boys: The Culture of the Gang* (Glencoe: Free Press, 1955).

2 Talcott Parsons, "Certain Primary Sources and Patterns of Aggression in the Social Structure of the Western World," reprinted in Mullahy (ed.), *A Study of Interpersonal Relations* (New York: Grove Press, Evergreen Edition, 1949).

3 Richard A. Cloward and Lloyd E. Ohlin, *Delinquency and Opportunity: A Theory of Delinquent Gangs* (Glencoe: Free Press, 1961).

4 William C. Kvaraceus and Walter B. Miller, *Delinquent Behavior: Culture and the Individual* (Washington, D.C.: National Education Association, 1959).

5 S. N. Eisenstadt, *From Generation to Generation: Age Groups and Social Structure* (Glencoe: Free Press, 1956).

6 Herbert A. Bloch and Arthur Niederhoffer, *The Gang: A Study of Adolescent Behavior* (New York: Philosophical Library, 1958).

7 Lewis Yablonsky, "The Delinquent Gang as a Near-Group," *Social Problems*, Vol. 7 (Fall 1959), pp. 108–117.

8 In a recent article Pfautz raised the question of whether Yablonsky's "near-group" concept is necessary. He suggests that Yablonsky's findings could be more productively recast into the theoretical traditions of collective behavior in general and social movements in particular. Certainly, Pfautz's point that this would widen the theoretical relevance of Yablonsky's findings is well-taken. There are two reasons for the authors' preference for the near-group concept rather than a collective behavior orientation: first, an immediate concern with indicating the point by point similarity between these observations and those reported by Yablonsky, regardless of the conceptual framework he uses in describing them, and second, the authors' feeling that in view of the fragmented and discontinuous state of the literature on the subject, it is at present more important to compare and relate studies of adolescent collective deviant activities to one another than to more general sociological issues and concepts. Harold W. Pfautz, "Near-Group Theory and Collective Behavior: A Critical Reformulation," *Social Problems*, Vol. 9 (Fall 1961), pp. 167–174.

9 James F. Short, Jr., "Street Corner Groups and Patterns of Delinquency," A Progress Report from National Institute of Mental Health Research Grant, M-3301 (Chicago, March 1961), p. 20.

10 Alva Collier, Personal Communication (Los Angeles, 1961).

11 These field observations precisely conform to what Zelditch has called Type I information. This consists of incidents and histories, and treats as data the meanings assigned to and explanations given for activities as well as the behavior itself. Morris Zelditch, Jr., "Some Methodological Problems of Field Studies," *American Journal of Sociology*, Vol. 67 (March 1962), pp. 566–576.

12 Albert K. Cohen and James F. Short, Jr., "Research in Delinquent Subcultures," *Journal of Social Issues*, Vol. 14, No. 3 (1958), p. 34.

13 William W. Wattenberg and James Balistrieri, "Automobile Theft: A 'Favored-Group' Delinquency," *American Journal of Sociology*, Vol. 57 (May 1952), pp. 575–579.

14 T. C. N. Gibbens, "Car Thieves," *British Journal of Delinquency*, 7–9 (1957–1959), pp. 257–265.

15 Parsons, *op. cit.*

16 Cohen, *op. cit.*

17 Gibbens, *op. cit.*, p. 262.

18 Wattenberg and Balistrieri, *op. cit.*, p. 575.

19 A. L. Porterfield, "Delinquency and Its Outcome in Court and College," *American Journal of Sociology*, Vol. 48 (1943), pp. 199–208; Ivan F. Nye and James F. Short, Jr., "Scaling Delinquent Behavior," *American Sociological Review*, Vol. 22 (1957), pp. 326–331.

20 Cohen and Short, *op. cit.*, p. 26.

21 David Matza and Gresham M. Sykes, "Juvenile Delinquency and Subterranean Values," *American Sociological Review*, Vol. 26 (October 1961), pp. 712–719.

22 J. A. Pitt-Rivers, *The People of the Sierra* (Chicago: University of Chicago Press, Phoenix Edition, 1961).

23 Ruth Benedict, "Continuities and Discontinuities in Cultural Conditioning," reprinted in Mullahy (ed.), *A Study of Interpersonal Relations* (New York: Grove Press, Evergreen Edition, 1949).

24 Erik H. Erikson, *Childhood and Society* (New York: W. W. Norton, 1950).

25 Harold Finestone, "Cats, Kicks and Color," *Social Problems*, Vol. 5 (July 1957), pp. 3–13.

26 *Ibid.*, p. 5.

Juvenile Delinquency in the Middle-Class Youth Culture

EDMUND W. VAZ

1 Robert Dubin, "Deviant Behavior and Social Structure: Continuities in Social Theory," *American Sociological Review*, 24 (April, 1959), 152.

2 The basic idea is taken from Albert K. Cohen, *Delinquent Boys*, Glencoe, Ill., Free Press, 1955, p. 60.

3 See Bernard Blishen, "The Construction and Use of an Occupational Class Scale," *Canadian Journal of Economics and Political Science*, 24 (November, 1958), 519–531.

4 See also the work of F. Ivan Nye and James Short, Jr., "Scaling Delinquent Behavior," *American Sociological Review*, 22 (June, 1957), 326–331. Also, John F. Scott, "Two Dimensions of Delinquent Behavior," *American Sociological Review*, 24 (April, 1959), 240–243.

Automobile Theft: A "Favored-Group" Delinquency

WILLIAM W. WATTENBERG AND JAMES BALISTRIERI

1 Frank E. Hartung, "White-Collar Offenses in the Wholesale Meat Industry in Detroit," *American Journal of Sociology*, XLI, No. 1 (1950), 25–32. See "Comment" by Ernest W. Burgess, "Rejoinder," by Frank E. Hartung, and "Concluding Comment," by Ernest W. Burgess, on pp. 32–34 of the same issue.

2 William W. Wattenberg and David Faigenbaum, "Completed Delinquent Careers" (Detroit: Crime Prevention Bureau, Detroit Police Department, 1949). (Mimeographed.)

3 William W. Wattenberg and James J. Balistrieri, "New Offenders, 1948" (Detroit: Youth Bureau, Detroit Police Department, 1950). (Mimeographed.)

4 L. E. Hewitt and R. L. Jenkins, *Fundamental Patterns of Maladjustment* (Springfield: State of Illinois, 1946).

5 Robert J. Havighurst and Hilda Taba, *Adolescent Character and Personality* (New York: John Wiley & Sons, 1949), chap. xiii.

Patterns of Drinking and Abstinence

GEORGE L. MADDOX AND BEVODE C. MCCALL

1 For additional comments on the concept of pattern of drinking see E. M. Lemert, *Alcohol and the Northwest Coast Indians*, University of California Publications in Culture and Society, Vol. 2, No. 6, pp. 303–406, Berkeley: University of California Press, 1954.

2 On the concept of self see Y. A. Cohen, *Social Structure and Personality*, New York: Holt, Rinehart and Winston; 1961, pp. 189ff. Also, E. Goffman, *The Presentation of Self in Everyday Life*, New York: Doubleday, 1959.

3 The credibility of reported amounts and frequency of drinking was not investigated. Both the tests of reliability of the questionnaire and impressions from interviews with students provide a basis for confidence in the consistency of responses. Subsequently, however, it should be understood that references to student behavior refer to reported behavior, not observed or confirmed behavior.

4 Riley and Marden, using data based on a representative sample of the adult population in the United States, developed by the National Opinion Research Center, found that one in two women in contrast to one in four men were abstainers. See J. W. Riley, Jr. and C. F. Marden, "The Social Pattern of Alcoholic Drinking," *Quart. J. Stud. Alc.*, 8: 265–273, 1947. These data have been corroborated by studies in single states. See M. A. Maxwell, "Drinking Behavior in the State

of Washington," *Quart. J. Stud. Alc.*, 13: 219–239, 1952. Also, H. A. Mulford and D. W. Miller, "Drinking in Iowa," Sections I–V. *Quart. J. Stud. Alc.*, 20: 704–726, 1959; 21: 26–39, 267–278, 279–291, 483–499, 1960. Straus and Bacon found twice as many women as men abstainers in a comprehensive study of drinking behavior in American colleges. See R. Straus and S. D. Bacon, *Drinking in College*, New Haven: Yale University Press, 1953.

5 The notion of a "double standard," especially when applied in discussions of morality, frequently implies an unequal treatment of presumed equals. The presumption that men and women are equal is consistent with a strong equalitarian bias often encountered in the writing of Americans. It is not the point here to argue whether or not men and women are actually equal in some absolute sense. The important point is that the cultural definitions of appropriate male and female roles in our society are defined as different. From this point of view a "double standard" is adequately described as a different cultural definition of male and female roles. See, for example, T. Parsons, "Age and Sex in the Social Structure of the United States," *American Sociological Review*, 7: 604–616, 1942. Also, M. Mead, *Male and Female*, New York: New American Library, 1955, pp. 184–285.

6 The functions of age peer groups in facilitating the acculturation of the children of foreign-born parents in the United States has often been noted. This situation illustrates in extreme form the importance of peer groups in bridging the gap between family training and acquiring the social skills required for adequate participation in the host society. In courtship and marriage, social and political beliefs and behavior, and in occupational selection, the peer group has frequently had a marked influence on the behavior of its members. See, for example, M. B. Sneidler and M. J. Ravitz, "A Jewish Peer Group," *American Journal of Sociology*, 61: 11–15, 1955.

7 For a summary of this characterization and a critique of it, see F. Elkin and W. A. Westley, "The Myth of Adolescent Culture," *American Sociological Review*, 20: 680–684, 1955.

8 The discussion of social stratification in the following paragraphs draws especially on the work of Weber, and Warner, Meeker and Eells. See M. Weber, "Class, Status and Party," in R. Bendix and S. M. Lipset (eds.), *Class, Status and Power*, New York: Free Press, 1953. Also, L. Warner, M. Meeker, and K. Eells, *Social Class in America*, Chicago: Science Research Associates, 1949. See also the critical discussion of issues and bibliography in this field in H. W. Pfautz, "The Current Literature on Social Stratification: Critique and Bibliography," *American Journal of Sociology*, 58: 391–418, 1953.

9 For example, see Pfautz, *ibid*. Also, G. P. Stone and W. H. Form, "Instabilities in Status: The Problems of Hierarchy in the Community Study of Status Arrangements," *American Sociological Review*, 18: 149–162, 1953.

10 See, for example, J. A. Kahl and J. A. Davis, "A Comparison of Indexes of Socioeconomic Status," *American Sociological Review*, 20: 317–325, 1955. Also, T. Parsons, "An Analytical Approach to the Theory of Social Stratification," *American Journal of Sociology*, 45: 841–862, 1940.

11 The notion that the "upper class" drink like "ladies and gentle-

men" in contrast to the more rowdy and less glamorous drinking among the "lower class" is reported in J. Dollard, "Drinking Mores of the Social Classes," in *Alcohol, Science and Society*, Ch. 8, pp. 95–104, New Haven: Quarterly Journal of Studies on Alcohol, 1945. For a characterization of drinking by the "country club crowd" in contrast to those who drink in roadhouses and bars see A. B. Hollingshead, *Elmtown's Youth: The Impact of Social Classes on Adolescents*, New York: Wiley, 1949, pp. 321 ff.

12 Havighurst develops this point of view in detail. See R. J. Havighurst, *Developmental Tasks and Education*, Chicago: University of Chicago Press, 1949. See also H. Hyman, "The Value Systems of Different Classes; A Social Psychological Contribution to the Analysis of Stratification," in R. Bendix and S. M. Lipset (eds.), *Class, Status and Power*, New York: Free Press, 1953.

Juvenile Delinquency Among Middle-Class Girls

NANCY BARTON WISE

1 Richard I. Perlman, "Delinquency: The Size of the Problem," *Reference Papers on Children and Youth*, White House Conference on Children and Youth, 1960, p. 245; Edward E. Schwartz, "Statistics of Juvenile Delinquency in the United States," *Annals of the American Academy of Political and Social Sciences*, Vol. 261 (1949), p. 15; David Bogen, "Juvenile Delinquency and Economic Trend," *American Sociological Review*, Vol. 9 (1944), p. 182; Benedict S. Alper, "Teen-Age Offenses and Offenders," *American Sociological Review*, Vol. 4 (1939), p. 172; Ernest W. Burgess, "The Economic Factor in Juvenile Delinquency," *Journal of Criminal Law, Criminology and Police Science*, Vol. 43 (1952), pp. 36–37; Mary Huff Diggs, "The Girl Runaway," *Current Approaches to Delinquency*, Yearbook of National Probation Association, 1949, pp. 65–75; or see any textbook in delinquency for comparable remarks, for instance, Martin H. Neumeyer, *Juvenile Delinquency in Modern Society*, Third Edition, Princeton, N.J.: Van Nostrand, 1949, pp. 40–41; Sophia Robison, *Juvenile Delinquency, Its Nature and Control*, New York: Holt, 1960, p. 9; Harry Manuel Shulman, *Juvenile Delinquency in American Society*, New York: Harper & Row, 1961, p. 468.

2 For data on comparability of male and female sex delinquency among teen-agers see: Alfred C. Kinsey, Wardell B. Pomeroy, Clyde E. Martin, and Paul H. Gebhard, *Sexual Behavior in the Human Female*, Philadelphia: W. B. Saunders, 1953, p. 331; Austin L. Porterfield and H. E. Salley, "Current Folkways of Sexual Behavior," *American Journal of Sociology*, Vol. 52 (1946), pp. 209–216; Alfred C. Kinsey, Wardell B. Pomeroy, and Clyde E. Martin, *Sexual Behavior in the Human Male*, Philadelphia: W. B. Saunders, 1948, pp. 335–347; Ira L. Reiss, "Sexual Codes in Teen-Age Culture," *The Annals of the American Academy of Political and Social Sciences*, Vol. 33 (1961), pp. 53–62. For instances of female delinquency similar to male delinquency but officially treated

differently see: Fred J. Murphy, "Delinquency Off the Record," *Society's Stake in the Offender*, Yearbook of the National Probation Association, 1946, p. 185.

3 See, in particular, the discussions of middle-class values: in Albert K. Cohen, *Delinquent Boys—The Culture of the Gang*, Glencoe, Ill.: Free Press, 1955, pp. 84–102; August Hollingshead, *Elmtown's Youth*, New York: Wiley, 1949, pp. 441–447; of working-class values in: Walter B. Miller, "Lower Class Culture as a Generating Milieu of Gang Delinquency," *Journal of Social Issues*, Vol. 14 (1958), pp. 5–20.

4 Harry Manuel Shulman, "The Family and Delinquency," *The Annals of the American Academy of Political and Social Science*, Vol. 261 (1949), pp. 30–31; Albert K. Cohen and James F. Short, Jr., "Research in Delinquent Subcultures," *Journal of Social Issues*, Vol. 14 (1958), p. 28; Albert K. Cohen, "Middle-Class Delinquency and the Social Structure," paper read at the annual meeting of the American Sociological Association, 1957; Joseph W. Scott and Edmund W. Vaz, "A Perspective on Middle-Class Delinquency," *The Canadian Journal of Economics and Political Science*, Vol. 29 (August, 1963), p. 329; Ralph W. England, Jr., "A Theory of Middle Class Delinquency," *Journal of Criminal Law, Criminology and Police Science*, Vol. 50 (1960), pp. 538–540.

5 For a thorough discussion of this point see Nancy Jo Barton, *Disregarded Delinquency: A Study of Self-Reported Middle-Class Female Delinquency in a Suburb*, Unpublished Doctoral Dissertation, Indiana University, 1965, Chapter III; for detailed data see: Urie Bronfenbrenner, "The Changing American Child," *Reference Papers on Children and Youth*, White House Conference, 1960, pp. 1–5; Ernest W. Burgess and Harvey J. Locke, *The Family from Institution to Companionship*, New York: American Book, 1945, p. 26; Daniel R. Miller and Guy E. Swanson, *The Changing American Parent*, New York: Wiley, 1958, pp. 200–202; William Westley and Frederick Elkin, "The Protective Environment and Adolescent Socialization," *Social Forces*, Vol. 35 (1957), pp. 243–249; Margaret Mead, "The Contemporary American Family as An Anthropologist Sees It," *American Journal of Sociology*, Vol. 53 (1948), pp. 455–456; Paul Wallin, "Cultural Contradiction and Sex Roles: A Repeat Study," *American Sociological Review*, Vol. 15 (1950), p. 292; John P. McKee and Alex C. Sherriffs, "Men's and Women's Beliefs, Ideals and Self-Concepts," *American Journal of Sociology*, Vol. 44 (1959), pp. 356–363; David B. Lynn, "A Note on Sex Differences in the Development of Masculine and Feminine Identification," in Jerome Seidman (ed.), *The Adolescent—A Book of Readings*, Revised Edition, New York: Holt, 1960, pp. 260–272.

A Perspective on Middle-Class Delinquency

JOSEPH W. SCOTT AND EDMUND W. VAZ

1 David Riesman, Nathan Glazer, and Reuel Denney, *The Lonely Crowd* (New York, 1955), 30 ff.

[2] *Ibid.*, 79.

[3] *White Collar*, (New York, 1956), 24.

[4] See William H. Whyte, Jr., *The Organization Man* (New York, 1957).

[5] *Ibid.*, 150.

[6] Riesman *et al.*, *The Lonely Crowd*, 67.

[7] Edgar Z. Friedenberg, *The Vanishing Adolescent* (Boston, 1959), 1–38.

[8] Albert K. Cohen, "Teachers vs. Students: Changing Power Relations in the Secondary Schools." A public lecture at the University of California, Berkeley, Aug. 22, 1961. See also Whyte, *Organization Man*, 425 ff.

[9] John R. Seeley, R. Alexander Sim, and Elizabeth W. Loosley, *Crestwood Heights* (Toronto, 1956), 236.

[10] *Ibid.*, 245.

[11] Whyte, *Organization Man*, 426.

[12] *Ibid.*, 434. See also Seeley, *Crestwood Heights*, 116.

[13] James S. Coleman, *Social Climates in High Schools* (Washington: U.S. Department of Health, Education, and Welfare, 1961), 3 ff.

[14] James S. Coleman, "Academic Achievement and the Structure of Competition," *Harvard Educational Review*, XXIX, Fall, 1959, 339–51.

[15] See James S. Coleman, *The Adolescent Society* (Glencoe, Ill., 1961), 244 ff.

[16] *Ibid.*, 34.

[17] For some recent alternative views on middle-class delinquency see Robert H. Bohlke, "Social Mobility, Stratification Inconsistency and Middle Class Delinquency," *Social Problems*, VIII, no. 4, Spring, 1961; Albert K. Cohen, *Delinquent Boys* (Glencoe, Ill., 1955); Albert K. Cohen, "Middle-Class Delinquency and the Social Structure," a paper read at the annual meetings of the American Sociological Society, 1957; Albert K. Cohen and James Short, "Research in Delinquent Subcultures," *Social Issues*, XIV, no. 3, 1958.

[18] Robert Dubin, "Deviant Behaviour and Social Structure: Continuities in Social Theory," *American Sociological Review*, XXIV, April, 1959, 152.

[19] The basic idea is taken from Cohen, *Delinquent Boys*, 60.

[20] Coleman, *Adolescent Society*, 23.

[21] C. Wayne Gordon, *The Social System of the High School* (Glencoe, Ill., 1957), 119–22.

[22] Some of the terms used by middle-class adolescents seem to serve as a convenient technique of immunization actually inhibiting the development of a delinquent self-conception. The innocuous term "joyriding" seems simply to define the use to which the car is put and mirror the motives of the boys. Furthermore, the automobile offers multiple functionally related services for the middle-class adolescent. A status symbol, it enhances the success of dating and also presents easily taken opportunities for engaging in sex behaviour.

[23] Coleman, *Adolescent Society*, 121.

[24] Richard A. Cloward and Lloyd W. Ohlin, *New Perspectives on Juvenile Delinquency* (New York: Columbia University School of Social Work, 1959, mimeo.).

[25] Coleman, *Adolescent Society*, 124.

26 Gordon, *Social System of the High School,* 113–14.
27 Whyte, *Organization Man,* 425.
28 Seeley, *Crestwood Heights,* 99.

Social Mobility, Stratification Inconsistency and Middle Class Delinquency

ROBERT H. BOHLKE

1 Albert K. Cohen and James F. Short, Jr., "Research in Delinquent Subcultures," *Journal of Social Issues,* 14 (No. 3, 1958), pp. 32–34; Clarence Dean, "Delinquency Rise Found in Suburbs," *The New York Times* (July 7, 1958), pp. 1 ff.; James P. Dixon, Jr., "Meeting Human Needs," in *Goals for Americans,* New York: Prentice-Hall, Inc., 1960, pp. 259–260; Ralph W. England, Jr., "A Theory of Middle Class Delinquency," *Journal of Criminal Law, Criminology and Police Science,* 50 (March–April, 1960), p. 535; William C. Kvaraceus and Walter B. Miller *et al., Delinquent Behavior,* Washington, D.C.: National Education Association, 1959, pp. 76, 85–86; "Report on Juvenile Delinquency," *Hearings before the Subcommittee of the Committee on Appropriations, House of Representatives,* Eighty-Sixth Congress, Second Session, Washington, D.C.: U.S. Government Printing Office, 1960, p. 116; Walter C. Reckless, *The Crime Problem,* New York: Appleton-Century-Crofts, Inc., 1961, p. 367; Harrison E. Salisbury, *The Shook-Up Generation,* New York: Harper & Row, 1958, pp. 109–110; Maurice R. Stein, *The Eclipse of Community,* Princeton: Princeton University Press, 1960, p. 252.

2 Cohen has noted that the evidence ". . . consists entirely of the impressions of police, court workers, social workers and school authorities, but there is enough consensus among these people to create a strong presumption that such an increase has actually occurred." Albert K. Cohen, "Middle-Class Delinquency and the Social Structure," paper read at the annual meeting of the American Sociological Association, August, 1957, mimeo., p. 1. There appears to be one shred of indirect evidence. Assuming that automobile theft represents a type of delinquency associated with youth from better-than-average homes, for which some evidence exists (see William W. Wattenberg and James Balistrieri, "Automobile Theft: A 'Favored-Group' Delinquency," *The American Journal of Sociology,* 57 (May, 1952), pp. 575–579; and Albert J. Reiss, Jr. and Albert Lewis Rhodes, "Social Class Distribution of Juvenile Delinquency," paper read at the annual meeting of the American Sociological Association, August, 1960), there are indications that automobile thefts have undergone a greater rise than all delinquencies in recent years. See Negley K. Teeters and David Matza, "The Extent of Delinquency," Philadelphia: Temple University, n.d., mimeo., pp. 9–10; also "Types of Delinquency," *Youth Service News* (July, 1960), pp. 8–9 (bulletin published irregularly by the Division of Youth, New York State, Albany, N.Y.). For some evidence from another

society see a study of London juvenile offenders in which the authors conclude that "In London between 1952 and 1957, we find the association between delinquency and low social class becomes much less apparent." W. R. Little and V. R. Ntsekhe, "Social Class Background of Young Offenders from London," *The British Journal of Delinquency*, 10 (October, 1959), p. 134. For changes in English society that may be related to an increase in middle class delinquency see David Lockwood, *The Blackcoated Worker*, London: George Allen & Unwin Ltd., 1958; and Peregrine Worsthorne, "Class and Conflict in British Foreign Policy," *Foreign Affairs*, 37 (April, 1959), pp. 419–431, and particularly pp. 423–427.

[3] Kvaraceus and Miller *et al.*, *op. cit.*, pp. 83–84.

[4] *Ibid.*, pp. 78–79; Cohen and Short, *op. cit.*, pp. 32–33. Cf. Reckless, *op. cit.*, pp. 4, 367.

[5] Kvaraceus and Miller *et al.*, *op. cit.*, p. 79; Cohen and Short, *op. cit.*, p. 33.

[6] Cohen and Short, *op. cit.*, pp. 33–34.

[7] Jessie Bernard, *Social Problems at Mid-century*, New York: The Dryden Press, 1957, p. 424. This idea, briefly mentioned by Bernard is not explicitly set forth as an explanation for a rise in middle class delinquency, but it seems reasonable to so categorize it.

[8] Bertram M. Beck, "The School and Delinquency Control," *Annals of the American Academy of Political and Social Science*, 302 (November, 1955), p. 66. The relationship of new suburban communities to an increase in middle class delinquency is implicit rather than explicit.

[9] England, *op. cit.*, pp. 535–540.

[10] Several sociologists seek to explain middle class delinquency by other formulations. See Bernard, *loc. cit.*; Herbert Bloch and Arthur Niederhoffer, *The Gang*, New York: Philosophical Library, 1958, pp. 7–17, 180–182; Albert K. Cohen, *Delinquent Boys*, Glencoe, Ill.: The Free Press, 1955, pp. 162–169; Harold L. Wilensky and Charles N. Lebaux, *Industrial Society and Welfare*, New York: Russell Sage Foundation, 1958, pp. 194–201. However, these analyses are not directed toward explaining an increase in middle class delinquency. The latter work, in elaborating Cohen's thesis only to reject it, does suggest one other interesting hypothesis—the increasing feminization of the male role among the middle class. See *ibid.*, pp. 195–196.

[11] Bernard, *op. cit.*, p. 413.

[12] *Ibid.*, pp. 10–11; also see Daniel Seligman, "The New Masses," *Fortune*, 60 (May, 1959), pp. 106–111 ff.; "The Rich Middle-Income Class," *Fortune*, 54 (May, 1954), pp. 94–99 ff. Cf. *Economic Growth in the United States*, New York: Committee for Economic Development, 1958, pp. 12, 28. For a dissenting view on the "income revolution" see Gabriel Kolko, "Economic Mobility and Social Stratification," *The American Journal of Sociology*, 63 (July, 1957), pp. 30–38.

[13] By *nouvelle bourgeoisie*, or "new middle class," we have in mind people born of lower income working class parents and who themselves today hold blue collar jobs but whose yearly income is now in the middle income range. One analysis estimated that in 1953, 60 per cent of the 15,500,000 families in the $4,000–$7,500 income bracket were headed by blue collar workers. See "The Rich Middle Income Class," *Fortune*, 54 (May, 1954), p. 97. When we will have occasion

to speak of the "old middle class" we will be referring to white collar workers, and particularly clerical and salesworkers who are usually defined as lower middle class. We do not mean "old" in terms of age, for obviously such people would not now have children of high school age. When we use the term "middle class" we will also be referring to the "new middle class." When the term middle class is not enclosed in quotations we will be referring either to the "old middle class" or to traditional middle class culture. We hardly need note that our "new middle class" and "old middle class" are not comparable to these terms as employed in C. Wright Mills, *White Collar*, New York: Oxford University Press, 1951. For one study of the culture of the "new middle class" see Bennett M. Berger, *Working-Class Suburb*, Berkeley and Los Angeles: University of California Press, 1960.

14 Kvaraceus and Miller *et al., op. cit.*, pp. 76–86.

15 A recent study concludes that ". . . 'social mobility' is a complex multidimensional concept consisting presently of an indeterminate but substantial number of components." Charles F. Westoff, Marvin Bressler and Philip C. Sagi, "The Concept of Social Mobility: An Empirical Inquiry," *American Sociological Review*, 25 (June, 1960), p. 385. Also see Seymour Martin Lipset and Reinhard Bendix, *Social Mobility in an Industrial Society*, Berkeley: University of California Press, 1960, pp. 64–68, 265–277; S. M. Miller, "The Concept of Mobility," *Social Problems*, 3 (October, 1955), pp. 65–72; Peter Blau, "Social Mobility and Interpersonal Relationships," *American Sociological Review*, 21 (June, 1956), pp. 290–295.

16 The term "stratification" seems preferable in this context to the term "status," used by a number of sociologists, because of the variant meanings of the latter. See Leonard Broom, "Social Differentiation and Stratification," in Robert K. Merton, Leonard Broom and Leonard S. Cottrell, Jr., editors, *Sociology Today*, New York: Basic Books, Inc., 1959, pp. 429–441; Gerhard E. Lenski, "Status Crystallization: A Non-Vertical Dimension of Social Status," *American Sociological Review*, 19 (August, 1954), pp. 405–413. Cf. the concept of "status ambiguity" as delineated in Lockwood, *op. cit.*, pp. 125–133. Also see the concept of "status-discrepancies" as used in Lipset and Bendix, *op. cit.*, pp. 64–66.

17 As Mayer notes, discrepancies in the several hierarchies of stratification are most likely to occur in periods marked by cultural and social change. See Kurt Mayer, *Class and Society*, Garden City: Doubleday and Co., 1955, p. 27. The shift from an economy of scarcity to one of abundance that has taken place in American society since 1940 represents just such a period.

18 In a personal conversation with the writer, Leonard S. Cottrell, Jr., after having read the original version of this paper, expressed the view that the spread of delinquency to a metropolitan New York county could probably be explained by a combination of Miller's inter-class diffusion theory and this writer's stratification-inconsistency theory. In the course of his comments Cottrell spoke of a leadership vacuum in the high schools which the aggressive "new middle class" tended to fill, with the "old middle class" youth becoming followers and adopters of the deviant patterns exhibited by the former. If Cottrell's impressionistic analysis is correct his comments on leader-

ship seem to relate to changes in socialization techniques that have altered the middle class personality. Bronfenbrenner, for example, notes that the shift to 'love-oriented' socialization techniques among the middle class "may . . . have the effect of undermining capacities for initiative and independence, particularly in boys." Urie Bronfenbrenner, "The Changing American Child," Ithaca, N.Y.: Dept. of Child Development and Family Relationships, Cornell University, n.d., mimeo., p. 6. For a somewhat different view but one with implications for middle class delinquency see Daniel R. Miller and Guy E. Swanson, *The Changing American Parent*, New York: John Wiley and Sons, 1958, p. 211.

[19] Cohen, *Delinquent Boys*, p. 159. Cf. Wilensky and Lebaux, *op. cit.*, p. 194.

[20] Cohen and Short, *op. cit.*, pp. 32–34.

[21] The "atypical" work, Walter C. Reckless, *The Crime Problem*, New York: Appleton-Century-Crofts, Inc., 1955, pp. 235–236, sees juvenile delinquency in economically developed countries like the United States as resulting in part from the interpersonal struggle for position in a highly mobile society. Cf. the third edition of the same work, 1961, pp. 4, 367. One paper reports data of some relevance to this matter. Glaser and Rice, in noting an inverse relationship between unemployment and juvenile delinquency, conclude "As economic insecurity is reduced, we may still expect criminality to be associated with status insecurity or other sources of anomie." Daniel Glaser and Kent Rice, "Crime, Age, and Employment," *American Sociological Review*, 24 (October, 1959), p. 685. Material published on social stratification and juvenile delinquency in Britain, although not exhaustively surveyed, appears also to have ignored this question. See D. V. Glass, editor, *Social Mobility in England*, Glencoe, Ill.: The Free Press, 1954; David C. Marsh, *The Changing Social Structure of England and Wales, 1871–1951*, London: Routledge and Kegan Paul Ltd., 1958, pp. 257–261. For a summary of British studies on juvenile delinquency see Barbara Wootton, *Social Science and Social Pathology*, London: George Allen and Unwin Ltd., 1959, Chapter 2, *passim*, and pp. 100–104, 107–110. This gap in the sociology of delinquency is particularly interesting inasmuch as the first comprehensive work on social mobility, published originally in 1927, noted a relationship between vertical mobility and criminality. Pitirim A. Sorokin, *Social and Cultural Mobility*, Glencoe, Ill.: The Free Press, 1959, pp. 526–529. The most recent work devoted exclusively to social mobility does not mention juvenile delinquency. See Lipset and Bendix, *op. cit.*

[22] Bruno Bettelheim and Morris Janowitz, *Dynamics of Prejudice*, New York: Harper & Row, 1950; Joseph Greenblum and Leonard I. Pearlin, "Vertical Mobility and Prejudice: A Socio-Psychological Analysis" in Reinhard Bendix and Seymour M. Lipset, editors, *Class, Status and Power*, Glencoe, Ill.: The Free Press, pp. 480–491. Two recent works have questioned this relationship. Lipset and Bendix, *op. cit.*, p. 71; Fred B. Silberstein and Melvin Seeman, "Social Mobility and Prejudice," *The American Journal of Sociology*, 65 (November, 1959), pp. 258–264. For interesting contradictory results from Northern and Southern samples see Thomas F. Pettigrew, "Regional Differences

in Anti-Negro Prejudice," *The Journal of Abnormal and Social Psychology*, 59 (July, 1959), pp. 32–33. Cf. Melvin M. Tumin, *Desegregation*, Princeton: Princeton University Press, 1958, Chapter 8.

23 A. B. Hollingshead and F. C. Redlich, *Social Class and Mental Illness*, New York: John Wiley and Sons, 1958; Mary H. Lystad, "Social Mobility Among Schizophrenic Patients," *American Sociological Review*, 22 (June, 1957), pp. 288–292; A. B. Hollingshead, R. Ellis and E. Kirby, "Social Mobility and Mental Illness," *American Sociological Review*, 19 (October, 1954), pp. 577–584.

24 J. Roth and R. F. Peck, "Social Class and Social Mobility Factors Related to Marital Adjustment," *American Sociological Review*, 16 (August, 1951), pp. 478–487.

25 Jerzy Berent, "Fertility and Social Mobility," *Population Studies*, 5 (March, 1952), pp. 240–260. For reservations about this thesis, as well as for other references, see H. Yuan Tien, "The Social Mobility/Fertility Hypothesis Reconsidered: An Empirical Study," *American Sociological Review*, 26 (April, 1961), pp. 247–257.

26 E. E. Lemasters, "Social Class Mobility and Family Integration," *Marriage and Family Living*, 16 (August, 1954), pp. 226–232.

27 Daniel Bell, editor, *The New American Right*, New York: Criterion Books, 1955.

28 *Op. cit.*, p. 295. For additional evidence supporting Blau's generalization see Tumin, *loc. cit.* For both supporting and conflicting evidence see Eugene Litwak, "Occupation Mobility and Family Cohesion," *American Sociological Review*, 25 (February, 1960), pp. 9–21, and "Voluntary Associations and Neighborhood Cohesion," *American Sociological Review*, 26 (April, 1961), pp. 258–271.

29 Blau advances his hypothesis in terms of occupational mobility which, of course, may be correlative with a change in income, but the latter is obviously not dependent upon the former.

30 Some evidence to support the use of this concept in speaking of middle income people of working class background will be found in Thomas Ktsanes and Leonard Reissman, "Suburbia—New Homes for Old Values," *Social Problems*, 7 (Winter, 1959–60), pp. 187–195. Another report on the middle income "group" is contradictory on this point. See Seligman, *op. cit.*, pp. 109, 111.

31 Cf. Irwin W. Goffman, "Status Inconsistency and Preference for Change in Power Distribution," *American Sociological Review*, 22 (June, 1957), p. 276; Gerhard E. Lenski, "Social Participation and Status Crystallization," *American Sociological Review*, 21 (August, 1956), p. 459. If this analysis is correct it raises the interesting question of how the parents manifest such stress. I would hypothesize that among the adults the anxieties would be reflected in such deviant behavior as frequent husband-wife quarreling, gambling, alcoholism, excessive TV viewing (See Leonard I. Pearlin, "The Social and Psychological Setting of Communications Behavior," unpublished Ph.D. dissertation, Columbia University, 1957, as reported in Robert K. Merton, *Social Theory and Social Structure*, Glencoe, Ill.: The Free Press, 1957, p. 181, footnote 35), psychoneurotic disorders and psychosomatic complaints. Other possible outlets for adults would be "community feuding" over such matters as school bond issues, educational methods, and

fluoridation, as well as the expression of intolerance toward those belonging to different ethnic groups and toward those with liberal political ideas.

32 Merton, *op. cit.*, p. 140.

33 Merton has noted that in his initial discussion of deviant behavior he used monetary success to represent the major cultural goal "only 'for purposes of simplifying the problem . . .'" *Ibid.*, p. 181.

34 Richard A. Cloward and Lloyd E. Ohlin, *Delinquency and Opportunity: A Theory of Gangs*, Glencoe, Ill.: The Free Press, 1960.

35 *Ibid.*, pp. 90–97.

36 See the Duncans' very significant analysis of income, occupation, and residential distribution by census tracts in Chicago in 1950, midway in the course of the income revolution Otis Dudley Duncan and Beverly Duncan, "Residential Distribution and Occupational Stratification" in Paul K. Hatt and Albert J. Reiss, Jr., editors, *Cities and Society*, Glencoe, Ill.: The Free Press, 1957, pp. 283–296. E.g., ". . . the clerical group has an income equivalent to that of operatives but the educational level of managerial workers" (p. 288); and ". . . although clerical workers are often grouped with professional, managerial, and sales workers as 'white collar,' in terms of residential distribution they are more similar to the craftsmen and operatives than to the other white-collar groups" (p. 289). In this connection also note the narrowing differential in income between operatives and clerical workers over the past 30 years. Even though the data are probably not strictly comparable see Mills, *op. cit.*, p. 280; and Everett M. Kassalow, "Occupational Frontiers of Trade Unionism in the United States," paper presented before the Industrial Relations Research Association, December 29, 1960, mimeo., p. 18. The latter notes that since 1950 there is evidence suggesting a reversal of this trend, but such a qualification ignores the fact that large numbers of people in the white collar and blue collar categories are likely to be characterized by stratification inconsistencies. See Carol Barry, "White Collar Employment: II—Characteristics," *Monthly Labor Review*, 84 (February, 1961), pp. 145–146, Tables 6 and 8, for national data which suggests discrepancies between education and income for clerical workers and operatives in 1959.

37 Albert K. Cohen and James F. Short, Jr., in a personal communication, commenting on the original version of this paper, formulated an interesting alternative explanation which sees the "old middle class" youth rather than the *nouvelle bourgeoisie* as the chief contributors to middle class delinquency. They theorize that the latter might contain "large numbers of aspiring and 'over-conforming' young people who begin to attract the favorable attentions of school teachers and administrators, and representatives of other institutions because of their industry and achievement, frugality and 'good behavior.'" The "old middle class" youth, they argue, may perceive the *nouvelle bourgeoisie* as a threat to their status and react in an anti-middle class manner. This idea has much merit, and the writer is in agreement with Cohen and Short's closing comment wherein they note that both theories may be ". . . valid under certain conditions and for certain types of persons, or for persons with certain problems within the middle class. We need to know the extent of middle class delinquency

and the segments of the middle class which account for such delinquency. It is possible that the latter may have changed, without an overall change in the volume of middle class delinquency in recent years. Present data do not permit an answer to these questions."

38 Starke R. Hathaway and Elio D. Monachesi, *Analyzing and Predicting Juvenile Delinquency with the MMPI*, Minneapolis: The University of Minnesota Press, 1953; William C. Kvaraceus, "Juvenile Delinquency and Social Class," *The Journal of Educational Sociology*, 18 (September, 1944), pp. 51–54; Edward E. Schwartz, "A Community Experiment in the Measurement of Juvenile Delinquency" in *Yearbook of the National Probation Association*, 1945, New York: National Probation Association, 1945, pp. 156–161; Wattenberg and Balistrieri, *op. cit.*

39 The precise definition of "middle income" would have to be determined. However, to establish a frame of reference, a range of $4,000–$7,500 in 1953 dollars, or $5,000–$10,000 in 1959 dollars, seem to be reasonable approximations.

40 F. Ivan Nye and James F. Short, Jr., "Scaling Delinquent Behavior," *American Sociological Review*, 22 (June, 1957), pp. 326–331.

41 There is need for the development of a standardized scale that will measure the degree to which a given family's culture approximates traditional middle class culture. It is rather interesting that sociologists have not produced an instrument which seems as basic to much of their research as the intelligence test is to psychological research.

42 Oliver Moles, Ronald Lippitt and Stephen Withey, *A Selective Review of Research and Theory on Delinquency*, Ann Arbor, Michigan: Institute for Social Research, University of Michigan, 1959, pp. 173–174.

43 Herbert Blumer, "Sociological Analysis and the 'Variable,'" *American Sociological Review*, 21 (December, 1956), pp. 683–690.

44 R. R. Dynes, A. C. Clarke and S. Dinitz, "Levels of Occupational Aspiration," *American Sociological Review*, 21 (April, 1956), pp. 212–215; LaMar T. Empey, "Social Class and Occupational Aspiration," *American Sociological Review*, 21 (December, 1956), pp. 703–709; Bernard C. Rosen, "The Achievement Syndrome," *American Sociological Review*, 21 (April, 1956), pp. 203–211; Richard M. Stephenson, "Mobility Orientation and Stratification," *American Sociological Review*, 22 (April, 1957), pp. 204–212; Alan B. Wilson, "Class Segregation and Aspirations of Youth," *American Sociological Review*, 24 (December, 1959), pp. 836–845.

45 Stephen Abrahamson, "Our Status System and Scholastic Rewards," *The Journal of Educational Sociology*, 25 (April, 1952), pp. 441–450. A. B. Hollingshead, *Elmtown's Youth*, New York: John Wiley and Sons, 1949; W. Lloyd Warner, Robert J. Havighurst and Martin B. Loeb, *Who Shall Be Educated?* London: Kegan Paul, Trench, Trubner and Co., 1946.

46 The comments of Cohen and Short regarding my original paper (see footnote 37 above) raise the interesting possibility that the "old middle class" youth may perceive the school as being biased in favor of the *nouvelle bourgeoisie* youth.

47 For an account of a research study that employed a sophisticated approach to this variable see Reiss and Rhodes, *op. cit.*

[48] See footnotes 42 and 43 above.

[49] S. Stanfield Sargent, "Assessing Community Attitudes and Social Relations" in Muzafer Sherif and M. O. Wilson, editors, *Emerging Problems in Social Psychology*, Norman, Oklahoma: University Book Exchange, 1957, pp. 265–276.

[50] See footnote 36 above.

[51] U.S. Bureau of the Census, *U.S. Census of Population: 1950, III*, Washington, D.C.: Government Printing Office, 1952, Chapter 4. Baltimore is mentioned only because the writer has the data for this city in his files.

[52] E.g., spending for a middle class social life, saving for a college education for the children, paying for middle class housing, purchasing the other material symbols of middle class life, and providing spending money for the teenager so that he in turn can compete for status in the teenage socio-cultural system which, with its radios, record players, records, clothing folkways, dating patterns, etc., represents a new consumer market increasingly being exploited in our economy. On this last point see Dwight W. McDonald, "A Caste, A Culture, A Market," *The New Yorker*, 34 (November 22, 1958), pp. 57 ff., and (November 29, 1958), pp. 57 ff.

[53] Although the writer places the emphasis on the clerical workers he recognizes the need for studying the effect of the various "mixes" on the families in other occupational groups. For one ingenious attempt to study the effect of "occupational mix" see Reiss and Rhodes, *op. cit.* This research, however, deals only with the relationship of the "mix" to the incidence of delinquency among the youth of three occupational categories; it does not seek to get at the effect(s) of the "mix" on family relationships. It does add in one other important variable—the incidence of delinquency in the residential areas of the various occupational groups.

[54] Cf. Merton, *op. cit.*, p. 177. Also see footnote 37 above. And in a personal communication Ralph W. England, Jr., made the same point.

[55] One observer has noted that the explanation of the diffusion of delinquent patterns to middle class adolescents ". . . is one of the main tasks confronting community sociologists." Stein, *op. cit.*, p. 252.

[56] Clyde E. Dankert, "Automation," *Dartmouth Alumni Magazine*, 48 (February, 1956), pp. 16–20; Arnold M. Rose, "Automation and the Future Society," *Commentary*, 21 (March, 1956), pp. 274–280; George P. Schultz and George B. Baldwin, *Automation: A New Dimension to Old Problems*, Washington, D.C.: Public Affairs Press, 1955.

[57] James R. Bright, "Does Automation Raise Skill Requirements?" *Harvard Business Review*, 36 (July–August, 1958), pp. 85–98. Cf. results of installation of electronic data processing in 20 offices in private industry. United States Dept. of Labor, *Adjustments to the Introduction of Office Automation*, Washington, D.C.: Government Printing Office, 1960, pp. 3–6, 33–41. Also see U.S. Congress, Joint Economic Committee, *New Views on Automation: Papers Submitted to the Subcommittee on Automation and Energy Resources*, 86th Congress, 2nd Session, Washington, D.C.: Government Printing Office, 1960.

[58] Ida Russakoff Hoos, "When the Computer Takes Over the Office," *Harvard Business Review*, 38 (July–August, 1960), pp. 102–112; Rich-

ard W. Riche and William E. Albi, "Office Automation in the Federal Government," *Monthly Labor Review*, 83 (September, 1960), pp. 933–938.

59 One student of labor takes the point of view that automation has had a greater impact on white collar work than on blue collar work. Jack Barbash, *What's Ahead for Labor*, Ann Arbor, Michigan: Bureau of Industrial Relations, The University of Michigan, 1960, pp. 8–9.

60 E.g., a recent news dispatch summarizing a Bureau of the Census report notes "that after taking inflation into account median incomes [of families] rose from $4,000 to $5,400 . . ." between 1947 and 1959, and that in 1959 about 40 per cent of the nation's families were in the $5,000 to $10,000 bracket. "U.S. Family Incomes Increase in 12 Years," *The New York Times* (January 7, 1961), p. 22.

61 This paper has obviously not been concerned with "complete" upward social mobility—that is, social mobility characterized by a relatively high degree of consistency among the several dimensions of stratification. However, it appears plausible to hypothesize that even this phenomenon may be accompanied by tension and thus be productive of deviant behavior. Here is one instance where Merton's model is perhaps deficient; in other words, conforming behavior may generate deviance. To illustrate, the blue collar worker may become a white collar worker, learn middle class culture and gain social acceptance from the middle class, but his "successful" transition may require physical, emotional and economic "expenditures" that produce strain within himself and within the family unit which, in turn, produces deviant behavior. And, one symptom of the tension within the family unit could well be delinquent behavior on the part of the son. Cf. Melvin M. Tumin, "Some Unapplauded Consequences of Social Mobility in a Mass Society," *Social Forces*, 36 (October, 1957), pp. 32–37, for other possible dysfunctions of social mobility.

A Theory of Middle Class Juvenile Delinquency

RALPH W. ENGLAND, JR.

1 Juvenile Court Statistics: 1956, Children's Bureau Statistical Series, No. 47, U.S. Children's Bureau, Washington, D.C., 1958.

2 Herbert A. Bloch and Frank T. Flynn, *Delinquency: The Juvenile Offender in America Today*, Random House, New York, 1956, p. 29.

3 F. Ivan Nye, James F. Short, Jr. and Virgil J. Olson, "Socioeconomic Status and Delinquent Behavior," *Amer. Jour. of Soc.*, 63: 381–389 (Jan., 1958), note 3; Frank E. Hartung, "A Critique of the Sociological Approach to Crime and Correction," *Law and Contemp. Prob.*, 23: 703–734 (Autumn, 1958), p. 730.

4 Talcott Parsons, "Age and Sex in the Social Structure of the United States," *Amer. Soc. Rev.*, 7: 604–616 (Oct., 1942).

5 Talcott Parsons, "Certain Primary Sources and Patterns of Aggression in the Social Structure of the Western World," *Psychiatry*, 10: 167–181 (May, 1947).

[6] Herbert A. Bloch and Arthur Niederhoffer, *The Gang*, Philosophical Library, New York, 1958, Ch. 5.

[7] *Consumer Reports*, "Teen-age Consumers," 22: 139–142 (March, 1957).

[8] Statistical Abstract of the United States: 1958, U.S. Bureau of the Census, Washington, D.C., p. 519.

[9] *Newsweek*, 49: 104–105 (April 1, 1957).

[10] *Statistical Abstract, op. cit.*, p. 519.

[11] Consumer Magazine and Farm Publication Rates and Data for May 27, 1959, pp. 400, 411–419. Circulation figures for *Datebook, Teens Today* and 16 are not currently listed in *Rates and Data.* A "Teensters' Union" has recently been organized by *Modern Teens* magazine, ostensibly "for the improvement of teen-age society."

[12] A crude measure of the increased public attention to our youth can be obtained by a count of *Readers' Guide to Periodical Literature* entries under *Youth—United States.* For the respective two-year periods of May, 1945 to April, 1947; April, 1951 to March, 1953; and March, 1957 to February, 1959 the number of entries was 24, 42 and 60.

[13] Albert K. Cohen, *Delinquent Boys: The Culture of the Gang*, Free Press, Glencoe, Ill., 1955.

[14] *Rates and Data, op. cit.*, pp. 65–74.

[15] *Consumer Reports, op. cit.*, p. 139.

[16] William A. Wattenberg and James T. Balistrieri, "Automobile Theft: A 'Favored-Group' Delinquency," *Amer. Jour. of Soc.*, 57: 575–579 (May, 1952). In studying 3,900 cases of juvenile auto theft in Detroit, the authors observed that not only were the boys from somewhat better neighborhoods than other delinquents, but were well socialized in their peer-group relationships. The 'favored-group' characteristic has reportedly been observed also in Britain. See, T. C. N. Gibbens, "Car Thieves," *Brit. Jour. of Delinquency* (April, 1958).

Index